Created and Directed by Hans Höfer

INSIGHT GUIDES
DenMaRK

Edited by Doreen Taylor-Wilkie

Editorial Director: Brian Bell

APA PUBLICATIONS

DENMARK

First Edition
© 1991 APA PUBLICATIONS (HK) LTD
All Rights Reserved
Printed in Singapore by Höfer Press Pte. Ltd

ABOUT THIS BOOK

The stereotypical Denmark is a "land of fairytales and fun." As editor of this book, Scottish journalist **Doreen Taylor-Wilkie** believes this smallest Scandinavian country has a great deal more to offer. She has set out to prove the point by showing Denmark and the Danes at home, at work and play, their great national pride, rich cultural life and interest in the arts, and the paradox of their affection for their Queen allied to a strong sense of equality. In addition to editing *Insight Guide: Denmark*, Taylor-Wilkie has written about Funen and its Archipelago and North Jutland.

Taylor-Wilkie first visited Jutland, Denmark's westernmost peninsula, in the early 1980s and, to get the true feel of this farming country, stayed with her young daughter on a farm near Velje. Since then, she has visited Copenhagen many times, travelled all over Denmark − part of it on a bicycle − and marvels at the diversity to be found in a nation of 5 million people.

The writing team

Rowlinson Carter, who lived in Scandinavia for several years, combines the knowledge he gained then with a love of history and a relish for the robust deeds of those great seafarers, the Vikings. A regular contributor to Insight Guides, Carter drew heavily on the old Viking sagas in chronicling for this book Danish history up to the present century.

Robert Spark's enduring affection for Denmark dates back to the 1950s and, though he finds that the country has changed considerably over the years "and not always for the better," he finds his favourite features of "closeness to the sea, rolling countryside, good food, placid islands and the Danes themselves" are still there. Spark, who is the author of a motoring guide to Denmark, has contributed three sections, West and South Jutland and Ålborg.

Australian **Geoffrey Dodd** tried tree-felling and cattle-farming before turning to journalism. For this book, he has written about farming, fishing and industry. He has worked in London and Denmark and returned to Denmark in 1985 on the toss of a coin, when friends there and in Canada both suggested he join them. He freelances for many publications and lives on a small-holding. This dual role makes him typical of the many Danes who, whatever their choice of job, continue a link with their farming past.

Penny Visman, who has written about Sealand, is usually based in Britain but makes the most of extra travel when she "not so reluctantly" accompanies her husband on oil-industry assignments overseas. By far the most civilised of these, she says, was three years in Denmark with Dansk Olie Naturgas.

Michael Metcalfe has lived and worked in the Nordic area for much of the 1980s, first as Reuters' chief correspondent for Scandinavia and now as Northern Europe correspondent for *Business International*. This puts him in a good position to disentangle 20th-century Denmark for the history section, and also to write the chapters on Greenland and the Faroe Islands, those far-flung areas to the northwest of the mainland.

Vivien Andersen has been called "more Danish than the Danes." As a Londoner married to a Dane, Andersen is the ideal person to hold both an insider's and an outsider's view of the country. She has written two chapters, the introductory essay on the

Taylor-Wilkie   *Carter*   *Spark*   *Dodd*   *Visman*

Danes themselves and "Culturally, Small is Beautiful", which describes the lively Danish arts scene. Andersen, an inveterate traveller, now lives in Scotland, where her husband is director of the Danish Cultural Institute in Edinburgh.

It is no surprise to find **Hugh Matthews** writing the chapter on Århus because he is regularly involved in Denmark's musical and band life, and the city's international festival is famous for both. A Briton, he has lived in Denmark for 12 of the past 15 years. He also wrote the chapter on beer.

The Danes involved in this book are headed by **Jo Hermann**, who has worked in Copenhagen as a book editor and in Houston, Texas, as a television journalist. She is now back in Copenhagen, involved in the arts world. Along with fellow Copenhagener **Stephen Rosenmeier** (writer of the chapters on churches and castles), she drew up the original outline for the book and continued to provide invaluable guidance throughout its long gestation period. Hermann also wrote the chapters on ecology and East Jutland, and assembled the initial picture selection.

Ulla Plon was well placed to write in detail about Copenhagen: as a student, she absorbed herself in town planning studies and remains concerned about the city's balance between preserving old buildings and succumbing to "international glass offices". Now the Scandinavian correspondent for *Time* magazine, she lives outside Copenhagen with her journalist husband, Julian Isherwood.

Lars Ole Sauerberg is a native of Fredericia just across the Lillebælt, from Odense on Funen, where he is Pro Vice-Chancellor of Odense University. He settled in the middle of the old city with his dentist wife and family and, in his words, "began a life of child-rearing, tooth-pulling and academic chores." He wrote the chapter on his adopted city.

Hanne Goldschmidt is also an academic and classical scholar. For this book, she writes about another favourite, the Queen, stimulated by her daily view of the Royal Guard passing her window.

Thomas Rosenmeier is a Bornholmer and a teacher of Danish and English on this charming east coast island. Like all islanders, he has spent times in "exile" in Copenhagen to complete his education and still wonders whether "being a happy illiterate here at the Gates of Eden was worth giving up for the hectic life of the city."

Many of the best pictures of Denmark's scenery come from **Bert Wiklund**, Denmark's leading nature photographer. Wiklund lives in Brande in Central Jutland where his archive (currently 80,000 pictures) is constantly growing, and travels all over Europe and Africa. **Marianne Paul** is a young photographer, presently at Copenhagen's Academy of Fine Arts. In addition to photography, she designs book covers and advertisments.

The editor wishes to thank press officer **Britt Sander** and her colleagues at the Danish Tourist Board in London for their encouragement and help in checking facts and reading parts of the text. The book was guided through a variety of computers by **Jill Anderson** and was proofread and indexed by **Pinta Carlsberg**.

A note on place names

In this edition, we have used the familiar Anglicised versions of certain place names. Thus Jylland is written as **Jutland**, Fyn as **Funen** and Sjælland as **Sealand**.

Andersen   *Matthews*   *Hermann*   *Plon*   *Paul*

History

Features

Places

Maps

"We are red, we are white, we are Danish Dynamite," chanted the fans in 1986 when Denmark reached the final rounds of football's World Cup. They painted the Dannebrog (Danish flag) on their faces, and stormed the matches with enthusiasm and pride. They were not hooligans, but *roligans* (*rolig* meaning calm), out to prove to the world that little Denmark was just as good, if not better, than any of the big nations. After all, five million Danes produced the world's best bicycle riders and badminton players, beer and bacon, so why not the best footballers?

The Danes are immensely proud of their "Danishness" – whatever that may be. Every respectable house (and there are one million of them) has its own flagpole. The Dannebrog is hoisted for all private and public celebrations, as well as on 15 June, Valdemar's Day, which commemorates the scene of battle during which the Dannebrog fell from the heavens to the feet of King Valdemar in 1219, thus spurring him on to win the war against the pagan Estonians. The Dannebrog decorates every birthday table, anniversary song sheet and Christmas tree in the land.

The Danes not only have the oldest national flag in the world but also the oldest monarchy, of which they are equally proud. Christian IX (died 1843) has often been called the Father-in-law of Europe, since his children ascended thrones in Denmark, Britain, Russia and Greece.

Making merry: In the 19th and early 20th centuries, the writers of the Romantic period sought to divert people's attention from the prevailing state of national bankruptcy and created a legacy of songs which praised the countryside, and the changing seasons, and the mother tongue. These are still very popular today, and at no time more so than on Midsummer's Eve, when people gather around bonfires, listen to speeches, eat, drink and sing "We love our country, but at midsummer most," and the national Anthem *Det er*

et yndigt land, which means, "This is a lovely/sweet/cute land."

The Danes never miss an opportunity to sing together. Baptisms, confirmations, weddings, wedding anniversaries, 40th, 50th, 60th and 70th birthdays all provide occasions for big dinners in the local church hall, Forsamlingshus (community centre) or hotel, where the hosts will be honoured with songs specially written for the occasion to a popular melody. Nobody is expected to know the words, and song sheets are distributed in

between courses, emerging from imaginatively created containers.

When the speeches are also included, the meal can last for a good six hours – but, then, partying is a serious business. Christmas starts early in December with a series of Christmas lunches and culminates in impressive blow-outs on the 25th and 26th, when guests are glued to the table from 12 noon until well into the evening. On New Year's Eve the Danes eat boiled cod as a kind of cold shower, and January editions of women's magazines are full of diets. This pang of conscience does not last, however, and is soon lost to the cycle of Carnival buns in February, Easter Eggs, summer barbecues and picnics, and Martinmas duck.

Apart from the big family celebrations, the Danes do not eat out. The luxury tax on restaurants is prohibitive, so these lively spirits are not evident to the casual visitor. After work and at weekends, the Dane retreats to his house and garden in the suburbs, which was probably built in the 1960s or 1970s (70 percent of Danish housing is post-World War II), or even further away to his allotment garden, where the garden shed has been transformed into a cosy weekend cottage.

Cosiness, the nearest approximation to the Danish word *hygge*, is what life is really all about. In winter you will find the average

Danish family in front of the TV set, probably watching a re-run of *Fawlty Towers* or some other British sitcom; with a vacuum flask of coffee, cakes and beer, and candles aglow as a final atmospheric touch.

In the summer the scene is transferred to the terrace outside the house or summerhouse, without the candles, and maybe with the addition of some neighbours to gossip with. Danes love a good talk, as long as it is not serious. The tax burden, currently reinforced by the economic squeeze called "Kartoffelkuren" (the potato cure) is number one topic. To an outsider, that may seem a serious topic but the Danes know they have

just as much influence on their tax situation as on the weather, so they try not to take it too seriously. In any case, they have been brought up to keep a low profile, not to seek or gain attention by having different ideas, and definitely not to stand out in a crowd.

Those who have objected both to the tax system and to the pressure to conform have probably left the country. The south-east of England, for example, has a colony of 50,000 ambitious, non-conformist Danes. The rest probably agree that his uniformity, sometimes even called mediocrity, is a small price to pay for the achievement of an egalitarian state, with social welfare second to none, based on a liberal democratic market economy.

Farm to factory: In 1940 one-third of the population was engaged in agriculture. In the 1950s the figure was a quarter, and today it is only 7 percent. Industrial development has been explosive. Half the total population is in the work force, including 80 percent of women between the ages of 20 and 54. Most work in the public service sector, which provides care, education and a security network from the cradle to the grave and allows all able-bodied adults to participate in the labour market.

With the advent of the dual-income family in the 1960s the Danish landscape changed irrevocably and today 60 percent of all Danes live in owner-occupied one-family houses in suburbs radiating from the medieval cores of the villages and towns. The farmers have come in from the land, bringing with them their skills, their work ethic, their traditions and their attitudes.

Danes are proud of their "Lilleput" land, which has managed to achieve an economic miracle at the same time as a social miracle, without exploiting anyone except the patience of the World Bank. They are proud of the mark they have made in the world of design, the construction industry, agricultural produce and hi-fi equipment. Every respectable Danish home is furnished with good quality, architect-designed furniture and, if they can afford it, a Bang & Olufsen TV set. They are proud of their liberalism, and their lack of racism (although the Danish reputation for the protection of minorities has become a little tarnished recently with the advent of their own guest-worker and refugee problems).

They are proud of the double-life they lead as members of the Council of Nordic Nations and as members of the European Community, balancing elegantly between the two camps. On the world stage they do not hesitate to exploit their smallness by expressing a minority view, usually to stir the conscience of the big powers, but they are also privately aware of the fact that nobody will take much notice, except their own newspapers. They don a protective shield, starting every argument with "Even though we are a little nation…" to defuse a counter-attack, or by a guarded aggressiveness.

They are also, perhaps justifiably, somewhat afraid of their big neighbours to the south and north, especially in the summer, when the otherwise peaceful roads are jammed with Germans coming north to seek the pleasant, unspoilt countryside and beaches, and Swedes and Norwegians coming south for a good time with their easygoing neighbours. The Danes have never forgotten that Sweden took Skåne, Blekinge and Halland (most of Southern Sweden) from Denmark in 1660, nor have they forgiven Germany for grabbing Holstein and Schleswig in 1864, not to mention their occupation in World War II.

Nevertheless, the Danes nowadays take a pragmatic approach, and try to safeguard their territory by prohibiting the purchase of holiday homes by foreigners. They have also consciously dropped all the outer signs of formality in which their neighbours excel. The formal mode of address "De" (*Sie* in German) has more or less been abolished. Clothes are ultra-casual, with open-necked shirts worn in most offices, and dark suits reserved for weddings and funerals.

The Danes are a people without extremes, which is perhaps why they are often just called "nice and friendly, if a little boring."

There are few prohibitions and relatively little crime. Their passion for equality has brought them far, and they don't want to stick their necks out to make life more exciting if that means upsetting the apple-cart. The 19th-century poet Hans Vilhelm Kaalund summed up the attitude:

Feet on the ground, feet on the ground
So I always heard it sound
when my soul so light and bright
swung itself into the height
Life's revenge will catch you soon
if you try to reach the moon
Feet on the ground, feet on the ground
So the triumph hymn of life should sound.

Left, Denmark has its share of immigrants. **Above**, role reversal is common – many Danish fathers take pride in looking after their children.

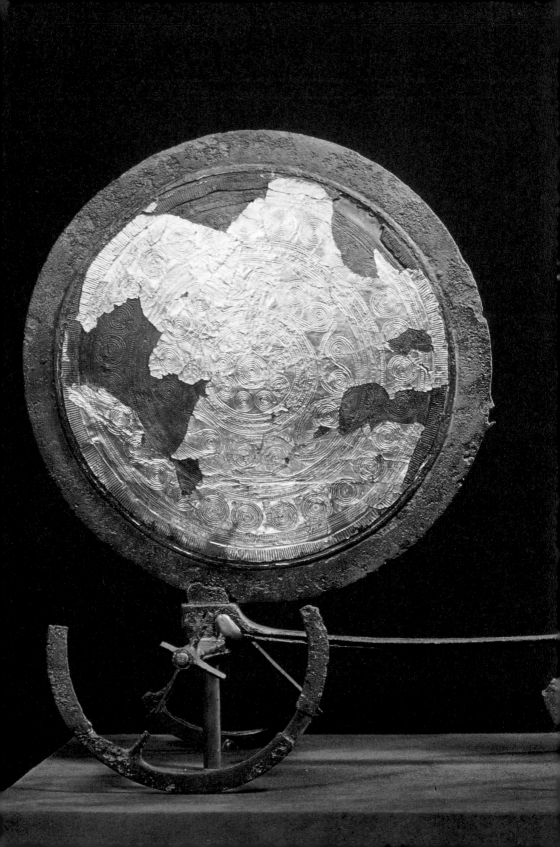

Until Scandinavia introduced itself to the rest of the world in the alarming guise of the rampaging Vikings, very little was known about the remote north, and even that tended to lack the ring of truth. The past remained unusually cloaked in mystery until well into modern times. While the sands of Egypt offered up papyrus and clay tablets providing intimate insight into the lives and thoughts of people who lived more than 1,000 years before Christ, nothing was reliably known about Danes and their Scandinavian cousins until they materialised as Vikings. As that news was mainly recorded by priests on the run from their depredations, the initial impression formed was not sympathetic.

When at last archaeology prised open the past, the evidence came trickling out in strange and wonderful ways. The earliest signs to date of human activity in Denmark were recognised in a pile of animal bones which, 80,000 years ago, had been tossed into a sand pit like so much litter.

To the unpractised eye, bones are bones. These bones, however, had not only survived what normally happens to old bones but also, amazingly, the crushing pressure of successive ice ages moving first one way and then the other over the site. That these particular bones should then have come to the attention of someone who knew what they meant completes a chain of improbable events next to which winning the proverbial million dollars on a Las Vegas fruit machine cannot hold a candle.

Murder inquiry: The flukes go on. A body dug up in the 1950s was thought at first to be prime evidence of a recent murder: the male victim had close-cropped hair, stubble on his cheeks and was naked but for a woollen cap. Police suspicions concentrated naturally on the rope around his neck. It transpired, however, that the luckless fellow had actually been dead for about 2,000 years, which made it a case for archaeologists rather than policemen. He joined the clues to Denmark's past, many of them objects recovered from the

seabed and – more litter – from the piles of domestic rubbish dumped by ancient Danes on the shore where they spent their summers.

The story of Denmark unfolds against a modest backdrop. Its highest mountain, if that's the word, would struggle to be seen against the Manhattan skyline. The deepest waterfall plunges all of 48 inches (122 cm), or so it's said. The country is only 224 miles (360 km) long and not much wider; it could be swallowed 16 times by Texas alone. Such puny dimensions are especially ironic be-

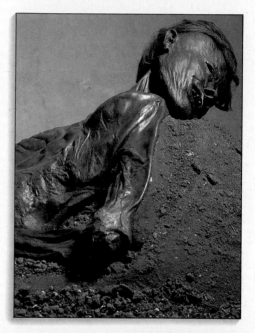

cause Scandinavia is flavoured with the image of rugged Viking-types plodding through wild terrain on primitive skis, fording raging rivers and grunting at the oars as they swept down slab-sided fjords – Norway or Sweden, in fact.

Odder still, then, that modern Denmark, a benign and gregarious place, has replaced its Viking past with dairy and pork products, Tivoli Gardens and Hans Christian Andersen. Denmark's history, however, is out of all proportion to the tiny stage. The Danes wielded a powerful influence over Western and Eastern Europe. They were instrumental in the creation of the English, French and

Preceding pages: the Sun Chariot in the National Museum. **Left,** stone axes in the same museum. **Right,** the Graubelle Man, some 2,000 years old.

Russian empires, initially by opening eyes to the potential of sea-power. The Danes like to think that it was their injection of a virile backbone into the bloodstock of the English that made the difference between the feeble warriors the Romans and then the first Danes encountered and the later empire-builders. By this somewhat tortuous logic, they therefore lay claim to moulding the English-speaking world. In France, the hell-raising Danes became paragons of piety, building cathedrals and dutifully joining the Christian crusades against Muslim infidels.

Throughout the predatory migrations criss-crossing Europe, the Danes clung with singular tenacity to the land of their ancestors. Their line of kings stretches back unbroken, at least over 900 years, to one Gorm the Old, making Denmark one of the world's oldest kingdoms. Tracing the line of kings is by no means straightforward. Denmark's first historian, Saxo, thought there may have been more than 50 Danish kings before the Viking Age, and an 11th-century German, Adam of Bremen, gave up in exasperation when he tried to make sense out of the royal succession: "Whether of all these kings or tyrants in Denmark some ruled the country simultaneously or one lived shortly after the other is uncertain."

Occupying forces: The Danes lost wars, and at times bled themselves dry on improvident military adventures, but they have never surrendered their independence to foreign invaders. It is not quite true, as some historians have claimed, that the Danes have always been entirely their own masters. There was a nadir after the Viking glories when intruders occupied parts of every Danish province. The closest the country came to total capitulation, though, was the Nazi occupation during World War II, when "independence" rested on a slender semantic subtlety. The Danish flag, which according to legend descended from heaven, undoubtedly gave other European countries the idea of adopting a national flag.

At the turn of the 15th century, the Danish-led Kalmar Union was the largest unified kingdom in Europe, covering not only Norway and Sweden but also Finland, Iceland and Greenland. The last alone, still Danish but now self-governing, is four times the size of France. Denmark once ruled Germany as far south as Hamburg, and their shared border right into modern times was a recurring trouble spot, latterly as that well-known, double-barrelled diplomatic nightmare, Sleswig-Holstein. Lord Palmerston once said that this thorny issue had only ever been fully understood by three men: "The first was Prince Albert, who is now dead. The second is a German professor, who has since gone mad. The third is myself, and I have forgotten the details."

Contemporary Danes are usually reticent about, or even slightly embarrassed by, their imperial pedigree. It suits them better now to be thought of as beacons of responsible, decent common sense. They are not, on the whole, as stridently sanctimonious as their Swedish and Norwegian neighbours, not nearly so keen on a state forever poised to rescue its citizens from shameful weaknesses like tobacco and alcohol. Danes had to fight off a long line of despotic monarchs to secure their civil liberties and they are not disposed to surrender them. If there is a price to be paid – if someone seizes on individual rights as a licence to build pornography into a major industry, for example – so be it.

The modern Dane, then, is a fairly amiable soul frequently to be found with a glass of beer in one hand, a cigar in the other and a *bon mot* for most occasions. This is all a far cry from ancestors whose worst fate was to die in bed. They felt obliged to go to their graves in a happy frame of mind, no matter what. "It shall hereafter be recorded in histories," said a royal eulogy, "that King Halfer died laughing."

The cause of Halfer's death is not specified, but it was as likely as not some hideous war wound. Adam of Bremen observed of Danish criminals that they much preferred the axe to any other form of punishment, such as imprisonment or flogging. "As for groans, complaints and other bemoanings of that kind, in which we (Germans) find relief, they are so detested by the Danes, that they think it mean to weep for their sins, or for the death of their dearest relations."

Cheerful fatalism was sometimes carried to what sounds like extreme lengths. In one instance, a warrior thrown to the ground in an armed wrestling match noticed that his opponent in the process had dropped his sword. He offered to wait in the same position while the other man retrieved his weapon to administer the *coup de grâce*. He kept his word.

R.M. Molesworth, sent to Denmark as "Envoy Extraordinary" by King William III of England in 1689, thought the Danes had already lost their warlike nature. Their chief characteristic, he decided, was "gross Cheating", a severe indictment in view of the fact that it was largely formed by his difficulty in buying a goose at what he considered to be an edible age. The locals, he complained, liked them "big and old". Poor Molesworth was paranoid every time he went out shopping. "In their Markets they will ask the same price for stinking Meat, as for fresh; for lean, as for fat..." Whenever he showed interest in some article for sale, the shopkeeper would immediately change his mind and say he was

like the Vistula, Dneiper, Elbe, Danube and Rhine, and indeed there is reason to believe that even before the Viking Age the Danes were sending furs and slaves (as well as amber) east in exchange for gold and bronze.

The first recorded voyage to Scandinavia was by the astronomer, Pytheas of Marseilles, in about 325 BC. His account no longer survives, but in its time it influenced generations of writers, including Strabo (63 BC–AD 25) who described priestesses on a peninsula, presumably Jutland, who sacrificed prisoners of war and foretold the future not in tea-leaves but in blood and intestines. This society, he said, had been discovered by a Roman expedition which had sailed around

going to keep it for himself. Molesworth would have scorned the thought that Denmark could ever become an artful trading nation, not least as the exporters of widely admired pork products.

Despite its northern isolation, there must have been some contact between Denmark and the Ancient World, because amber found only in the Baltic region has turned up in Stone Age remains in Greece and even in Egyptian jewellery. The country was close to the well-worn trading routes along rivers

C.A. Lorentzen's famous painting of the coming of the Dannebrog, Denmark's national flag.

Jutland on the orders of the Emperor Augustus in AD 5.

Ptolemy produced a remarkably accurate description of the "four islands of Scania" (Denmark plus Sweden) in the second century AD, but one wonders where Pliny got his information about a purported animal whose solid legs (i.e. no knees) forced it to sleep upright or, at best, leaning against a tree. The same creature was obliged to walk backwards when grazing – it would otherwise trip over an over-sized upper lip.

A more reliable picture begins to take shape through the observations of Christian missionaries in Charlemagne's time. Flights of fancy nevertheless continued to circulate well into the Middle Ages, like one about a tribe of Amazons, larger and more impressive than some of the lesser women, who merely had beards. The Amazons produced beautiful daughters but their sons, unfortunately, were born with the heads of dogs.

In the 19th century, the new science of archaeology, to which the Danes Christian Thomsen and Jens Worsaae made a substantial contribution, began to assemble a more credible picture of Denmark's prehistory. The beginnings are difficult to trace because the Arctic ice cap shifted remorselessly one way and then the other. When the ice retreated northwards, men followed the thaw to hunt

and fish. When it crept south again, they were forced to retreat to more temperate zones. Parts of Jutland escaped the ice, but elsewhere there was little chance that evidence of early human activity could survive in places which, for thousands of years at a time, were first frozen solid and then awash when the ice melted.

It was during one of these prolonged retreats of the ice that hunters who had moved in to occupy an area near the Gudenå River in North Jutland sat down to eat some deer they had killed. The marrow in the bones was a prized delicacy, and with practised hands they split open the bones to get at it. The

remnants were thrown aside into a pit. The discarded bones lay there as apparently meaningless litter until, in 1912, archaeologists detected that they had been split as could only have been done by human hands. Dating techniques were employed to determine the age of the bones and put it at 80,000 years. It was altogether an astounding conclusion to what must have been at the time an agreeable but hardly exceptional meal.

Archaeology needs such luck in Denmark at least until it reaches the end of the last Ice Age, about 10,000 years ago. That gradual event was a mixed blessing when it happened. Although the thaw made much more inland territory habitable, seas swollen by melting ice flooded the low-lying coastal plains which, as they were warmed by the Gulf Stream, had previously been the most congenial spots for settlement.

As the surge of tides over thousands of years would normally have obliterated all signs of an inundated coastal settlement, divers working in about 10 ft (3 metres) of water in 1976 were initially not sure what to make of unexplained humps in the seabed off Tybrind on the island of Funen. Marine excavation confirmed more than they dared hope for: they had chanced upon a fishing village which had existed 6,000 years ago. They brought up a dug-out canoe 26 ft (8 metres) long and 30 inches (80 cm) wide which had a fire hearth built into the stern and still contained stones, evidently the ballast for some voyage along the Baltic coast, possibly to catch eels, in about 4100 BC.

The canoe, restored and now exhibited at the Moesgård Prehistoric Museum in Århus, was only part of the story which unfolded around Tybrind. There had once been, it transpired, a village with a road leading down to a port. The houses had perished, but there were still signs of the stone roadway and of mooring posts. The settlement had evidently been inhabited for well over a millennium: it offered up a wealth of artefacts including pottery, stakes, bows, spears, wooden arrowheads and various implements, including fish hooks, made out of antler and bone. Human remains were found: a woman and child in a grave and the scattered bones of at least four other people.

In 1987, Korshavn in North Funen produced another exciting find: a boat similar in design to the Tybrind example but older by

1,000 years or so. Apart from the German frontier, which in its present state is 40 miles (65 km) long, Denmark is surrounded by sea and, furthermore, stands like Gibraltar at the junction of the strategic North and Baltic Seas. The need to exploit the sea, and in times of danger to defend the sea approaches, put a premium on maritime skills. Boats are therefore key items in Danish archaeology, and more than 250 dug-out boats have been recovered. Many ended their working lives as coffins pushed out to sea. The 2,000-year-old Hjortespring boat on display in the National Museum in Copenhagen is significant as a prototype of later Viking design.

Burial chambers: A more benevolent and stable climate in the latter part of the Stone Age (13000 to 1800 BC) brought about rapid progress on land as well. Changing burial practices are the milestones of cultural development. The most familiar relics, of which no fewer than 23,000 examples are still to be seen, are stone cairns, or "dolmens", a number of upright stones topped by a huge capstone. The mechanics of getting the capstone into position inspired the sort of debate surrounding the construction of the Egyptian pyramids. In any case, the dolmens imply a considerable degree of technical skill on the part of the builders. Their design became ever more ambitious until they were oblong chambers capable of holding more than 100 bodies, the approach being through stone-lined passages.

The Stone Age farmers who ended up in dolmens spent their summers at the coast. Refuse from one summer after another piled up, an unplanned treasure trove for future archaeologists. These kitchen middens, as they are called, have revealed a varied diet of birds, shellfish (especially mussels and oysters), seal and game. Food was cooked and stored in large jars which could be made to stand upright by pushing their pointed bases into the ground, a design that probably originated in the Aegean. Nights were lit by blubber burnt in crucibles.

The Bronze Age, normally put at around 1500 BC, opened Denmark's frontiers. Furs, slaves and amber went out; bronze and bronze objects came in. Local craftsmen proved

adept at copying the imported items and were soon producing fair imitations of bronze swords and other articles, right down to the decorative motifs.

In some respects, though, the Danes resisted change. They stuck to religious beliefs which, in common with a religious movement then convulsing Egypt, was rooted in sun worship. The sun god was courted with the trombone tones of a curved horn known as the *lur*, still to be seen on packets of Danish butter. The finest surviving tribute to the sun is unfortunately only a contemporary model of the original object, a huge gilded disc which, mounted on six wheels and drawn by a gilded horse, would have been carried

through the fields to bring down a blessing on the crops.

In common with the rich classes almost everywhere, Danes who profited from the boom in commerce insisted on taking the trappings of success to their graves. They were buried with their finest weapons in oak coffins whose tannin helped to preserve not only the clothes they were buried in but also nails and hair. A young girl, interred at Egtved in eastern Jutland, was found to be wearing a short, woollen skirt wound twice around her hips, a short-sleeved jacket and a belt decorated with a large bronze disc. Her hair and nails were carefully groomed. Men

Left, reconstructed dug-out canoes at the Stone Age village of Hjerl Hede in Jutland. **Above**, return to the past at Hjerl Hede.

generally wore kilts with shoulder straps, cloaks and tall, woollen caps.

Cold comfort: A dramatic change in the climate occurred in about 500 BC. While Athenians basked in warm sunshine as they built the Parthenon, temperatures dropped suddenly in Denmark. For some time previously, Denmark and even Norway had enjoyed a climate rather milder than has been experienced since. Among the first casualties were the clothes worn since the Bronze Age. Kilts and short skirts were out, trousers and underwear came in. Building had to be more substantial, not only for humans but also for animals which had previously been left to graze outdoors all year round.

idea that they had a murder inquiry to attend to. All the bog people seem to have met violent deaths, not least the famous Grauballe Man (in the Moesgård Museum in Århus) whose throat was very comprehensively cut.

The manner of these deaths suggests a religious ritual, probably a sacrifice to the fertility goddess for a good harvest and to ward off pestilence. Rings and necklaces found with some of the bodies were symbolic of the goddess concerned. From around the same period is one of the country's most exciting archaeological digs near Roskilde. An unusually large long-house, discovered in 1986, offered a tantalising prize of jewellery and other valuable artefacts. It was no

The solution was the long house with thick earth walls and a roof supported on a central row of wooden posts. The animals stayed at one end, radiating warmth in what almost qualifies as an early form of central heating.

The water in Denmark's peat bogs has an acid and iron content which is responsible for vivid confirmation of people's physical appearance in the Iron Age which succeeded the Bronze. Hermetically sealed in peat, the bodies of some 160 "bog people" have been extracted in an extraordinary state of preservation; the most notable was the Tollund Man, the fellow who, on being removed from the turf near Silkeborg, gave police the

ordinary residence, which led archaeologists to wonder whether it was Denmark's long-lost capital, the home of the early Vikings.

It is at this point that Danish history is transformed. Instead of being drawn from inanimate objects, it comes alive with people who have names like Harald Bluetooth, Sweyn Forkbeard, Magnus the Good and Eric the Very Good. The names are sometimes a clue to their character but in any case, thanks to the scalds, they are able to speak.

Above, Archaeological Research Centre, Lejre. **Right**, working holiday at Lejre. **Following pages**: beautiful Viking Age golden horns .

RELIVING THE IRON AGE IN LEJRE

A week in an Iron Age long house, wreathed in smoke, with the only light filtering hazily through a low door, may not seem the most inviting way to spend a holiday. Yet modern Danish families queue up to try out this primitive life at North Sealand's Iron Age village.

The village is part of the Historical Archaeological Research Centre at Lejre, just west of Roskilde (off road 21/23) and people who choose a holiday in the Iron Age are the raw material for the Centre's research into ancient ways of life.

The Centre opened in 1964 with the aim of re-creating a landscape of the past. The underlying theory was that, by imitating primitive methods of farming and living, Lejre could discover what effects different forms of cultivation had on the ground. This became a cross-check to deductions drawn by archaeologists working on sites from similar periods. It is also often faster. It may take archaeologists thousand of hours to trace patterns of life in a hut from the erosion on a clay floor. The Lejre Centre need only leave a family to fend for itself in the Iron Age village for a couple of weeks to find they live to a totally different pattern.

Lejre was founded by its first director, Hans-Ole Hansen. Hansen had been interested in primitive hunting weapons and household implements since his boyhood and he had already helped build a long house at Allerslev, south of Lejre.

After Danish Television took an interest in that project, the Carlsberg Foundation offered Dkr 500,000 (around £50,000) to expand the new "science" of recreating the past. With more volunteers, Hansen set about building the Iron Age village, using only traditional tools and building methods. It has houses, paved streets and wells, surrounded by a high wooden stake fence, as authentic as the Lejre builders could devise.

The Centre now covers many other periods of Danish history, ranging from a late Paleolithic Stone Age site to the reconstruction of 18th and 19th-century workshops and a "land labourer's"

house of the same period. Its summer season includes training in forgotten techniques, and demonstrations of past technologies and crafts, for schools and seminars as well as more casual visitors. Nevertheless, in this curious mixture of academic institution, museum and visitor centre, the Stone Age village and its dedicated holiday-makers are the greatest attraction.

The houses, which crouch low, are copies of excavations from various parts of Denmark, with side walls around 3 to 4 ft (1 metre) high, and sloping, shaggy, thatched roofs. Inside they are dark and draughty. The reaction from modern families, used to double-glazing and central heating, is astonishment. But the houses are soon crowded with food supplies, tools, a hand spinner, tanning hides, and piles of wood for the central fire. Above hang drying plants, hunks of smoked meat and cheeses, and drying clothes, almost as smoky.

Lack of light affects the families most, and the need to bend, both to avoid the "smoke loft" and to duck under the door. It is not so much that Iron Age people were small but that they spent most of their lives doubled over. Some modern Iron Age dwellers choose contemporary garments and the Centre can provide Iron Age food, primitive cooking utensils, and instruction in using them.

All this is fascinating to the 100,000 or so visitors who may have no ambitions to live as our ancestors did but enjoy taking the Centre's marked route back into the past. The tour lasts around three hours and is 2 miles (3 km) long. In the old workshops potters make copies of prehistoric Danish pottery, fired in Dätgen kilns, sunk into the hillside; weavers copy Iron Age garments and others experiment with, and teach the skills of, natural dyeing.

There is a sacrificial bog, prehistoric dancing, and the nearest modern strains to ancient crops. These usually come from the Middle East and Pakistan and are planted on ground tilled with an ard, an ancient plough. Most interesting of all are the long-nosed pigs which snuffle through the ground, a cross between wild boar and domestic pig. There are Gotland sheep, ancient species of goats and hens, Iceland cows (nearest modern relative of the Iron Age cattle) and a sturdy little horse that looks like a Shetland pony.

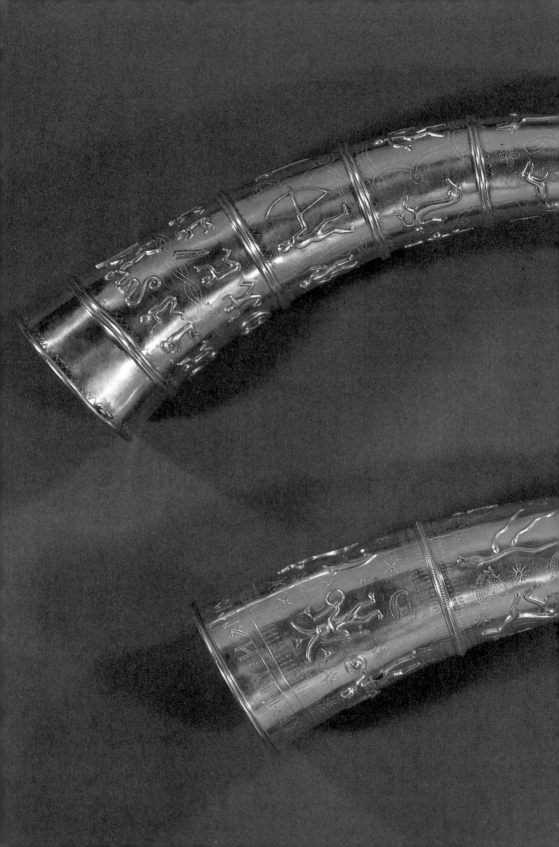

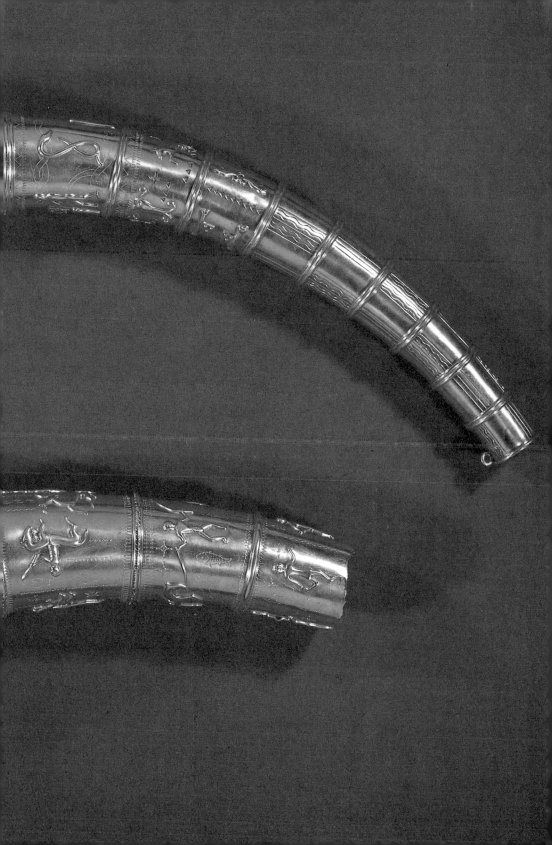

THE VIKINGS AT LARGE

In 789, the Vikings descended like bolts from the blue to refute dubious theories about strange folk living in the north. The sheriff of Dorset in England was one of the first to be enlightened.

The Vikings arrived unannounced in three ships of a design markedly different from anything seen in English waters before. The language they spoke among themselves made no sense at all, but strangers had been turning up at English ports since Phoenician times and the sheriff assumed that the purpose of the visit was, as usual, trade. He invited them to the royal manor house to determine by one means or another what they wanted and what they could offer in exchange. He was being naive. The Vikings battered him to death, bundled everything of value into their ships, including some of the startled population, and disappeared.

If the Vikings found the sheriff of Dorset naive, they rejoiced in the blind faith which left rich pickings for the taking in isolated, undefended monasteries. In a Christian society, monasteries were protected by their sanctity. To the robustly pagan Vikings, this was absurd, as the bodies of monks strewn around the plundered Lindisfarne monastery in Northumberland testified when the Vikings called again four years later and sailed away in ships loaded to the gunwales. One or two other monasteries suffered a similar fate before the Vikings left England alone for about 40 years while they explored opportunities elsewhere. When the raids resumed, they were organised like annual summer outings.

The tempo of raids had every monastery in England, Ireland and France praying for deliverance from the wrath of these "Northmen" and, specifically, from their throat-cutting. The Muslims in Spain and in North Africa did more than pray. When Vikings captured Seville in 844, they fought back. The Vikings suffered a notable reverse, and those taken prisoner were too numerous to be dealt with on the city's gallows. They were hanged – and left hanging – from trees.

There may have been some method in the way the Vikings cultivated their atrocious reputation. Small raiding parties, no matter how daring, would always have been vulnerable while moving about among a large and truculent native population. If the mere suspicion of their presence was enough to make everyone scatter, their work was made that much easier and they would probably have been well clear before effective countermeasures could be organised. Vikings who fell into English hands had nothing to look forward to: scalping was routine and some wretches were flayed, their skins being nailed to church doors. As years went by, however, a growing number of raiders decided against going home for the winter and struck up a *modus vivendi* with the locals.

It meant nothing to victims whether their tormentors were Danes,

Norwegians or Swedes, and of course Vikings did not sit down patiently to explain distinctions which, in any case, would have been far from clear in their own minds. Even "Viking" is vague; the original form probably referred to "men of the creek" but in the 9th and 10th centuries it took on the unequivocal meaning of "sea robber". There were then so many peripatetic chieftainships in Scandinavia, and so much intermarriage between the leading families, that any thought of national identities in the modern sense would be inappropriate.

Moreover, many accounts of Vikings on the warpath were by priests in no position to press questions on their pursuers. The early chronicles are therefore full of Norsemen (implicitly Norwegians) who were actually Danes, and "Danes" who were almost certainly Norwegians. Only in the very broadest terms, then, can it be said that the Vikings who pushed eastwards by land into Russia and ultimately to Constantinople were predominantly "Swedes", while "Norwegians" sailed west to Scotland, the smaller British isles and Ireland, thence leapfrogging via Iceland and Greenland all the way to America. The "Danes" busied themselves in Germany and, in competition with "Norwegians", in England and France.

The impulse which caused the Vikings suddenly to abandon their isolation has been debated with the same uncertainty surrounding the tags of nationality. One of the theories put forward is that lustful pagan polygamy produced more people than the land could support. Although the tradition of dividing land equally among legitimate and illegitimate sons (in prolific numbers) would have placed a greater strain on the notoriously unyielding terrain of western Norway than on Denmark, the argument that land hunger drove the Vikings abroad is generally plausible. Less so, however, is the romantic view that the Vikings – slightly flawed, perhaps, but no more than that – were on some kind of pre-ordained mission as exemplars of egalitarianism, artistic sensitivity, good government and other qualities which mankind had been lacking since Pericles.

The Viking explosion has also been interpreted as a pagan revolt which very nearly finished off Christianity when it was on its knees in Europe, between the fall of the Roman Empire in the West and the spiritual resurgence generated by the Crusades. That threat, at least, was removed when the Vikings embraced Christianity and ploughed into their new cause the same zeal which, under pagan colours, had so recently caused universal panic. Mass conversion to Christianity was actually effected at home less by theological dialogue than by the thrust of a sword.

The adventures of an admiral named Hastings indicate that the Vikings were not over-awed by the mystical powers of the "White Cross", as they called Christianity. He entered the Mediterranean in about 857 with a fleet of about 100 vessels with a view to investigating and if at all possible plundering Rome. As it happens, the city he approached while it was celebrating the feast of Christmas was not Rome at all but Luna, the ancient Etruscan city.

Nevertheless, the defences looked formidable so he "had recourse to that perfidy which a Northman never scrupled to employ against an adversary." He sent word to the Bishop that he merely wished to repair and replenish his battered fleet, but he also dropped the tantalising hint that he had grown tired of seafaring and might be inclined to consider Christianity "in order to find that repose in the bosom of the church which he had had so long sighed for." The Bishop leapt at the prospect of such an unexpected baptism but

regretted, having administered it, that the new convert would not be allowed to enter the city. He could, however, camp outside, and the Italians warily agreed to supply him with provisions and other necessities.

The loud wailing which soon reached the Bishop's ears from the camp was explained as a lament for Hastings who had suddenly fallen ill and was not expected to live. The messenger advised the Bishop that Hastings had intimated that he would leave all his booty to the church (the ships had profitably called at Spain, North Africa and the Balearic islands en route) provided the Bishop conceded a Christian burial within the city. Shortly afterwards, crestfallen Viking pall-bearers filed into the city with the coffin and set it down in the cathedral.

The Bishop himself was leading the service for the repose of the admiral's soul when the coffin flew open and, sword drawn, Hastings ran the Bishop through. The pall-bearers thereupon drew their weapons and Hastings, pall-bearers and reinforcements were quickly masters of the city, "which they set fire to, after committing their usual acts of ferocity". Hastings then loaded his already creaking ships with more booty and sailed for home, "not forgetting to take with him the handsomest women of Luna."

The normal authorities can only guess that Hastings was a Dane, but Denmark has undisputed title to the legendary Jomsburg Vikings, a *corps d'élite* founded by a certain Palnatoki in the reign of Harald Bluetooth (941–91) and featuring such luminaries as "Bui the Thick" and Vagn, "the most unruly and turbulent youngster who ever sailed on a Viking cruise." They were based in an island camp on the Baltic coast of Germany, probably at what is now Wolin. The camp seems to have been run along the lines of a boarding school as may have been devised in Sparta. No one was admitted until proving that "he did not fear to face two men equally as strong and well armed as himself." In any case, no one under 15 or over 50 was allowed in (the turbulent Vagn, Palnatoki's grandson, excepted) and certainly not any female. No one was allowed to leave for more than one night without Palnatoki's personal permission.

When the spotlight of recorded history suddenly floods the Danish stage, it reveals what had been happening in the shadows since the days when the inhabitants were mainly occupied by spearing reindeer with flint weapons and chasing seals at the edge of the ice. The country was well on its way to becoming a recognisable nation, the scores of warring chieftainships having forged some degree of unity under the time-honoured threat of hostile neighbours.

In this case, the principal threat was Charlemagne and his Christian hordes to the south. A king named Godfred first threw up the celebrated Danevirke defensive line across the Jutland peninsula, but others like Horik pushed beyond that until in 811 Denmark had established its southern border at the Eider River.

Astonishing speed: Also in the shadows, as we have seen, the Scandinavians as a whole had been applying themselves to ship design, the development of a strong keel capable of securing a substantial mast being the key to long sea voyages. The standard long boat was about 60 ft (20 metres) long, powered by 30 oars and a sail, but still so light that its crew could when necessary drag it across land. They could attain the astonishing speed of 10–11 knots in bursts and, as a hinged rudder on one side of the stern would fold up under impact, they could be driven on to a beach at full tilt. At this watershed in history, the emergence of the dreaded Vikings, the navy which made it possible was already a *fait accompli*.

Marvellous tales pour from the pages of the Sagas. The rows of empty shelves in the library are suddenly crammed with information. The writers responsible for the transformation drew on the oral traditions of the scalds. Although they were expected by the kings who employed them to make the most of their victories and fine personal qualities and skip over the other stuff, they managed by innuendo and plain cheek to present a remarkably balanced picture.

Left, the romanticised view – modern "Viking" in so-called traditional costume in the Viking play *Rolf Krake*.

The famous King Knud (Canute in English), whom we shall soon be meeting, provides a glimpse of the royal relationship with scalds. It came to his notice that a visiting Icelandic scald, one Toraren Praisetongue, had produced some unauthorised verses about him. He ordered Praisetongue to present himself the following day and recite these verses – or be hanged. Perhaps Praisetongue made some hasty revisions, but in any case the king found the verses very acceptable, especially the bit about:

Knud wards the land, as Christ,
The shepherd of Greece, doth the heaven.

Revision or not, Praisetongue not only saved his neck with this inspired passage but was rewarded on the spot with 50 marks of silver. The verses were ever afterwards known as "The Head Ransom".

The manner in which the first wave of Vikings pounced out of the north on an unsuspecting Europe is covered in the feature on pages 38–39. It recounts how these early terrorists (or cultural ambassadors, as romantics would have it) increasingly chose to remain in the lands they scourged, and that in itself led to a different kind of problem. In England, the well-groomed Danes (they bathed on Saturdays) made a greater impression on English women than was good for them, which contributed to a war which resulted in Sweyn Forkbeard, then king of Denmark, conquering virtually the whole of England and incorporating it in a Danish empire in 1014.

War over the women of England is a lovely idea but, alas, altogether too simple. Denmark was actually suffering an economic crisis because the changing map of Europe had closed the long-used oriental trade route along the Volga, depriving Denmark, the western terminus of that route, of markets for its amber, furs and slaves in the east and cutting off its supplies of Arabic silver. At the start there had been plenty of substitute wealth in the unguarded monasteries of Europe, but there was a more efficient way of extracting foreign assets. It revolved around conquest, occupation and the collection of tribute from the cowed natives. The name given to this institutionalised blackmail has a resonant historical ring: Danegeld.

Forkbeard the Conqueror has rather unfairly been eclipsed in history by a distant kinsman, William, who in 1066 (i.e. less than 50 years after Forkbeard's conquest) arrived in England with the descendants of Vikings who had settled in Normandy. Forkbeard was a pagan but he produced a son and heir who earned the accolade of being "the first Viking leader to be admitted into the civilised fraternity of Christian kings." The son, Knud, was said to be "of great size and strength, and very handsome except that his nose was thin, high and slightly bent. He had a light complexion and fair, thick hair, and his eyes surpassed the eyes of most men, in beauty and in keeness."

Knud was already king of England (as King Canute) when he succeeded his brother two years later and became king of Denmark as well. In England, the most familiar incident in Canute's reign is the exact opposite of what actually happened. He placed his throne on the beach but it was not to defy the incoming tide. It seems he was bored with obsequious courtiers who kept on saying that he was master of the universe etc. He sat on the beach and let the waves engulf him precisely to demonstrate that he was not master of the seas, whatever they said.

Chess games: Knud fares almost as badly in Danish folklore, which depicts him as a shocking loser at chess. It seems he was playing a game with his kinsman, Ulf the Jarl, during a lull in a campaign against Sweden and Norway when he made an ill-considered move and lost a knight. Knud put his knight back on the board and said he wanted to try a different move. This was too much for Ulf, who overturned the board and walked out. "Runnest thou off, Ulf the Coward?" the king taunted. Ulf turned at the door, shouted "Thou didst not call me Ulf the Coward when I came to thy help when the Swedes were beating you like dogs," and went to bed.

In the morning, Knud told his shoe-lad to get rid of him. The lad found his intended victim at prayer in St Luke's Church, the cathedral in Roskilde, and thought it was the wrong place and time for a summary execution. A Norwegian named Ivar the White had no such qualms, however, and ran his sword through him, "whereby Ulf the Jarl met his bane." The monks in charge were appalled at the sacrilege but felt better about it when Knud granted the church "great lands so that it became a big lordship."

Knud's conscience – the popular version of events continues – drove him to seek forgiveness for this outrage from the Pope. In reality, he had political reasons for the visit, which coincided with the coronation of Conrad IV as Holy Roman Emperor. Knud needed support for – or at least acquiescence in – his plans to expand his empire. In modern terms, then, the meeting was an informal "summit", and by publicly posing with these powerful personages Knud hoped to convey the impression that he was one among equals. He made a great show of it, insisting on taking a place in the coronation procession at Conrad's side.

He planned to run his empire, which already incorporated Norway, parts of Sweden and a number of outposts along the Baltic coast, from a capital in England. The enterprise was cut short, however, by his untimely death when he was only 37, so the full potential was never realised of a man who bows out as, genuinely, the father of Christianity in Denmark, and, unjustly, as a pompous idiot or poor loser at chess.

Knud's various sons and heirs were not equal to keeping his imperial dream alive. One of them, Hartha-Knud, kept a united England and Denmark going for a while but dropped dead from drink at a wedding feast in Lambeth. According to the chronicler of the period, "He never did anything royal." The English throne went to Edward the Confessor, the Danish to Magnus the Good of Norway.

On his death-bed in 1047, he passed Norway on to Sven, the Danish son of the chess casualty, Ulf. Sven "held the whole history of the barbarians in his memory, as it were in a written book" and fathered 19 children, only one of whom was legitimate and anyway died in infancy. Sven's notable qualities – "handsome, tall and strong, generous and wise, just and brave but never victorious in war" – seem to have eluded his offspring. One of them, Harald, was known as "the Hen".

On the feeble note of royalty relegated to the level of poultry, the imperial Denmark of the Viking Age petered out. Many Danes remained in the colonial outposts and were assimilated. Those who went home retreated into a domestic madhouse, with rivals drowning one another (the preferred method was to wrap the chosen victim in heavy chains and throw him into deep water) and difficult clergymen being forced to sit in prison wearing funny hats.

Knud IV, great-nephew of his illustrious namesake, had the idea of re-conquering England. A fleet of 1,000 ships assembled for that purpose and waited a whole summer for Knud to show up and lead them across the North Sea. He didn't, and they went home. Knud earned the distinction of becoming Denmark's first saint, partly because at his funeral, having been murdered in church,

a third of it lost to Denmark's *bête noire*, a tribe of Baltic Slavs usually referred to as "the heathen Wends" who had based themselves on the island of Rugen. Valdemar was fortunate in being able to call on the Bishop of Roskilde to find a solution to the loathsome tribe.

Absalon, Bishop of Roskilde, is rare in history as being equally comfortable in the role of bishop, statesman, warrior, literary patron and admiral. He took to the Wends with a vengeance, storming their supposedly impregnable temple stronghold and rubbing in the humiliation by requiring the Wend priests to assemble and watch him demolish their gigantic wooden god, the four-headed

"two days' unceasing rain stopped, the sun shone in a blue sky and all present joined in a *Te Deum*." Modern authorities in these matters are not impressed. "Little justification for his being made a saint," sniffs one.

Violent departure: Never were the Danish nobility more certain of avoiding the old Viking stigma of death in bed than in the decade of civil war after 1147. Valdemar I only narrowly avoided a violent departure before rising to survey a kingdom in tatters,

Above, Viking festival in Britain's Isle of Man, once one of many Viking strongholds in their far-flung empire.

Svantovit. Reduced to splinters, Svantovit was handed around to the Danish troops to be used as firewood. Absalon then marched on to the Wend capital, Garz, and did the same to the seven-headed Rugeivit. The Wends could take no more. They agreed to immediate baptism as Christians and surrendered their island, which was thereafter part of the bishopric of Roskilde.

Absalon next applied himself to the defence against pirates of a fishing village called Havn. The fortified village was first known as Kaupmanna Havn (Chapmen's or Merchants' Haven) and later as København (Copenhagen). The stronghold which

Absalon built in 1168 was on the site now occupied by the Christiansborg Palace and it is fittingly his statue – on horseback, battle-axe in hand but a bishop nevertheless – which stands nearby. Although he was somewhat overshadowed by the energetic bishop, Valdemar was always a popular king who, on his death, "was lamented by all Denmark for which he fought more than 28 battles in heathen lands and warred against the pagans to the glory of God's church so long as he lived."

With the Wends out of the way, Valdemar II pursued the Estonians with the same venom. He very nearly over-reached himself at the battle of Lyndanise. His attack with an armada of 1,000 ships on the city of Reval was all but lost when a red banner with a white cross in the centre floated down from heaven. It provided just the tonic the Danish forces needed to turn the battle around and win. The "Danish Cloth" (*Dannebrog*) was adopted as the national flag, setting a precedent for the flags which would later flutter over every country in the world.

Valdemar II turned Reval into a fortress, which was tantamount to annexing the Baltic as a Danish lake. Just when it looked as if Valdemar was within reach of emulating the great Knud's empire, he made a poor choice in asking Count Henry of Schwerin to join him and his son on a hunting trip to Lyo, a small island south of Funen. The date was 6 May 1223. "In one day," a contemporary historian notes grimly, "this Empire, and with it the hegemony of the North, crumbled to dust." Count Henry, it seems, nursed a secret grudge over some confiscated property. He crept up to the tent where Valdemar and his son were sleeping, and marched them off to the dungeon in Danneberg, his castle on the Elbe in Germany.

The unfortunate Valdemar was not released until two years later, and only then on humiliating terms. The ransom was 45,000 marks in silver, all the Queen's jewellery, arms and equipment for 100 knights, the whole Danish empire bar Rugen. He had to provide hostages and take an oath to keep the peace. He had to seek a special dispensation from the Pope to be released from the vow. The Pope listened to the circumstances and agreed that it had been taken under unreasonable duress.

Valdemar was therefore free to seek revenge with a clear conscience but the results were disappointing. He lost an eye at the battle of Bornhoved and decided that he would rather study law. His *Liber Census Daniae*, drawn up in 1231, is the Danish Domesday book.

Tottering throne: Valdemar's four sons all became Kings of Denmark in turn, but the throne was by then hollow. "At the death of Valdemar II," the Ryd Monastery annals say, "the crown fell off the head of the Danes. From that time forth they became a laughing-stock for all their neighbours through civil wars and mutual destruction, and the lands which they had honourably won with their sword were not only lost but caused great disasters to the realm and wasted it."

For a century afterwards, most kings had only the consolation of not dying in bed. The alliance between church and state in particular broke down, the church threatening kings with ex-communication, the kings replying, for instance, by throwing the Archbishop of Lund, Jacob Erlandson, into a dungeon. He was chained and forced to wear a cap made out of fox tails.

The only respite from this mayhem was in the royal personage of Eric Klipping, who ascended the throne at the age of 11. In 1282 he enacted Denmark's Magna Carta at Nyborg. Parliament was to meet once a year and no one was to be imprisoned without trial. Ultimately, the high-minded Eric fared no better than his contemporaries. His misfortune was also to go hunting. Exhausted after a hard day in the field, he slumped in a barn and was found the following morning with 56 wounds to the body.

Norway was behind the assassination. The perpetrators were greeted there as heroes and made the subject of sentimental ballads. Their agent in Denmark was identified as Archbishop Jens Grand, who was accordingly thrown into a dungeon as "the lowest criminal with every circumstance of ignominy until December 1295, when he escaped." Pope Boniface VIII took a different view of him, declaring him a martyr because "there was many a saint in heaven who had suffered less in the cause of God." Norway and Denmark embarked on a long war over the affair.

Denmark's difficulties were altogether too much for Christopher II, "the most faithless and useless ruler Denmark has ever had." He was made to step aside (he died in "extreme poverty") while the monarchy was carved up among a number of foreign princes, notably Count Gerhard III of Holstein, who also fell victim to a murderer who crept up on him in his sleep. Denmark badly needed a saviour.

Valdemar IV, only 20 or so when he ascended the throne, was determined to make himself "Restorer of Denmark" and, while being forced to sell Estonia to settle debts and to cope with the ravages of the Black Death, conceived an elaborate plot which would win back England. He threw his hat into the ring of the Hundred Years' War, offering to help out France by invading

but, for the poor, the ordinary kinds of fish were an unaffordable luxury.

The Frenchman interpreted the herring as divine intervention, a fish so small and numerous that Lent could be properly observed even by the most wretched peasant. Danish and German fishermen were drawn to the Sound in scenes which anticipated the Californian gold rush, 40,000 boats at a time scooping up the herring. The fish were in any case a budget-saving godsend for the king, whose revenue from the tax imposed on catches exceeded the revenue available from all other sources put together.

Flush with money, Valdemar gave full vent to ambition. He began by capturing

England with 12,000 men for 600,000 florins. His son, he thought, could usefully marry a French princess.

As the scheme came to nothing, the 600,000 florins did not materialise, but Valdemar received a windfall from a quarter which no one could have anticipated. Fantastic shoals of herring appeared in the Sound, so tightly packed that, according to a Frenchman who witnessed the phenomenon, "one may cut them in two with a sword." Everyone was obliged to eat fish during Lent

Above, each year Viking plays are held at Frederikssund, north of Copenhagen.

Visby, a rich Hansa town in Gotland, off the east coast of Sweden, and proclaimed himself "King of the Goths", a title still borne by Danish monarchs. The Hanseatic traders recognised the threat and took the 77 cities they controlled into union with Sweden, Mecklenburg and Holstein. Valdemar's campaign ground to a halt and he was forced to seek asylum abroad. In future, the victorious allies declared, they would have the last say over who ruled Denmark. They had no objections when Margrethe, Queen of Håkon VI of Norway, proposed her five-year-old son, Oluf.

Margrethe had been married to the much

older King Håkon when she was 10; she was only 17 when she gave birth to her first and only son, Oluf. As the precocious power behind Håkon's throne, she was in the perfect position to hone her natural political abilities. Steering the baby Oluf on to the Danish throne was merely her opening shot. The addition of the Norwegian crown to Oluf's head was automatic on the death of his father in 1380. Her move on Sweden began when Oluf turned 15 and, on his mother's recommendation, started calling himself "the true heir to Sweden". The claim was based on his hereditary connection with the dispossessed Folkung dynasty and infuriated King Albrecht, who occupied that

her grand-nephew, Eric of Pomerania, who met the requirements of the Norwegian Council and was proclaimed hereditary sovereign. Eric was seven. Sweden, however, still eluded her net.

Oluf's contentious claim to the Swedish throne had rested, as stated, on the Folkung pretender, Bo Jonsson Grip, and when Grip died Margrethe persuaded the Swedish nobles to transfer all his fortresses and most of his land to her in exchange for future guarantees of their privileges. The nobles therefore acknowledged her as Sweden's "sovereign lady and rightful master" but there was still Albrecht to contend with. He went off to recruit a mercenary army in

throne on what he considered to be legitimate grounds.

Margrethe's designs on Sweden were taken aback by Oluf's death in 1387 when he was only 17. His mother – "a dark complexion and somewhat masculine in appearance" – stepped into his shoes and within a week assumed titles like "Our Sovereign Lady, the Guardian of the Realm" and "The Right Heir and Princess of Denmark." The Norwegian lords were speedily impressed into recognising her as their "mighty lady and master" although this was in clear contravention of the Norwegian law of succession. She settled misgivings in this respect by producing

Germany but was routed soon afterwards by Swedish and Danish forces at Falköping.

Albrecht was dragged off the battlefield in chains and Margrethe fulfilled her long desired goal. "God," said a contemporary chronicle, "gave an unexpected victory into the hands of a woman." To which another added, "All the nobility of Denmark were seized by fear of the wisdom and strength of this lady."

The union of the three countries was formally enacted with Eric's triple coronation at Kalmar in 1397, appropriately enough on Trinity Sunday. Eric was then 14. In theory, the three countries were equal; in practice,

Denmark was very much the senior partner. Norway's participation at the coronation seems to have been through the Bishop of Orkney, and he was an Englishman.

The coronation became "the most intensely discussed single event in Nordic history" because of a contradiction in two documents drawn up at the time. One proclaimed that the three realms would forever be united under one king, the other that, after Eric, the countries could individually choose a king from his direct descendants or, if they weren't any, from elsewhere. The immediate effect, though, was the creation of an empire which stretched from the Gulf of Finland to the Varanger Fjord on the Polar

schemes. She was on her boat in Flensborg, trying to unravel a war he had started with Holstein, when she died, thus surrendering "the greatest personal position ever achieved in Scandinavia."

In spite of her prodigious achievements, very little is known about her personally. There is a glimpse of her in straitened circumstances as Håkon's young bride in Norway, a letter begging him to arrange credit with a Hansa merchant in Oslo so that she could pay the servants, but little else has survived. The effigy on her tomb in Roskilde cathedral depicts her as eternally, enigmatically young.

Eric stumbled along, trying to undermine

Seas and south to the Eider. It included the islands of Orkney, Shetland, Faroe, Iceland and Greenland. It was twice the size of the German empire.

Young Eric turned out to be "rash, violent and obstinate", and Margrethe spent much of her time trying to repair the damage caused by his ill-considered and badly carried out

Far left, an altarpiece from Skt Olai Kirke in Helsingør showing a bishop ministering and giving alms to a party of lepers. **Left**, a frescoe in the church at Lolland which is said to be a rare depiction of Queen Margrethe. **Above**, an ivory crucifix in Herlufsholm Kirke, near Næstved.

the power of the Hanseatic League and developing Copenhagen as a royal seat. He managed to antagonise his subjects in all three kingdoms and, in a pointed anticlimax to the optimism at Kalmar, he threw in the towel. The manner of his departure at least adds a little romance to this disappointing monarch. He went off with his favourite mistress to Visborg Castle in Gotland and there established himself as, of all things, an efficient and prosperous pirate. One of the demands made of his successor, his nephew Christopher, was to suppress these piratical exploits. Christopher declined to do so, quipping: "Uncle must live too."

Christian II (1513–23) brought "genius and madness" to the throne although by then Sweden had backed out of the Kalmar union and was running its own affairs. As crown prince and his father's regent in Norway, he had averted a similar move towards independence there by murdering the Swedish-Norwegian nobleman Knut Alvsson. His death, according to Ibsen, plucked the heart out of Norway, which for a long time afterwards was reduced to little more than a Danish province.

Norway continued to trouble him, however, because it harboured pockets of Hansa authority in cities like Bergen. It was in Bergen that Christian was attracted to the daughter of a Dutch market woman and asked for a dance. "In that dance," sighs the chronicler Arild Huitfeldt (echoing Valdemar II's decision to take Count Henry of Schwerin along on his hunting trip), "he danced away the three kingdoms of Denmark, Norway and Sweden."

Dove tale: Christian actually married the 13-year-old Isabella of Burgundy, an arrangement which cemented links with the House of Habsburg and the Emperor Maximilian, her grandfather. The "little dove" (Dyveke), as he called the Dutch girl, was kept at hand, however, a few miles outside Copenhagen. When Maximilian heard about the arrangement, he demanded the little dove's immediate expulsion from Denmark. Christian's response was to move her and her mother even closer – in fact, to a house around the corner from his palace. It seems that living in the city centre, Dyveke may have caught the eye of the governor of Copenhagen castle, one Torben Oxe.

There is some doubt as to what happened. Oxe may have made advances and been rebuffed. He may then have conspired to make her eat a bowl of poisoned cherries. In any case, in the fourth year of Christian's reign, the little dove died. Oxe was arrested and, over the pleading of the queen, who

went on her knees before Christian, was sentenced and executed.

The affair was not merely a domestic melodrama but a symptom of Christian's attempts to tug his kingdom into the Renaissance era taking place elsewhere in Europe. These necessitated a high degree of monarchical authority, which could only be at the expense of the nobility. Moreover, his upbringing had given him both bourgeois sympathies and a hostile suspicion of the nobility, as exemplified by Torben Oxe.

Some authorities believe that Oxe was wholly innocent or, at least, that the case against him was never proven.

The real consequences of the dance in Bergen, however, were not so much the ill-fated affair but the looming figure of the mother, Sigbrit. A former student of alchemy and medicine, she came to believe that she possessed telepathic powers which gave her remote control over the King. Of common stock herself, her hatred of the nobility spurred Christian's bourgeois reservations. The idea of a king reaching over the heads of the nobility to lend a hand to the commoners is one that has inspired Danes to

Preceding pages: *Dawn: Luther at Erfurt*, by Joseph Noel Paton. **Left,** manuscript of Valdemar II's Jutland Code, of 1241, granting legal rights. **Right,** Christian II.

regard him as a prophet of the benign state.

Christian's ability to curb the power of the Danish nobility turned ultimately on events in Sweden, where "Sten Sture the Younger" (his real name was Nilsson) was hoping to claim the Swedish crown on the back of mass support for his strongly expressed nationalism. He had already seized and installed himself in a castle when Christian advanced on him with a force of German, French and Scottish mercenaries. Sten Sture was defeated twice, the second time dying of wounds while retreating to Stockholm. His widow, Kristina Gyllenstierna, kept the resistance going from Stockholm but in the end she capitulated and on 4 November 1520

Christian was crowned king of Sweden.

The Bloodbath: Christian had been supported all along by the Holy Roman Emperor, which angered the Protestant movement brewing in Uppsala. Three days after his coronation, he proceeded to secure his position with "a stroke of truly machiavellian ruthlessness." His opponents were rounded up in the Great Square near Stockholm Castle, charged with heresy, and executed. Eighty-two lost their heads, including two bishops and the scions of many noble families.

The killings did not stop with what came to be known as the "Stockholm Bloodpath";

similar trials were held in other places on his way back to Denmark until the number of victims exceeded 600. It was a journey "marked by gallows and executions."

Visiting the Netherlands, Dyveke and Sigbrit's birthplace, Christian was hailed as a great European monarch. He met Erasmus and they talked about Luther. When Erasmus criticised the violence that had been stirred up by the reformer, Christian ventured that "mild measures avail nothing; the medicine that gives the whole body a good shaking is the best and surest."

It was a telling remark from one who was closely identified with the Holy Roman Emperor, the dispute over Dyveke notwithstanding, and a portent of the Reformation ahead. Christian had summoned a Lutheran preacher to his court in 1519, only two years after Luther nailed up his thesis at Wittenberg, and while the preacher made some converts among the Danish upper classes, the king was not yet ready to follow.

Christian continued to give a good shaking instead to the Danish nobility but he was soon in trouble both at home and in Sweden where Gustav Vasa, some of whose family had died in the Stockholm Bloodbath, led the Swedish miners in a revolt which saw him elected to the Swedish throne. Christian was helpless to do anything about it.

In Denmark he faced growing resentment over extortionate taxation and could no longer rely on his old ally, the church, not only because of the Bloodbath but also because he had confiscated the profits of a papal legate who had been doing a roaring business in indulgences. He tried to excuse the Stockholm atrocity by putting the blame on the man he had just appointed Archbishop of Lund. The bewildered archbishop was burned at the stake.

In December 1522 his excesses drove 18 Jutland nobles, including four bishops, to offer the throne to Christian's uncle, Frederik, Duke of Holstein. Friendless in Denmark, Christian sailed for the Netherlands with his wife, children and Sigbrit, where he hoped to rally support from the Holy Roman Emperor. "In fact," says Professor T.K. Derry, "the union of the three crowns came to a final end with the sudden eclipse of this highly gifted, but despotic and unstable ruler."

In the Netherlands Christian "became so

poor that he had to pawn his jewels, his faithful queen died in 1526, and his three children were taken from his custody to be made Catholics." In the circumstances, then, he understandably leapt at an invitation from Norwegian bishops to assume the crown of Norway independently. Aided by his brother-in-law, the Emperor Charles V, he set sail with 10,000 men and laid siege, indecisively, to Akershus in Oslo.

He was in turn encircled by Danish and Hanseatic reinforcements who, in the end, sent him into solitary confinement in Sønderborg Castle on the island of Als. With nothing else to do, he walked round and round his table wearing a path in the stone

others preferring his older brother, the future Christian III, a Lutheran. Solving the impasse was not made easier by the arrival of Count Christopher of Oldenburg in Denmark with an army, financed by the Hanseatic mayor of Lübeck, who demanded the restoration of Christian II.

Surprisingly, perhaps, the imprisoned king still enjoyed considerable support in Copenhagen, if only among the peasants he had championed, and the so-called Count's War dragged on for two years, the last civil war in Denmark's history.

Few kings have reached their throne by such a blood-stained path as Christian III whose victorious army entered Copenhagen

flags of the floor which is still there for visitors to see. He outlived two successors, Frederick I and Christian III, and died at 77, having spent eight years of his life in exile and 27 in prison.

Frederik, the uncle who succeeded Christian II, fudged the developing religious division by tolerating both camps. On his death, though, the issue came to a head, with part of the Council in favour of Prince Hans, who was being brought up as a Catholic, the

Left, an influx of Dutch artisans brought these characteristic breeches to Amager. Above, still hopeful of a return, Christian II in exile.

in 1536. By that time, the citizens (still faithful to Christian II, or more probably to their redoubtable burgomaster Ambrosius Bogbinder, a childhood friend of the king) had long waited in vain for help from Charles V. For months Christian's ruthless German general Johan Rantzau drove back any emaciated citizen who attempted to escape, and Bogbinder equally ruthlessly suppressed talk of surrender. In the end, the Copenhageners were reduced to eating dogs and cats, small birds, frogs and even rats, and made their bread from soaked leather. By July 1536, when the people of Copenhagen filed out of the city bare-headed and with white sticks to indicate surrender, there was nothing left to eat but "the leaves on the trees."

The new Lutheran king was now the most powerful man in Denmark. Every other citizen from noble to peasant had bled along with the scarred country, and the hold of the Hanseatic League was gone for ever. Despite his power and unlike his relentless general who counselled vengeance, the young king treated Copenhagen generously and decreed that peace was to be restored in his name. In this way, his nickname as "The Clergyman King" seems less surprising than his early activities might have indicated.

Though his German-Holstein advisers advocated an absolute monarchy, in the early

preachers such as Hans Tausen, a renegade monk, were permitted to preach, though the Catholic hierarchy did not always make their mission easy. When Tausen himself was imprisoned by the Bishop of Viborg, he continued to preach to huge crowds through the prison bars. Despite the bishops, he became Frederik's own chaplain and, later under Christian III, Bishop of Ribe.

Apart from his zeal for religious reform, at the end of the tangle of civil war Christian III had an even more pressing need: to pay Rantzau and his German troops. The two coincided neatly and, as it did with King Henry VIII of England across the North Sea, the wealth of the Catholic Church, its mon-

days at least, Christian III knew he needed the support of the nobility and the ordinary people to bring about the reforms his Lutheranism demanded. He was wise enough also to listen to Mogens Gøye, Frederik I's chief counsellor, and the strong man of Jutland, who counter-balanced the Germans and urged moderation in the king's move against the Catholic bishops.

The revolt against the Catholic Church had started in the reign of his father Frederik I and, as governor of the Duchies (Slesvig-Holstein), Christian had early adopted the new faith. By 1526 Frederik declared the Danish Church independent. Lutheran

asteries and estates provided a strong second motive for dealing swiftly with the bishops.

A secret nocturnal council decided "in God's name to take these bishops by the scruff of their necks" and, during that night, Christian III rounded up the bishops, including the astute Joachim Rønnow, who had earlier appeared to support Frederik I's reforms but retained his true colours and was found hiding on a beam in his palace. Only the Bishop of Børglum, Stygge (Ugly) Krumpen, escaped and he was flushed out of a baker's oven a few days later. The country's last Catholic archbishop fled the country without a finger being raised on his behalf and Danish troops marched north to implement the same changes in Norway. Norway, Christian then declared, would "henceforth be and remain under the Crown of Denmark …and it shall henceforth neither be, nor be called, a kingdom in itself."

The Catholic Church was dead in Denmark, Rantzau's soldiers were paid, and the people of Copenhagen, so recently humiliated, were glad to witness the downfall of their bishops. The Reformation was sealed by a council of 1,000 nobles, merchants and peasants (but no clergy) which agreed to confiscate Church lands and to the establishment of Lutheranism. Magnanimous in victory, Christian III also declared an amnesty

again became a royal councillor, after he had demonstrated his conversion by marrying and fathering six sons and six daughters.

With the reduction of the role of the Catholic Bishops, who had been members of the royal council and held positions of power as great as those of the nobility, the latter were less interested in office in the new church. Lutheran bishops and clergy were not, as their Catholic brethren had been, exclusively drawn from the nobility. Tradesman and peasants took a part in church affairs. The new Bishop of Sealand, Peder Plade (known as Palladius) was the son of a shoemaker, yet he along with Bugenhagen was pre-eminent in shaping the new doctrines.

for offences committed during the civil war, the blame for which was now firmly and conveniently laid at the bishops' door.

The bishops could be thankful that Christian felt no need to treat them in the way his Viking predecessors might have dealt with subjects who offended. Only Bishop Rønnow remained a captive for life. The rest were gradually released and provided with lands. Oluf Munk, the last Catholic Bishop of Ribe,

Left, herring market at the height of the season. **Above left**, Christian II's daughter, Christine, once a prospective bride of Henry VIII of England. **Above right**, religious reformer Hans Tausen.

The Danish Reformation was undoubtedly German inspired, with most of Denmark's reformers looking to German universities for their religious education and the king bringing in a German, Johannes Bugenhagen, a disciple of Luther, to organise the new Reformed Church. But this ecclesiastical reformation turned into a national and patriotic revival. Danish became the language of the church, with hymn books, services and the Bible being translated into Danish, in a surge of national feeling that looked ahead to a similar period of national pride in the 19th century. Post-Reformation Denmark was distinctly Danish.

ABSOLUTE MONARCHY TO END OF EMPIRE

"Looking at the list of Danish monarchs for the last five hundred years is a little like watching a long volley in tennis," says Donald Connery in his entertaining book *The Scandinavians*, his point being that one Christian is followed by the next Frederik and vice versa.

Christian III reigned for 23 years and, with finances enormously improved by the confiscation of Church property, he presided over the recovery from civil war and instituted the centralisation of power which was to become a characteristic of the tennis volley ahead. The economic benefits of this period were not evenly spread, however. The peasants were as badly off as ever, and many of the smaller land-owners, as well as the nascent urban middle class, were long made to suffer for having taken the wrong side in the civil war.

Christian III's son, Frederik II, felt emboldened to launch his largely mercenary army against Sweden, where his counterpart, Eric, was often distracted by his ultimately futile desire to marry Queen Elizabeth of England. "There was a tremendous killing," wrote Eric of one of the battles. "The water in the river was coloured red as blood… We stuck into (the Danes) like a herd of wild boars, sparing none…" Eric went mad before the war ended. He stabbed one of his nobles to death personally, had others butchered in prison, married his mistress in private and then insisted on having her crowned in public. In the end he was put away and died nine years later of arsenic poisoning. Peace was restored at Stettin in 1570, not an inch of territory passing one way or the other.

Frederik's successor, Christian IV, was "a man of action rather than reflection, brave, artistic, and interested in all kinds of practical concerns; he is the one sovereign of the long Oldenburg line who not only became a popular hero in his lifetime but has been widely and on the whole gratefully remembered by posterity." Professor Derry's fulsome appraisal is slightly qualified by other historians, one of whom adds that he was also "vitiated by a pleasure-loving nature, prone to excesses."

His family life has been called "full-blooded": his first marriage produced three sons, his second (a morganatic union with a young noblewoman) another son and six daughters. When the second wife was banished for adultery, he consoled himself with her chambermaid. "The quarrels between his natural children, among themselves and with his legitimate children, caused the King much grief and misery," it is recorded.

Christian changed the face of Denmark and of Norway, not merely with many of their finest public buildings but also with new towns, whose names often boasted the royal connection. The name of the Norwegian capital, Oslo, was changed to Christi-

ania, a new town on the west coast became Christiansand (now Kristiansand). He trebled the size of the Danish navy with ships he helped to design, sent explorers off to find the Northwest passage, personally sailed around the North Cape into the White Sea and chartered companies to develop trade with the Far East. He was fond of the grand gesture. On visiting his brother-in-law, James I of Britain, his present was a warship.

Single combat: Like Frederik before him, Christian came round to thinking that he was ready for a war with Sweden. When the Council demurred, reminding him that the previous one had been expensively fruitless,

Christian threatened to declare war in his independent capacity as Duke of Slesvig-Holstein. He had his way but, though the Danes captured two of Sweden's main fortresses and laid siege to Vaxholm, Stockholm's defensive fortress, again the war was not decisive. At one point, possibly with a view to economising, the Swedish king challenged Christian to settle the dispute in single combat, adding: "Herein if you fail we shall no longer consider you an honourable king or soldier." Christian scorned the challenge from "a paralytic dollard" and advised him to stay at a warm fireside with his nurse. In the negotiated peace of Knaerod, 1613, Denmark restored some of the captured Swedish territory. But, for six years, Sweden lost its major western stronghold, Älvsborg and its major trading station at Gothenburg until the country paid a crippling ransom to the Danes. On balance, this was a victory for Denmark over its neighbour – but one never to be repeated.

Christian allowed himself to be drawn into the Thirty Years' War and suffered crushing defeats first by Germany and then by a rejuvenated Sweden. He was in the thick of the fighting himself and was on the quarter-deck of his flagship when a gun exploded. Shrapnel struck him in 23 places, including an eye, but he picked himself up off the deck and ordered the fight to continue.

He felt let down by the Danish nobility and his son-in-law, Ulfeld, when ultimately forced to sue for peace on what he considered humiliating terms. He saw out the last years of his 52-year reign in the company of the loyal chambermaid, being described as "a Renaissance prince whose sense of beauty found expression in buildings which have long outlived the collapse of his political ambitions."

The practical politics behind the glitter of Christian's reign was a steady erosion of the power of the nobility. The power did not pass downwards to the people, however, but in the other direction, into the hands of the king. Frederik III paid lip service to the idea of redistributing their powers more democratically. Having promised a constitution to that effect, he did nothing and the changes were "never heard of any more after that day and the Estates of Denmark did not meet again for nearly two centuries."

There was a new constitution, however, a

secret one, and it is not hard to imagine why Frederik wished to keep it under wraps until his death. It did away with any pretence: power was to be invested absolutely and exclusively in the monarchy. The Danish people were left hugging their chains, according to Molesworth, "the only comfort left them being to see their former oppressors in almost as miserable a condition as themselves, the impoverished nobles being compelled to grind the faces of the poor tenants for their own subsistence."

Absolute monarchy: At the mercy of the crown, Denmark was doubly unfortunate in the untalented procession of individuals who wore it. Christian V, according to a calmly

and body" as a boy, went from bad to worse. "With his drunken comrades he visited bars and public-houses, where His Majesty used to break glasses, bottles, and furniture to pieces and throw them out of the windows."

A German doctor, Johann Friedrich Struensee, was retained as Court Physician to put Christian right. The Queen, Caroline Matilda, a sister of George III of England, was at first distrustful of this "atheist, of dissolute life and elegant manners" who, furthermore, was "spoilt by women". Nor could his professional skills reverse her husband's slide into "hopeless imbecility". She was not yet 21.

Struensee charmed the King into granting

balanced view, was "weak, shallow and vain." Frederik IV was practically illiterate when he ascended the throne at 28 although he later learned to read and enjoy poetry. Christian VI's "whole appearance was unsympathetic; his voice and face were equally disagreeable." His queen was, if anything, worse: "sulky and fretful". Frederik V died of drink; Christian VII, "depraved in mind

Preceding pages: Denmark was not always a small country – the wider boundaries in 1629. **Left,** Christian III, known as the clergyman king because of his religious reforms. **Above,** Christian IV's Round Tower in Copenhagen.

him wide powers of state, and the Queen into bed. Struensee decreed, wisely, that adultery and unchastity were no longer offences, but that was only one of 1,069 Cabinet orders through which in 16 months he attempted to overhaul Danish society. He introduced freedom of the press, exercised tight budgetary controls, and laid down qualifications for holding public posts which had previously been sinecures for men of influence.

His zealous reforms made enemies, not least because they were the work of a German who never learnt Danish and was "of a domineering character." A powerful group led by the Dowager Queen cornered the imbecilic king in his bedroom at 5 a.m. and made him sign an order for Struensee's arrest, the rest of the plan being to lock up Caroline Matilda in Kronborg Castle at Helsingør. Struensee was plucked out of bed and made to listen to a list of charges which included usurpation of royal authority, *lèse majesté* and injury to His Majesty's honour.

He was not given the benefit of his own legal reforms which, as well as legalising adultery, had abolished capital punishment for most offences and forbidden judicial torture. On 28 April 1772 the executioners first cut off his right hand, then his head. His body was drawn and quartered; the severed head mounted on a pole. As the king was in no condition to take over his duties, the Crown Prince Frederik stepped in as regent.

The Queen was imprisoned in the castle until rescued by a British man-of-war despatched by George III. Although depressed by separation from her infant daughter, she became a popular figure around the old Hanoverian castle where she lived until struck down by smallpox at 23.

In 1801, the British Navy again sailed under the guns of Kronborg Castle, on this occasion 20 ships of the line among 53 under Admiral Sir Hyde Parker and Horatio Nelson. Two days later the greater part of the fleet entered Copenhagen harbour and engaged seven dismasted Danish blockships, two ships of the line and several floating batteries and gunboats. The raw recruits and students manning the Danish defences put up what Nelson later described as the hottest fight he had ever known.

Brave crews: The cause was Denmark's ratification of an armed neutrality treaty with Russia, the latest in a series of steps to prevent Britain from searching neutral ships in case they were violating Britain's embargo on trade with the enemy, Napoleon. After five hours of desperate fighting, when six of his ships were aground, Nelson sent a message addressed: "To the Brothers of Englishmen, the Danes." In it, he offered to spare the defenders if they ceased fire. If not, he would be obliged to set on fire the batteries he had taken "with their brave crews."

Crown Prince Frederik, still the regent, agreed to a truce and was slightly taken aback when Nelson praised an 18-year-old Dane, Peder Willemoes, who, in a tiny gunboat, had attacked his flagship for four hours.

Nelson recommended that he be promoted to admiral for his pluck.

Hostilities broke out again in 1807 for much the same reasons as before. Napoleon and Alexander I of Russia ordered Denmark (together with Sweden and Portugal) to close its ports to England and to declare war. The British reply was to send a large fleet and 30,000 troops under the command of Lord Cathcart and the future Duke of Wellington with an ultimatum: either come out formally for England within eight days or Copenhagen would be bombarded.

The sequel is a black page in the history of the British Navy. The admiral concerned later faced a court-martial for cowardice in the face of the French fleet, but there was no fleet of any kind to threaten him in Copenhagen. The Danish Crown Prince almost certainly desired a rapprochement with England but, for one reason or another, it was impossible to meet the deadline. Copenhagen was bombarded for three days. The university and cathedral were destroyed, as were hundreds of houses. The city capitulated on 7 September.

All Danish ships and boats – more than 70 in all – their stores and ammunition were carried away to England. The Crown Prince, acting as regent to the notoriously mad Christian VII, promptly concluded an alliance with Napoleon, whereupon England declared war on Denmark. Napoleon sent French and Spanish troops to shore up Danish defences, and it is said that the incomprehensible sight of these troops marching past his window was the last straw for the deranged monarch. The hard-pressed Crown Prince, regent for more than 20 years, succeeded him as Frederik VI.

Shocked by the bombardment of Copenhagen, Denmark stayed with Napoleon while all his other allies deserted him, especially after the Russian fiasco. Denmark paid a terrible economic price for its stand and, by prolonging it, stood to lose even more through reparations at the Treaty of Kiel, 1814. In the event, bankrupt Denmark, having recently seen its proud navy carted off, then lost Norway to Sweden. The only faint consolation was that it retained Iceland, Greenland and the Faroes.

Right, a 19th-century courtyard typical of city life at the time.

It was almost as if Denmark's intellectual community redoubled its efforts to compensate for the diplomatic and military setbacks. The generation of 1810–30 produced a Golden Age of Danish literature with the names of Hans Christian Andersen and Søren Kierkegaard pre-eminent among them. Frederik VI, small of stature and sickly, had no real interest in literature.

With his passion for military matters somewhat irrelevant in the country's reduced circumstances, he turned his hand to establishing a public school system. He coincidentally bolstered the writers' campaign to advance Danish literature and language by speaking Danish, rather than German, at court, the first monarch to have done so for many centuries.

Encouraging the use of Danish in government and in the arts was very much the spirit of the European National Romantic movement, which regarded a common language, rather than geography, as the criterion of nationhood. While the promotion of the Danish language helped to restore self-esteem when it was at a low ebb, the emphasis on language ties created for Denmark more problems than it cured.

Buffer zone: The Norwegians were re-discovering their identity through language, too, but as far as Denmark was concerned Norway after 1814 was a lost cause. When the issue raised its head in the Danish-ruled Duchies of Slesvig and Holstein, however, the repercussions had Lord Palmerston, as we have seen, tearing at his hair. They lingered well into the 20th century. Slesvig and Holstein represented a kind of mixed buffer zone between "pure" Denmark and "pure" Germany. The German-speakers were politically dominant in both places: in Holstein as an overwhelming majority; in Slesvig because relatively few of the Danish-speakers, a majority in real terms, met the franchise qualifications. The Germans, on the whole, were prosperous town-dwellers,

the majority of Danes were peasant farmers.

Germany in 1830 consisted of a confederation of states and, following the overthrow of the Bourbons in France, they adopted liberal constitutions which were the envy of Danes in general and the German-speakers of Slesvig and Holstein in particular. The latter agitated for similar rights, implying that the two duchies would then become independent and, as such, might even abandon their Danish connection in order to join the German confederation.

Whatever reservations the Danish-speakers might have had about Copenhagen's reluctance to move with the times, they liked the prospect of German hegemony even less. For its part, Copenhagen could hardly agree to liberal reforms without extending them to the two duchies, in which case they could vote to go their own way.

At its heart, the issue polarised into a contest between Denmark and Prussia, an inexorable route to war, but it was caught up in broad cross-currents as well. The pan-Germanic movement was met on the other side by pan-Scandinavianism, a cause taken up by students under the influence of Nikolaj

Preceding pages: Denmark won the Battle of Egersund but lost the 1864 war to Germany. **Left,** the Painters' House at Skagen. **Right,** N.F.S. Grundtvig, founder of the folk high schools.

(N.F.S.) Grundtvig, who sought to develop a tolerant form of Christianity incorporating the virtues of Norse mythology, a combination which produced stirring hymns.

Grundtvig's educational ideas were the basis of Denmark's folk high schools, the first of which was established significantly in North Slesvig. They were intended for rural children, the school year being concentrated in the five winter months when they could be spared from the land. Traditional book learning was replaced by emotional discussion and community singing which sent pupils back to their farms with a lively pride in the nation's past and with a streak of idealism concerning the future.

High hopes rested with the accession of Christian VIII, who had shown himself to be a comparatively open-minded regent in Norway. These hopes were disappointed, not so much by royal truculence as the fear that too many concessions would jeopardise the autonomy needed to keep the situation in Slesvig-Holstein under control. Nevertheless, Christian virtually conceded the point in the last months of his life, and his successor, Frederik VII, sealed the matter. A witness has described how, on 29 January 1848, "in a silence so profound that the stroke of the pen could be plainly heard, the king signed the order with a firm hand, thereby abolishing absolutism."

Denmark was still without a real constitution, and reforms lay within the discretion of the ageing King Frederik. He tinkered with the way the country was run, occasionally making major advances such as the early introduction of universal elementary education. But he held back on the laws of land-ownership which might have improved the status and security of rural tenants who paid rent with their labour and a mass of workers, like dairy maids, who put in long hours for little more than their board and lodging. Censorship laws still required newspapers and magazines to be scrutinised by the police before they went on sale.

The reaction in Slesvig-Holstein was very much as predicted with some demanding freedom (including the right to determine future relations with Germany) and others the incorporation of Slesvig with Denmark. A flicker of armed rebellion in the Duchies was quickly put down by Danish forces, but their intervention attracted an overwhelming number of German troops under a veteran Prussian commander who overran not only the Duchies but also Jutland as far as Århus. King Oskar of Sweden thereupon offered a force of 15,000 Swedes and 3,000 Norwegians to repel the Germans. With Britain and later Russia taking a keen interest

– the balance of power in the Baltic was at stake – hostilities were suspended, resumed and suspended again.

Humiliating blow: Denmark's southern border remained the Eider River, originally fixed in 811 and still defended by ancient earthworks little different from what they had been then. They were no match in 1864 either for the new breech-loading Prussian needle-gun, against which the Danish forces offered muzzle-loaders, nor for the Prussian now orchestrating his country's affairs, Bismarck. The Chancellor had correctly anticipated that the great powers would not intervene on Denmark's behalf and was unyielding at the negotiating table. The

to dairying and cattle-breeding. The pork industry took pains to produce precisely the kind of streaky bacon popular on British breakfast tables.

The economic revolution was painful for many country dwellers, who had to choose between joining the drift towards towns or emigrating altogether. The growth of industry, and with it an urban proliteriat, made the lingering privileges of the land-owning classes anachronistic and untenable. With every election, the Left reduced the Conservatives' position in the Folketing until, in 1884, they held only 19 out of 102 seats, although they still formed the government.

The Conservatives went on about building

Duchies were surrendered into his hands, a humiliating blow to the Danish monarchy which thereby lost 40 per cent of all that remained of its territory in Europe after the departure of Norway and Skåne.

Danes responded by making the best of what was left. The Health Society set about reclaiming the hitherto useless wasteland of western Jutland and settling it with rural poor. North American and Russian grain flooding the European markets steered Danish agriculture away from traditional cereals

Left, an old etching of surveyors at work on land enclosure. **Above**, Vesterbrogade, *circa* 1865.

a ring of fortifications around Copenhagen (with the inference that the rest of the country could be sacrificed in the event of war), while the socialists agitated for legislation to benefit poorer workers. They edged towards a compromise which then took on its own momentum as the genesis of the Danish welfare state. In 1901, by which time the Conservatives were down to eight out of 114 seats, King Christian capitulated and invited the majority to form a government. Celebrations greeted the *systemskiftet* (change of system), the beginning of a democracy that was to make 20th-century Denmark one of Europe's most liberal nations.

FROM LAND TO TOWN: MODERN DENMARK

As Denmark moved into the 20th century, its social, political and economic structures were fluid and changing fast. The overtones of the long and often acrimonious constitutional row that had led to the *systemskiftet* (change of system) still lingered, and the great march from land to town had only just begun. The new industrial workers and smallholders swelled the ranks of the emerging Social Democratic Party and Radical Liberal Party, making them political forces to be reckoned with.

By 1915, reforms went further and the Social Democrats and Radical Liberals combined with the farm-based Liberal Democrats, to push through a monumental amendment to the Conservative constitution of 1866. This reform transferred the balance of power to the Folketing, abolished the electoral privileges of the upper chamber (the Landsting), granted the vote to women and servants, and introduced proportional representation. As a consequence, the old Right Party, its energy sapped by the constitutional row, was transformed into the modern Conservative People's Party.

This more polarised society was tested during World War I. Denmark, like Scandinavia as a whole, was determined to remain neutral, and had an extra incentive stemming from the country's crushing defeat at the hands of the German Confederation in 1864. At first, neutrality was under acute pressure from Germany, which forced Denmark to sow mines in the Great and Little Belts through which the British navy might enter the Baltic. King Christian apologised in advance to his kinsman, King George V of England. As Britain was in no position to resist near-certain German invasion of Denmark if the Danes refused, his predicament gained British sympathy.

Strains on both neutrality and supply lines grew as the war drew on and German submarine warfare sank a third of Denmark's merchant fleet. The country remained neutral, however, and was thus deprived of a seat at the Versailles conference which would have been the ideal forum for re-opening the question of Slesvig. As it was, the Slesvigers themselves had to petition the peace confer-

ence for the fulfilment of an 1866 promise of a plebescite

In the immediate wake of the war, internal tension grew. Extremist sentiments began to spread, especially among the working class, and industrial antagonism, worsening in 1919–20, led to a domestic political crisis.

After a brief but menacing period, a new government held controversial referenda separately in the northern and southern zones of Slesvig. The north returned a three-quarters majority for reunion with Denmark, but Danish euphoria was cut short by the second set of results in the south, which showed an even bigger majority the other way. The southern border was redrawn ac-

classes were on the rise, and the old ruling classes were in decline. Social and geographical mobility played its part in producing a more homogeneous society based on the precepts of welfare and middle-class morals and modern Denmark was born.

All this was due in large measure to social reform policies chiefly promoted by the Social Democrats and Radical Liberals, but in time adopted by most other parties. Their methods were taxation and social legislation, especially practised during the long-running coalition of Social Democrats and Radical Liberals from 1929 to 1940.

The Social Democrat leader Thorvald Stauning dominated this period. Cigar-

cordingly and Danes masked their disappointment by Christian X's ceremonial return to the Duchy on a white charger.

The great levelling: From 1924, the Social Democrats displaced the Liberal Democrats as the largest political party. Despite that, an absolute majority remained constantly out of reach so that the two parties held office in turn, supported respectively by the Radical Liberals and Conservatives.

Political fragmentation and the rise of Social Democracy had forever altered the landscape of Danish politics and, in turn, reflected an incipient levelling-out in Danish society. The former "lower" and working

maker and prime minister, he came to be associated with the crucial transition from middle-class rule to social democracy. With more than 30 years of political activity, he became one of this century's leading Danish politicians, symbolising the era between the Great Depression and World War II.

World economic depression in the 1930s hit hard in Denmark, which still depended on agricultural exports. Falling prices, followed by foreign curbs on Danish exports, had a disastrous effect on farmers and seriously hit the emerging manufacturing industries. Unemployment shot up to record levels and in 1933, the Social Democrats,

Radical Liberals and Liberal Democrats were forced to turn to sweeping emergency measures to avert national bankruptcy. They devalued the currency and curtailed the debt burden, banned strikes and lockouts, guaranteed farm prices and controlled production. They also continued foreign exchange and trade controls which had been introduced the previous year.

Nazi threats: Concerns over economic and social well-being were soon dwarfed by a growing anxiety over Hitler's rise to power just over the border in Germany. Nazi rearmament again threatened Denmark's neutrality – a double blow because money saved on army and armaments had been an impor-

invaded Denmark and Norway on 9 April 1940, these belated preparations proved of little avail. Organised military resistance was futile and, after a brief struggle, the Danish government yielded under protest. It did, however, secure a German agreement to respect Danish rule. The government's goal was to maintain neutrality and internal self-government but it was forced to concede to many German demands. Sealed off from the outside world, Danish farmers and manufacturers had also to adapt to the German market as their sole outlet if workers were to keep their jobs.

The agreement was the price the Danes paid to avoid a Nazi government and to

tant factor in laying the foundations of a modern welfare state. Under this German pressure and, spurred by the Danish government's reluctant decision in 1933 to accept the German offer of a non-aggression pact, Denmark's politicians felt obliged to close ranks. Slowly, preparations were made to upgrade its defences.

It was already too late. When Germany

Preceding pages: workers at a furniture workshop around 1870; Hans Vermeehren's painting of a late 19th-century shepherd. Left, soldiers protect strike breakers in Randers. Above, German tanks advance in to Denmark in 1940.

control local Nazism; but, as the war progressed, the Germans intensified their demands. The problem became one of how far the Danish government could yield without sacrificing the essential values and interests which it had remained in office to safeguard.

Limits to sacrifice: The issue of how much to sacrifice spawned an organised Resistance movement against the occupation forces. The movement gained early support from Britain but was strongly opposed by the Danish authorities, who felt their position and policy could be undermined. As the Germans began to experience their first serious reversals in the war, the situation deteriorated. Supplied by air-drops from the British, the Danish Resistance resorted to widespread propaganda and sabotage. Groups carried out more than 2,500 attacks on industry and 2,000 attempts to damage and destroy the railways. The Resistance's greatest successes were in Jutland and Funen, where German troop transports from Norway to the Normandy front were at times cut to a quarter of their schedules.

In response to the Resistance action, the Germans retaliated with ever harsher methods. In August 1943, the Danish authorities reached a point where they could no longer yield to German demands without destroying their position with the Danish popula-

1943, the Germans decided to "solve the Jewish question", but they failed. In a miraculous few weeks during that autumn – just before the Germans began their round up – the Resistance and thousands of other sympathisers smuggled no fewer than 7,000 Jews on to small fishing boats and other craft and across the Sound to Sweden. The 7,000 made up almost the whole Jewish population of Denmark and the Germans arrested only 202 Jews. The horrible fate of many of those unfortunate 200 in the concentration camps is proof of what the rest would have faced but for their astonishing escape.

In the war's closing stages, the old political leaders were obliged to seek contact with

tion. German military occupation forces took over executive power and the Danish government and monarch effectively ceased to function from 29 August 1943.

From that time, the Resistance leaders in the underground government, the Freedom Council, emerged with growing authority to direct the struggle against the Germans. Sabotage attacks and reprisals escalated in a period of lawlessness. The Germans rounded up Resistance members, policemen, military leaders and many others. Thousands were sent to concentration camps, while the luckier ones escaped to Britain and Sweden.

Jewish escape: The night before 2 October

the Freedom Council. Military personnel, released from internment, were placed under the Council's direct command to bring an infusion of new and trained men. By the time British troops entered Denmark on 5 May 1945, Denmark was a recognised ally of the victorious Allied Powers.

The relationship between the Resistance movement and the politicians was another matter; but, despite residual friction, a coalition government of political parties and Resistance leaders made the transition to peacetime. It restored all lawful authorities, and enacted comprehensive (if controversial) powers to punish collaborators.

The cold war: After five grim years of occupation, the Danes knew they could not return to the pre-war policy of isolated neutrality and weak defence. They had to seek security in an extended international partnership and solidarity with the West. Nevertheless, many still clung to the idea of the non-alliance policy of the inter-war years but this time within the framework of the United Nations. Denmark had joined that organisation immediately after Liberation and, though supporters of the plan realised that the United Nations might demand some form of stronger defence, the dream of neutrality still continued. The Cold War changed all that.

possible and the three countries chose their own paths. Sweden continued to maintain its non-aligned policy and, in April 1949, Denmark and Norway joined the Western defence alliance, the Atlantic Pact, otherwise called NATO. For the first time in 150 years, Denmark was assured of assistance in the event of any attack.

Even before it joined NATO, Denmark became part of the Organisation for European Economic Co-operation (OEEC), an offshoot of the Marshall Plan, now the OECD. Denmark was a founder member of the European Free Trade Association (EFTA) but, in January 1973, after a national referendum voted in favour, the country joined the European

The Soviet Union now stood out as the strongest naval power in the Baltic, only 20 miles (35 km) from the Danish coastline. To keep out of the Soviet orbit, Denmark was forced to abandon any ideas of neutrality within or outside the United Nations.

Along with Norway and Sweden, the country explored the possibilities of a Nordic defence union. From a Danish point of view, this would have continued the old non-alliance policy; but agreement proved im-

Left, Danish troops guard the German battleship *Prinz Eugen* as at the end of World War II. **Above**, Copenhageners welcome British airborne troops.

Community, together with Britain and Ireland. Despite reservations, particularly over sovereign rights, Denmark tirelessly supported closer co-operation and integration within the various organs of the European Community, and solidly backed the creation of a single internal European market by the end of 1992.

The breakdown of the defence negotiations was a serious blow to Nordic co-operation but, largely thanks to Denmark's Social Democrat prime minister, Hans Hedtoft, the three countries resumed discussions and formed the Nordic Council in 1952. The Council covers co-operation in

THE QUEEN

Queen Margrethe II, a statuesque blonde, is a popular and strong monarch who isn't afraid to involve herself in contemporary affairs. In contrast to her father, Frederik IX, whose traditional New Year's Eve radio and television broadcast seldom varied, she attracts attention and creates debate by choosing subjects near to her heart, and isn't afraid of scolding her listeners, sometimes for their smugness and intolerance, sometimes for their lack of self-confidence.

In 1987, for instance, she criticised their Jante mentality. "Jante is a fictional village in a novel by Axel Sandemose, which quite frankly I haven't read," she explains. "But the Jante attitude is very familiar: it's a don't-get-too-uppity attitude, don't get too big for your boots – keep your head down, nobody will notice you. It's perhaps not untypical of village life anywhere, but in Denmark it spills over from village life into the whole country."

Abroad, of course, she is a staunch ambassador for her people's talents. "Swedes can make things, but we can sell them," she says. "We are very, very good at marketing."

She was born on 16 April 1940, a week after the Nazis occupied Denmark, and was regarded as a welcome ray of light breaking through the darkness of war. No-one then imagined she would ever rule the country: the Danish constitution specified male inheritance of the throne, and it was not until 1953 that the law decreed that a woman could ascend if there were no male heirs. The constitutional change was ratified by referendum, so that Margrethe became the first Danish Queen to be elected by the population. She was 13 when she became heir-apparent, and she has two younger sisters, Benedikte and Anne-Marie.

From that moment, her education was meticulously planned. After graduation from the Danish gymnasium (upper secondary school) she studied national and international law at Danish and foreign universities. Apart from studying the "basics", she also found time to attend lectures in archaeology, a favourite subject, and to take part in fieldwork. Even military service was included: she served in the Women's Flying Corps, and the WAAF in England. Certainly, she could claim to be Europe's best-educated monarch.

It was, however, a tremendous upheaval for her to ascend the throne in January 1972, after her father's death. She was 31, married, the mother of two small boys and, despite her public duties, still found time to take care of her family, her interests and her private life. She quickly forged a personal style, not least in her relaxed media interviews.

Margrethe, who keeps herself politically informed, meets her government weekly and has a full round of social and diplomatic functions. But she doesn't hide the fact that she has a life outside the job. First comes her family: her husband Prince Henrik (French-born as Count de Laborde de Monpezat), and their two sons, Crown Prince Frederik (born 1968) and Prince Joachim (1969). Both parents follow their sons' education closely. The family has permanent residences at Amalienborg in Copenhagen and at Fredensborg in Northern Sjælland, where the Queen Mother, Queen Ingrid, also lives.

From her mother's family, the Swedish Bernadottes, she has inherited artistic talent. She has twice translated books into Danish, the first of these in partnership with Prince Henrik when, under a pseudonym, they published the Danish translation of Simone de Beauvoir's novel *Tous Les Hommes som Mortelle.* The second time was in 1988, when the Queen translated a Swedish novel, Stig Stramholm's *Dalen.* She was fascinated by J.R.R. Tolkien's *Lord of the Rings* and illustrated it, again using a pseudonym.

Her most ambitious work came in 1987, when she designed costumes and scenery for a TV production of Hans Christian Andersen's *The Shepherdess and the Chimney Sweep.* Here she worked as a member of a team of professionals, and is said to have loved it. Once, when her jewels were stolen during a visit to England, she drew detailed sketches of them to assist the police.

Even in circles where it is fashionable to speak condescendingly of royalty, the Queen's abilities are recognised. People joke that, if Denmark's few republicans were ever to end the monarchy, their first choice for president would be Margrethe Alexandrine Thorhildur Ingrid.

spheres from economic, social, and cultural affairs to communciations. Among other successes, it has led to an unrestricted labour market, a common passport area, equal social rights and benefits and identical legislation in many other fields. Recently, however, as European integration within the European Community has gained impetus, the Nordic Council's powers have begun to wane, and Denmark has urged its Nordic neighbours to seek European Commmunity membership during the 1990s.

Developing world: Along with its Nordic neighbours, Denmark has always promoted a spirit of reconciliation and rapprochement in her diplomatic dealings and has a strong

largest single political party (with the Liberal Democrats and Conservatives vying for second place). A succession of Social Democrat-led governments has left its imprint on the social landscape. Whether in government or opposition, the Social Democrats have influenced policy-making, directly or indirectly helping to shape the basic tenets of a modern welfare society.

Population growth and a zeal for improved living standards in the 1950s and 1960s contributed to a vigorous expansion in every sphere. Welfare policies brought retirement pensions and free medical and social services, along with a host of developments and improvements in other social areas. At the

interest in the problems of the developing countries. As well as providing generous development assistance in the way of aid and subsidised credits, many Danes have worn the blue beret of the United Nations peace-keeping forces, first in the Congo and Kashmir and later in the Middle East and Cyprus.

Since World War II, Denmark's main preoccupation has been the long and often painful process of consolidating the modern welfare state. During this time, the Social Democrats have held their position as the

Left, HM Queen Margrethe II. **Above**, guards at the Amalienborg Royal Palace.

same time, the Social Democrats initiated educational reforms, which led to the expansion of higher and adult education as well as increased public support for the arts.

Royal emancipation: In 1953 a constitutional revision, unanimously approved by all parties, brought the country's constitution into line with the mood of the time, by abolishing the Landsting (upper chamber) to leave the Folketing as the sole legislative body. At the same time, the revision introduced a much-applauded change in the rights of succession to what is the world's oldest monarchy. This allowed Margrethe, the popular daughter of King Frederik IX, to succeed to the throne. In January 1972, Margrethe became Queen and has continued a down-to-earth monarchy in true Scandinavian style (*see page 76*).

During the first difficult post-war years, the Danes had no choice but to retain stringent restrictions in order to safeguard the exchange rate and supplies of a country made poor by war. Even reconstruction and reorganisation had to wait until aid came from the Marshall Plan which the government used to introduce far-reaching liberalisation and expansion of the economy. Nevertheless, Denmark's dependence on international trading makes its balance-of-payments extremely vulnerable to world eco-

same time as radical modernisation has further boosted farming output. But, despite everything, agriculture keeps its important political position and it would be a bold government that ignored the powerful farming organisations and the strong agricultural voice in the Liberal Democrart and Radical Liberal parties.

Painful choices: In the 1990s, Denmark faces a number of painful yet pressing choices if it is to continue as one of the world's most affluent, comfortable and peaceful countries. For a nation with a population not much more than half the size of London, Denmark's 5 million inhabitants enjoy a standard of living almost unparal-

nomic trends and, again and again, the government in power has been obliged to introduce austere financial policies to restrict the expansion of consumption.

Under pressure from foreign competition and domestic costs, much of Danish industry has been forced to streamline itself and this has intensified in the run-up to the single market in 1992. Present day Denmark has become an industrial country, and industrial manufacturers now export more goods than farmers export food, although Danish bacon and pork products, as well as dairy products and other food, still play a vital role. The numbers on the farm have declined at the

leled in the rest of the world. Social welfare, health and education are among the best; homogeneity appears scrubbed clean of racial conflict; and society is one of the most open and free. But every balance sheet has its liabilities. Denmark in the 1990s is not the model of social harmony, middle-class well-being and political consensus traditionally associated with the world's oldest monarchy. Families stagger under a national debt equivalent to over 60,000 Dkr (around £6,000) per inhabitant, and living standards have begun to decline. Welfare, health and education buckle under the strain of government austerity and local cutbacks.

Hardest of all to believe in tolerant, liberal Denmark, with its strong sense of responsibility towards the weaker and less privileged, racism has begun to rear its ugly head in the peaceful cities and countryside, as the flow of refugees into Denmark swells. Only recently, the unthinkable happened when central government had to intervene in local politics to dissuade a municipality from holding a referendum on the level of immigration in its community.

The comforts of a "cradle-to-grave" welfare system – free medical care, education, child allowances, rent subsidies, pensions and almost full pay for those out of work, and more – worked well in the "boom years" of

of the 20th century. Many suggest that the present system – a host of small parties working, or not working, together on the basis of ever-shifting political alliances – is fast becoming untenable. In May 1988, the national elections produced the worst possible result for both the centre-right government and the opposition: political stalemate, with no single block the outright winner. A hung parliament, in which every piece of legislation would be hotly contested could not have come at a worse time.

It has led to a classic conundrum: can a government with responsibility but without power outflank an opposition with power but without responsbility? If it cannot, could it

the 1960s. They proved exorbitant in the harsher climate of the 1970s and 1980s and now swallow up almost 50 percent of Denmark's gross domestic product. The present centre-right coalition government, led by prime minister Poul Schlüter, and opposition parties alike are well aware of the debt problem but no-one has yet come up with a common platform to tackle the issue.

Danes are also debating the way in which Denmark is governed in the closing decade

Left, Turkish shops have added to the range of exotic foods. **Above**, physiotherapists hold a gymnastics class for disabled children.

herald a situation in which sober democratic processes in one of Europe's oldest democracies might buckle under the strain of stalemate and extremism?

To most Danes and to people who know the country's easy-going ways, the latter is unthinkable. The vital question is whether the government can muster crucial parliamentary votes to push through unpopular legislation that will tighten the communal belt. If it succeeds, a return to solvency could mean a restoration of the old traditions of social harmony in a country known and widely respected for its prosperity, tolerance, and largesse.

When the British say "Danish", they sometimes mean pastry; but, more often than not, they are thinking of bacon. Denmark has been shipping the staple of the British breakfast table across the North Sea for well over a century, in the process creating powerful shipping companies and a considerable skill in handling perishable foods.

Although Britain is still an important market for Danish bacon and other pork products, large amounts are sent to countries such as Japan and the United States. Dairy products, like milk powder, butter, yoghurt and cheese, are also important exports.

Agriculture was the mainstay of the Danish economy until the end of the 1950s, and the country's food exports to the United Kingdom, more than any other single factor, motivated Denmark's decision to join the European Community in 1972. The terms of the referendum which decided the issue made Danish membership conditional upon Britain's joining. Without the British food trade, Denmark was not interested.

Land reforms in the 18th century had brought freehold farming to Denmark, and consolidated scattered holdings into viable individual farms. By the time North America began shipping cheap grain to Europe in the late 19th century, the Danes were able to switch production from grain to livestock.

In a sense, it was a victory for free trade. Instead of applying tariffs to protect farmers from cheap grain imports, the structure of the farming industry changed to take advantage of the cheap grain. Before long, Denmark became a net importer of grain which was used to feed livestock and created an export of higher-priced livestock products.

The co-operatives: This laid the foundation for today's agricultural production, although another element was involved as well: the co-operative movement. The ideas behind the Rochdale consumer co-operative in England were soon adopted in Denmark with the formation of a consumer co-operative in 1866, a dairy co-operative in 1882, a bakery

in 1884, and a pig slaughterhouse in 1887.

In the following year, 244 new co-operative dairies were built, and the movement grew steadily. By the turn of the century it dominated both dairy and pigmeat production and processing, and had spread into eggs and poultry, grain trading, and farm equipment purchase. By 1909 there was even a co-operative bank, Andelsbanken.

It is difficult to over-estimate the role of the co-operatives in the development of Danish agriculture. They introduced quality standards and effective modern marketing methods, developed export markets and new products, even supported the arts and cultural development, and heavily influenced the democratic traditions which exist in Denmark today.

The discipline implicit in the co-operative movement was particularly important for animal health, and the strict supervision which made Denmark, with the Irish Republic, the only European Community countries able to export their farm produce to the United States, Japan, and other countries with particularly strict health regulations.

Today, in a situation where co-operatives

Preceding pages: Denmark is a land of rich agriculture. Left, sometimes the past shows in a grave mound. Right, butter-making by machine.

dominate every sphere of agriculture, their role has come under critical examination. Critics blame the movement for excessive complacency, for running an "old boy" network, ignoring the interests of grassroots members, even blocking progress by showing an unwillingness to support innovations.

Not unnaturally, the co-operatives defend their record, and their management skills. The business community, meanwhile, has shown that it is prepared to provide capital to finance a further expansion of the co-operatives, and capital will be needed on an unprecedented scale to continue the introduction of new processes and products.

Denmark had 80,000 farms at the end of

of the world's leading fishing nations, and a major exporter of fish and fish products.

Danish fishing vessels land nearly 2 million tonnes of fish a year, mostly cod, plaice, mackerel and herring caught in the North Sea, Baltic Sea and Kattegat regions. Even so, Danish processing factories sometimes have to import fish from other countries for processing and subsequent re-export. The vessels are generally smaller than those used in other countries (though the trend is towards bigger ships) and they operate mainly in the near to medium-distance waters, returning to port frequently to land catches while they are still fresh.

The ownership structure, and the way

the 1980s, compared with nearly 200,000 in 1960, and 140,000 in 1970. Most are farmed by the owner; only one farm in six has full-time employed labour. The average farm area is about 85 acres (35 hectares), with more than half used for cereals, 4 percent for fodder beet and 20 percent grassland.

Fisheries: For centuries, farming and fishing have been closely related in Denmark. Fishing was an important activity in slack periods on the farm, and an alternative source of income. All that is history. Like farming, fishing has become a skilled full-time occupation, and even if quotas have put limits on the total catch, Denmark is still one

crew members are paid, is different as well. Most of the small vessels are skipper-owned, and only the larger ships are operated by companies (which usually own only one ship). And in a maritime echo of agriculture's co-operative system, crew members are paid by results. Half the income from a voyage goes towards maintaining the ship itself, while the rest is distributed to a fixed scale. The skipper may get the biggest share, but even the cabin boy can find himself rich after a successful voyage.

Quotas, and periodic algae and industrial pollution, particularly in the Kattegat and Baltic, have seriously affected total catches in recent years and made fishing less profitable for many trawler operators and crews.

Traditionally, a quarter of the Danish catch by value is sold fresh or frozen but untreated. Ten percent is in the form of fishmeal and fish oil, and the balance is processed fish in one form or another, from frozen blocks of fillets to complete oven-ready meals. Danish fish products are exported to over 100 countries, but the European Community receives over half of the total export.

Aquaculture and mariculture: Today's quotas, and fears of further restrictions on catches, have stimulated the development of fish farms, and Denmark has an extensive

Wain (marine diesels), Atlas Industries (machinery), F. L. Smidth (a conglomerate built round cement technology), Schur International (packaging), Dronningborg (farm machinery) plus others founded in the second half of the 19th century. But, despite these pioneers, Denmark's first period of broad industrial growth did not come until the years between the two world wars – and even then budding industrialists received little encouragement. Danish agriculture was a model for the rest of Europe at the time, and farm mechanisation had hardly started. To most people, including the decision-makers of the day, the future lay in farming and food production. When, therefore, farm-

production of farmed trout in fresh water ponds. Before long, the industry expects to grow salt water fish in significant volumes as well, keeping them in coastal enclosures until they reach maturity.

Industrial success: There was an obvious link between Denmark's agricultural heritage and the country's potential position in the world for food processing machinery, but it took a long time for the country to realise its industrial potential. The scene was set by early starters such as Burmeister &

<u>Left</u>, mending nets at Esbjerg. <u>Above</u>, hand-painted Royal Danish porcelain.

er's son Mads Clausen decided in the depths of the 1930s Depression that he preferred engineering to agriculture, both his family and the neighbours feared that the young man was courting disaster.

Undaunted, Clausen began his business in a vacant loft room at the family farm, assembling refrigerator controls from parts which he had made locally. Of course, there's a happy ending – Clausen's firm, Danfoss, is now Denmark's biggest industrial employer, with a workforce of about 14,000 internationally. It is world leader in the production of heating and refrigeration controls – thermostats, compressors, special application hydraulics, electromotor gearing systems, and much more – with production plant in Sweden, Germany, the United Kingdom, Canada, the US and Japan, apart from Denmark.

The Depression years seemed to stimulate the inventiveness of many more young Danes. Lego, the toy company, was founded in 1932, while Bang & Olufsen, internationally famous for home electronics of exquisite design, started in 1925, and paint and lacquer manufacturers Dyrup began in 1928.

Overtaking agriculture: It was not until the end of the 1950s that industry overtook agriculture as the main contributor to the Danish economy in terms of exports, employment,

For lack of other raw materials, agriculture also provided the basis for other forms of production. Animal glands were the basis for insulin production by Nordisk Gentofte and Novo – since merged to form Novo-Nordisk, the world's largest insulin producer. (Today, of course, insulin comes mainly from biotechnical production, and is identical to human insulin, rather than the close approximation of porcine insulin.)

As industry developed, the search continued for other activities where skill and technology were more important than the raw materials involved. In particular, this approach stimulated the development of electronics, and more recently of computer soft-

and share of gross national product. It has continued to grow steadily since, in spite of the country's lack of raw materials and its very late industrial start.

Then, as now, industry meant manufacturing. Denmark lacks the raw materials that have helped to build major industrial companies in neighbouring Sweden. All significant inputs must come from abroad; the other side of that equation is that companies must export to meet the cost of raw materials.

Danish industry began mainly as a supplier to agriculture, making tilling equipment, the many metal fittings needed in pig sheds and dairies, plant for food processing.

ware. America's IBM has placed its European software production centre near Copenhagen, Commodore's international centre for LAN and networking is in Jutland.

Better late: Even Denmark's late start in manufacturing has been turned to good use, particularly in the production of furniture. The late start of industrial production meant that traditional crafts were preserved in Denmark long after they had disappeared in most other countries, and the Danes put these skills to good use when furniture production began to develop as an export business in the years after World War II. The industry has mechanised heavily since, and much furniture today is produced on computer-assisted design systems, but it was the fine work of traditional craftsmen that made its early successes possible.

Danish manufacturers have no doubts about why their furniture has won its special position, or why many industrial products do so well on international markets: the secret is design. Art, architecture, sculpture, handicrafts and industrial design are all very close to each other, both in practical production and in the education system.

Small but flexible: By any international yardstick, Danish industries are small, and less than 2 percent of Denmark's 7,500 industrial companies have 500 or more em-

switched quickly to adapt to changing conditions, or to meet the needs of a client at short notice. The lack of local raw materials, heavy taxation and comparatively high wage levels all make production in Denmark relatively expensive, and high volume production is just not competitive. Pigmeat in many different forms is the only true Danish bulk product. Industries have been forced to rely upon quality, spiced with a flexible approach and a willingness to produce to specifications in numbers not considered worthwhile by bigger producers.

Finding riches: To survive, the Danish manufacturer has to be a skilful niche player, and spot gaps that are of no particular interest

ployees, while more than 75 percent of them have fewer than 50. Yet the 5 percent which have 200 or more employees are responsible for about 23 percent of the country's industrial employment.

With all these small to medium-sized companies, there are very few able to boast an internationally-known brand name. The other side of the coin, according to the men who run the companies, is flexibility. Because they are small, production can be

Left, farmhouse holidays involve young and old. **Above**, Danish industry excels at designing and making hi-tech medical equipment.

to competitors in other countries.

A prime example of this is electronics. If you want a gadget to measure noise level, or blood gas, or something to monitor the condition of a patient in intensive care, you'll find it in Denmark. Equipment for people with a hearing disability is another niche the Danes have exploited successfully so that they are, collectively, the world leaders. Well over half Denmark's electronics production comes in the form of professional equipment, and almost 90 percent of it is exported. Some companies export 100 percent of their output. For them, the home market doesn't exist.

Danes drink beer anywhere, any time. They are the ones sitting in a hotel breakfast room with long frothing glasses on the table, plus a tiny tot of Gammel Dansk bitters as a pick-me-up. Some pubs open as early as 5 a.m. so that the thirsty Dane can get a beer on his way to work. During office meetings, it is not uncommon to find beer on the table, and the speed of working outside is often tuned to the pace of elbow and glass.

A true Danish beer drinker can open a bottle with the most unlikely instrument: the base of a disposable lighter, a screwdriver, the front-door key, or even another bottle and top. Skilled beer drinkers claim they can open a bottle with a folded newspaper and it is even said that, if a Dane has thirst enough, he can open a bottle with a soggy hot dog bun. First freeze the bun and then follow the usual techniques.

One of the worst things in Denmark is a brewery strike and on several occasions in the 1980s the brewery workers left their vats. For the duration of the conflict, no topic was more important whenever Dane met Dane on city street or country market place. In desperation, the Danes brought in beer from Germany and Belgium, and it was sold illegally on the streets during the annual Copenhagen Carnival.

Booze and burials: Beer has very deep roots in Danish culture. For centuries it was served morning, midday and evening – in the town as well as the country – and it was always at hand should thirst strike in the middle of the night. No feast or burial was complete without it. The Greek merchant Pytheas, who is believed to have visited western Jutland during the Neolithic period, noted that the inhabitants drank *mjød* (mead), a brew of honey and grain. This is the earliest record of Danish brewing but the result must have been very thick and sticky.

Snorri Sturlusson, the Icelandic saga writer, told of a Swedish chieftain who visited Lejre near Copenhagen and, after much beer with his Danish host, went outside and "slipped and drowned in the beer." Today,

Danes tell stories of Swedish drinkers who, lacking a good Danish head for strong beer, become drunk and disorderly – but then, as a well-known British saying has it: "They would say that, wouldn't they?" Nevertheless, great practice has meant that, though Danes drink a lot and drunkenness is sometimes accepted as an excuse for misbehaviour, most people frown on those who become embarrassing. Each year, during Denmark's biggest festival in Århus, the citizens argue fiercely about the rights and wrongs of

the Festival's great beer tent full of a jazz and free local brew.

The first use of hops in Denmark came in the middle of the 13th century when the phrase "hop garden" began to appear in records. A 1693 by-law in one Danish village laid down that every newcomer had to provide a barrel of beer. Similar 19th-century rules stipulated that a party must be held within a year of any change in a farm's status, be it sale, marriage, birth or death.

Sometimes beer was used as a punishment. Slander could be made good by the payment of one barrel of beer and the same fine was also levied on those who committed murder. No-one now knows whether this means that small offences were taken very seriously or that murder was lightly regarded. Nor was it sufficient to apologise for turning up late for a local festivity. It cost a quarter of a barrel of beer.

Women were not valued in beer as highly as men. When a farmer died, his widow had to supply a whole barrel in his honour. If she died first, he only had to provide half a barrel "and not a drop more."

The Danes drank enormous quantities of beer in the 16th and 17th centuries. Accounts and letters tell of "four pots" (almost a gallon) a day as normal rations for sailors and prisoners, though the beer must have been

that sugar had to be added at the table, as people today stir it into coffee or tea. The quality of the brew depended to a high degree on luck, and ingredients were often of dubious origin. Little was known until the 19th century about the natural science of brewing and, though people aimed for cleanliness, the danger of bacteria was unknown and the city surroundings were very unhygienic, with the streets little more than open sewers.

In early times, brewing beer could be compared to baking bread. It was made in cycles governed by the speed with which the previous supply ran out. But, though bread was the traditional domain of the farmer's

much weaker than it is today. Children were not allowed to drink the water in Copenhagen and the city wells were securely locked. Instead, they too drank copious quantities of light beer. The beer ration for sailors reduced considerably during the latter half of the 17th century, possibly because of the arrival of schnapps, of which they received half a pint (about a quarter of a litre) a week, served only at meal times.

Ancient beers would have been unpalatable to modern taste and, even later, few brews would have tasted as good as they do today. At a time when there was no way to keep it cool, the beer often became so sour

wife, beer was everybody's business. Once the hops had been picked and brought indoors, the whole household, including stable boys, maids and other servants, set about stripping the stems ready for the next brew. Of course, it became a party, calling for copious amounts of beer and, by the time the hops were ready for drying in the loft above, the labourers' hands were sticky-black and their bellies full of beer.

The brewing cycle started in March, on Easter Sunday at the latest, during a time when the moon was waning. The winter brew began around 9 December, to be ready for St Thomas's Eve on 20 December, and there were several more brews and festivities throughout the year. There was also gammel beer, Æl (old beer), which called for a much longer time to brew. Few today know or continue these rituals, though in one or two places groups have formed themselves into brewers' guilds to follow the old practices and their celebrations.

To improve the flavour, herbs have been (and still are) used to give beer a pleasant aroma and taste, and to keep it clear and fresh. Juniper berries and porse (bog myrtle) have long been popular and, today, an export beer from the Thisted Brewery in Jutland is called Porse Export.

The first brewery, Kongens Bryghus, is mentioned as early as 1454 and, though it no longer exists, the name has been taken over by Tuborg. Brewers in Copenhagen set up the Copenhagen Brewers' Guild in 1622, most probably with the aim of regulating quality and, in 1687, the Guild began a system of rotation so that each member brewed an equal amount.

The yeast used in brewing is very important to the flavour and a 19th-century discovery led to the formation of the industry as it is today. Carl Jacobsen, the founder of Carlsberg Breweries, is usually given the credit for developing an ideal yeast culture. In fact, Emil Christian Hansen was the revolutionary brewer who cultivated this special yeast, *saccaromuces carlbergensis*, for Carlsberg, to ensure a uniform, first-class brew. This has formed the basis of every Carlsberg brew since the mid-19th century but, instead of keeping Hansen's discovery a secret, Jacobsen, as head of the brewery, declared that anyone who wanted to use this special yeast could buy it, a concession that still continues.

The advent of Carlsberg's yeast so vastly improved standards that fewer farms brewed their own, and Danish brewing became an industry. Other large breweries started up at much the same time, including Wiibroe in Elsinore, Albani in Odense, Ceres in Århus, and the forebears of Odin in Viborg and Thor in Randers.

Most Danish beer comes in bottles, although draught beer is also sold widely.

Left, Carlsberg's famous dray horses leave the brewery in Copenhagen. Right, the message is the same in many languages.

Some drink it directly from the bottle; others prefer a glass, but no-one can agree what a real beer glass should look like. Many say the tall, narrow glass seen in the international Tuborg advertisements gives the best flavour. Draught drinkers often prefer short, tubby glasses with an inward-curving brim to keep the head in shape.

As beer tastes best when freshly poured, draught drinkers believe small glasses should be used and the traditional way of pouring it should take around eight minutes. The stream of beer is allowed to trickle down the edge of the tilted glass until that is half-full and then aimed at the centre.

All this tradition and mystique has come to

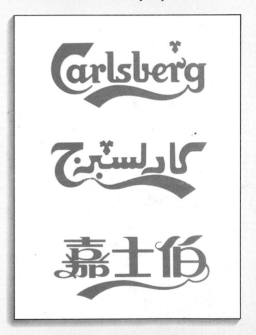

mean more than just beer. Carl Jacobsen, the founder of Carlsberg Breweries, also established the Ny Carlsberg Glyptotek, an important art museum in Copenhagen, and the Carlsberg Fund provides grants and endowments to support a wide variety of scientific and cultural activities.

Beer culture is also involved in the sponsorship of sporting events, including an annual six-day indoor bicycle race in Copenhagen. It might be hard to imagine why anyone should want to spend six days indoors to watch bicycles tearing round a wooden track – but then maybe the spectators are only there for the beer.

Denmark is not only a very small country, but the population of 5 million shares its language with no-one else, apart from perhaps the 4 million Norwegians to the north, whose language is closely linked to Danish. Danes may understand their Swedish neighbours off the east coast, but the Swedes claim not to understand a word of Danish.

So where does this leave Denmark? Isolated? Well, yes and no. Denmark is not an island, and its largest land mass (Jutland) shares a border with Germany. The lure of the south has always been stronger for the Danes than for other Nordic peoples and many great artists and writers have found that the development of their talent, and often also public recognition, have been possible only on the world stage. For that reason, the great neoclassical sculptor Thorvaldsen lived for 40 years in Rome; the most famous painter of the modern era, Asger Jorn, spent the pre-war years in Paris, and returned south after the war, first to the Low Countries and then to Italy. Denmark's two most famous names in literature, Hans Christian Andersen and Karen Blixen both made their names overseas, and Blixen even wrote in English.

For these and others, the narrow confines of Danish society, with its predominantly agricultural base and its *petit bourgeois* mentality, presented too many limitations and too few opportunities. Yet they were products of a society which allowed a baker's son (Christian Købke) to become an artist and a poor cobbler's son (H. C. Andersen) to become one of the world's greatest story-tellers.

State support: Modern artists do not, like their predecessors, have either to go abroad or to wait until they are dead to gain fame and fortune. A sizeable chunk of the national budget is allocated to the support of the arts. The state has not taken over the role of private benefactors, with artists and writers

Preceding pages: an example of Danish fabric design. Left, ballerina from the Royal Danish Ballet in a painting by Hans Voigt Stephensen. Right, a statue of Hans Christian Andersen in Town Hall Square.

"in residence" but funds are channelled into public productions and to making culture, both with a small and a capital C, generally available and accessible throughout the country. This policy is partly a natural feature of a welfare society, and partly based on the recognition of the lack of commercial viability of any Danish-language production, whether it be a book, film or play. The audience will always be limited to 5 million.

Of even greater significance, perhaps, the current policies are based on the underlying

egalitarian philosophy of N.F.S. Grundtvig, which has pervaded Danish society since the end of the 19th century and which was responsible for Denmark's abrupt transformation from a nation of peasant farmers to the highly sophisticated and industrialised country it is today.

Grundtvig (1783–1872) was a theologian and philosopher who pointed to the spoken, live word as the road to a humane and Christian community. In the name of enlightenment (the equivalent of the Danish word *Oplysning*, which also means information), he fathered the Danish folk high school movement, bringing general education, without exams, to illiterate agricultural workers. Education and culture continue to go hand in hand. The folk high schools still thrive and provide short courses for adults who are taking time off work.

Even more so, official policy recognises that frequent users of educational facilities are also those who are the greatest users of the arts and encourages a positive interaction between arts institutions and grassroots culture. Official funds are given not only to theatres, film, individual artists and Fine Art museums but also to libraries, folk high schools, open universities and evening classes, music and film clubs and schools, youth clubs and even sports clubs.

Literature, theatre and films: Of the most recent allocation of public funds to the arts, over 20 percent went to libraries. Sixty-five percent of adults, and nearly 80 percent of juveniles claim to use public libraries, and the lending rate averages 18 units per head of population, rising to nearly 30 for children. Thus, with 50 million books on the shelves of the public and school libraries, each book is lent out on average twice a year. Authors receive remuneration not for their lending rates but according to the number of volumes on the shelves. For example, Robert Fisker, the popular children's author, has nearly 300,000 copies of his books on the shelves

and is assured of a handsome income. Hans Christian Andersen (1805–75) may have created the Danish reputation for writing children's stories but it is now a very serious occupation, with 400 authors and 35 illustrators, and 10 percent of all titles published are for children.

In one recent year, 8,000 first editions were published, of which 20 percent were literary titles, and in the same year 2½ million books were sold to the libraries. Many of these must have been by Klaus Rifbjerg (born 1931), who has over 100 titles to his name and who is the most prolific writer of the post-war period. Starting with his (then) scandalous *Chronic Innocence* in 1958, he joined forces with the philosopher and essayist Villy Sørensen (born 1929) to establish a new literary movement through the periodical *Vindrosen*, which they edited from 1959 to 1963.

Both have since mellowed and survived the radical movement of the early 1970s, with Sørensen publishing a Utopian manifesto, *Revolt from the Centre,* in 1978 and Rifbjerg enjoying a comfortable position as literary editor of Denmark's largest publishing house. He still writes two novels a year.

Many other authors of this generation deserve to be mentioned and, even more so, to be translated. Hans Scherfig and Henrik Stangerup are a couple who have won audiences outside Denmark.

But in many ways it is the female writers who are attracting most interest overseas; Marianne Larsen (born 1951) and Pia Tafdrup (born 1952) are widely read poets. Unlike their illustrious compatriot Karen Blixen, who wrote in English, the novelists Dorrit Willumsen, Kirsten Thorup, Dea Trier Mørch and Suzanne Brøgger, all born in the early 1940s and all deeply involved in the women's movement, have taken up the very topical Danish themes of social change and its effects on social and sexual roles; their books are all available in translation.

Public funds of Dkr 603 million were allocated to the theatre in 1988. More than one-third went to finance the National Theatre, Det Kongelige Teater. This includes Gamle Scene, which stages opera, ballet and large-scale productions, and three other theatres Nye Scene, Grabrødrescenen and Comediehuset. It is a state institution and also home to the Royal Opera, the Royal

Ballet and the Royal Danish Orchestra. A quarter of the public funds covered the losses of the 20 other Copenhagen theatres, as well as the theatres in the three largest provincial towns, Århus, Odense and Ålborg.

These public sources provided Dkr 33 million for the touring companies and Dkr 9 million for children's theatre groups on tour, which also provide the repertoires for the numerous provincial theatre associations spread over the country. A further Dkr 49 million went to subsidise ticket sales, in the form of low-cost subscriptions, both for the permanent theatres and for seasons arranged by the local theatre associations (accounting for 20 percent of ticket sales).

which – the summer revues at provincial resorts – are equally popular.

Three major playwrights emerged around 1930; Kaj Munk (1898–1944), who was executed by the Germans, Carl Erik Soya (1896–1983) and Kjeld Abell (1901–61). The most recent talent, Leif Panduro (1923–77), wrote his witty psychoanalytical plays about modern Danish society for the more potent medium of television, punching through the screen at the self-satisfied, new middle classes in their cosy living rooms.

Academy Awards: The film industry receives generous funding for the production and distribution of new feature films and short films. A quarter of this budget is strictly

Not many of the productions offered are Danish in origin. Dramatists have been few and far between, apart from Ludvig Holberg (1684–1754), who is claimed by both Denmark and Norway. He wrote in the tradition of Molière, and his work has recently been much performed in honour of the 300th anniversary of his birth. Although Henrik Ibsen wrote in Danish, he was a Norwegian and his work is undeniably Norwegian in character. Danes of the same period were enjoying light opera, the modern version of

Left, Copenhagen Jazz Festival. **Right**, a gay cabaret in the capital.

allocated to productions for children and young people.

The oldest film company in the world still in operation is the Danish Nordisk Film Kompagni, founded in 1906. The works of Carl Th. Dreyer (1889–1968) for that company are still the subject of film festivals throughout the world. He was a master of psychological realism, from his 1925 *The Master of the House* to *Gertrud* in 1964. The film industry, dominated by the one production company, developed slowly due to lack of funds and relied on a series of comedies (*The Olsen Gang*) and television productions (*Matador*) to survive.

KAREN BLIXEN

Karen Blixen was an exotic Scandinavian "Scheherazade" and a fascinating Danish enigma. A baroness by marriage, who let it be known to the deeply democratic Danes that she wished to be addressed by her title both in conversation and correspondence. A brave hardworking woman, she found fulfilment in Africa after marrying her lover's twin brother; but he lost her fortune and gave her syphilis.

Her story is now world-famous, thanks to the success of the film *Out of Africa* in which Meryl Streep portrayed Blixen, cleverly capturing the Danish accent. However, under the pen-name of Isak Dinesen, Blixen had been established in the literary world since the success of *Seven Gothic Tales*, published in the US and Britain in 1934. Acceptance took a little longer in Denmark, where she was criticised for writing about the aristocracy in approving terms, and for her fastidiously correct, slightly old-fashioned idiom which was considered by some to be affected and arrogant. But as more became known of her life and literary motives her image underwent considerable change and she has long been revered as a "national institution".

Karen Blixen was born on 17 April 1885 into the Dinesen family who lived at Rungstedlund, a large house, north of Copenhagen, overlooking the Sound between Denmark and Sweden. With much more of the temperament of her artistic and adventurous father, who committed suicide when she was 10, she grew up constantly rebelling against the restraints of the strict bourgeois standards set by her mother. Her marriage of convenience to a Swedish relative, Baron Bror von Blixen-Finecke (after an unhappy love affair with his twin brother Hans) was in many respects a total escape and rejection of her upbringing. So was their subsequent emigration to Africa. Theirs was an unemotional marriage happily arranged between two good friends – she wanted his title and the respect she felt this would bring, and he wanted her money to start a farm in Kenya.

During her time in Kenya, Karen Blixen learned Swahili, developed an empathy with the African people and grew to love the country deeply. *Avant garde* for her time, she was regarded as "pronative" by the upper-class British, and remained largely an outcast of the colonial social scene. Neither when her marriage was dissolved in 1925, nor during the many crises of the coffee farm, did she feel any desire to return to Denmark. This was partly due to her love-affair with Denys Finch-Hatton, an English aristocrat, whom she enthralled by playing the role of story-teller as after-dinner entertainment. In 1931 her world in Kenya finally collapsed with the failure of the coffee farm and the death of Finch-Hatton who crashed while piloting his safari plane.

A young real estate developer, Remy Martin, bought her farm at auction to create a smart Nairobi suburb of expensive houses with a large golf and country club. He named both "Karen" in her honour.

She returned to Denmark to live with her mother and began her literary career as Isak Dinesen. After the success of *Seven Gothic Tales* she published her masterpiece *Out of Africa* in 1937. This was followed by *Winter's Tales* in 1942; *The Angelic Avengers* in 1946; *Last Tales* in 1957; and *Anecdotes of Destiny* in 1958. She became a celebrity both in Denmark and abroad, with a circle of admirers. Constant ill health cast a shadow over her success, but she did not allow it to curb too many of her activities, and she travelled a great deal. In 1959, just three years before her death, she made a lecture tour of the US, where she was feted everywhere she went.

Although most famous as Izak Dinesen, other pseudonyms were Peter Lawless, Osceola, Nozdref's Cook, Pierre Andrezel, and she also wrote under her own names, Tania (related to "Tanne" as she was called affectionately by her family) Blixen, and Karen Blixen, which is the name on her tombstone. She died on 7 September 1962 at Rungstedlund and, according to her wishes, was buried in the grounds.

It was her wish, too, that the Danish Academy, instituted in 1960, should have the use of the main wing of the house for their meetings, and plans are now in motion to create a museum there, devoted to her life and work.

Since 1982 the state has increased its allocation and this, coupled with the establishment of a film school, has resulted in a blossoming of the industry, running to some 15 productions a year. So far, this has culminated in Academy Awards two years running for the best non-English language film. *Babette's Feast*, directed by Gabriel Axel and based on a story by Karen Blixen, was the first winner, and *Pelle the Conqueror* triumphed the following year. It was directed by Bille August and based on a story by Martin Andersen Nexø (1869–1954), with the Swedish-born Max von Sydow in the role of the father.

Music: In 1976 legislation made financial provide permanent homes for the Odense Symphony Orchestra, Aarhus Symphony Orchestra and the Jutland Opera Company. Northern and Southern Jutland also have their own orchestras, and there are a number of smaller ensembles specialising in chamber music. Live performances are well attended, thanks to a heavily subsidised subscription system, which has brought ticket prices down to a level acceptable to the Danish public.

Great Danish names in the classical genre were a bit sparse before the turn of the century. The Romantic period produced writers of Lieder, operettas in the German tradition (Friedrich Kuhlau 1786–1832, fa-

provisions for the support of musical activities of all kinds and established a Music Council, consisting of the interested parties, to oversee the distribution of funds. The "classical" tradition is still able to attract the most funds, with the Royal Danish Orchestra, the Danish Radio Symphony Orchestra and Sjælland Symphony Orchestra in Copenhagen. In the provinces attention has focused on Odense and Århus, both cities having opened new concert halls in 1982 to

Left, Karen Blixen. **Above**, Meryl Streep and Robert Redford in a scene from *Out of Africa*, based on Blixen's own life.

mous for the score of *Elverhøj*) and ballet music, such as J.P.E. Hartmann (1805–1900), N. W. Gade (1817–90), and H. C. Lumbye (1810–74, also famous for the Viennese-style *Champagne Gallop*) mostly commissioned by August Bournonville, master of the Royal Danish Ballet School.

Turning from Romanticism, the Funen composer Carl Nielsen (1865–1931), placed Denmark firmly on the international map of serious music. Although influenced by Mozart and Brahms, he ignored contemporary developments and struck out on his own. From his first symphony in 1892 to his sixth and last in 1925, he was borne along by a powerful and dramatic internal driving force, rapidly abandoning inherited traditions of form. In addition to the popular symphonies, which were on the repertoire of orchestras from Stuttgart to San Francisco, he wrote three instrumental concertos, choral music, piano pieces and two operas.

Since Nielsen, Danish music composition has developed dramatically and, as the professional orchestras are state institutions, their remit includes the requirement to play new Danish work. Thus, audiences at home and abroad are familiar with the work of Rued Langaard (1893–1952), Vagn Holmboe (born 1909), Hermann D. Koppel (born 1908), Ib Nørholm (born 1931), and Per

popular music forms to "come out in the open," literally. In early July the annual Copenhagen Jazz Festival fills the streets, cafés and halls of the city. What Paris has been to American writers, Copenhagen has been, and still is, to American musicians. Here they find an informality and intimacy, combined with enthusiasm and talent, which has made Copenhagen the European Jazz Capital. In the 1960s artists such as Thelonius Monk, Duke Ellington, Charlie Mingus, Miles Davis, Mel Tormé, Woody Herman and Ray Charles were regular visitors and, when the Danish Radio Big Band was established in 1964, it attracted Ray Pitts, Thad Jones and others, who set up residence in

Norgaard (born 1931) whose opera *The Divine Circus* created considerable interest at the Edinburgh International Festival of Music and Drama in 1989. They are also getting to know the work of younger composers such as Poul Ruders (born 1949) and Hans Abrahamsen (born 1952).

The music season traditionally concentrates on the winter months but, in Denmark, concerts are held throughout the summer in the Tivoli Concert Hall in Copenhagen, as well as at music festivals throughout the country, culminating in the Århus Festival at the beginning of September.

Summer is also the time for the more

Denmark, wrote for, inspired, and conducted the band. Saxophonist Jesper Thilo, bass player Niels-Henning Ørsted Pedersen, the trumpeters Palle Mikkelborg and Jens Winther, all international players, had a common nursery – the Big Band.

Jazz has also influenced light and pop music and, as in most other western countries, there are strong movements of folk and rock, which have spawned a middle-of-the-road folk-rock movement of their own, with a peculiarly Danish flavour. The record *Midt om Natten*, produced by the rock star Kim Larsen in 1984, still has the highest sales of any record in Denmark, and the live concerts during the summer attract the young and, young at heart in their tens of thousands. Amongst the most famous venues are the Roskilde Festival (established in 1970) and the Tønder Festival.

The visual arts: Danish art has only recently attracted attention in other European countries. The first uproar occurred when the German newspaper magnate Axel Springer purchased a forgotten treasure of the Skagen art colony. Then, in the early 1980s, the English auction houses Sotheby's and Christie's appointed representatives in Denmark, and the Skagen artists began to fetch millions of krone on the international market. There was a scurrying in the attics of

1853), a painter who had made the obligatory study tour to Rome via Paris where he worked under David, who taught his pupils to study nature and to see with their own eyes. Eckersberg returned with this philosophy of "*voir beau et juste*" which he passed on to his own pupils, including Marinus Rørbye, Christen Købke, Wilhelm Marstrand and Constantin Hansen, the painters who formed the nucleus of The Golden Age.

The next group of importance became known as the "Skagen painters". This group collected around the artist couple Michael and Anna Ancher (1859–1935) and P. S. Krøyer (1851–1909) who, distancing themselves from stiff academic tradition and the

the old family homes, just in case the odd Krøyer happened to be lying around.

Two large-scale exhibitions followed. *Danish Painting of the Golden Age* was the title of an exhibition at the National Gallery in London in 1984 and, three years later, a combined Scandinavian effort resulted in *Dreams of a Summer Night* at the Hayward Gallery, also in London.

"The Golden Age" (approximately 1815–48), was fathered by C. W. Eckersberg (1783–

constraints of the capital, settled in Skagen. Attracted by the light at the northernmost tip of Jutland and by the motifs of the seascapes and local fishing population, they painted gloriously naturalistic works in the last decades of the century. A similar movement emerged on the island of Funen, with Vilhelm Hammershoi (1864–1916) the most famous painter of this group.

Another half century passed before the next wave of significant artists emerged, culminating in the group called COBRA (including artists from **C**openhagen, **Br**ussels and **A**msterdam). The group was established by the Dane, Asger Jorn (1914–73) and

Left, *Babette's Feast*, a Danish film success. Above, a painting by Martinus Rørbye (1803–48) one of the early Skagen painters.

moved from the inspiration of Expressionism in France to simplicistic abstract art and the influence of the Norwegian, Edvard Munch. Another, more naturalistic artist of the period was the painter and sculptor Henry Heerup (born 1907), who also influenced the sculptor Robert Jacobsen (born 1912) and Svend Wiig Hansen (born 1922).

In the 1960s the School of Experimental Art produced artists such as Per Kirkeby (born 1938) and fostered the graphic art movement which is so strong today and which allows the younger, less wealthy art fan to purchase "originals" by artists such as Palle Nielsen and Arne Haugen Sørensen. It is difficult to be objective about contempo-

decorative works which will always be available to the public, regardless of its museum-going habits. The first such work was a ceramic mural created by Asger Jorn in 1959 for Statsgymnasium (Upper Secondary School) in Århus. Paul Gernes decorated the County Hospital in Herlev, and Svend Wiig Hansen the Technical University in Lundtofte, Copenhagen.

There are two types of art museum in Denmark, the general and the specific. The admirer of modern art will find international collections at the Louisiana Museum in North Sealand and at the Aalborg and Aarhus Art Museums. On the other hand, some Danish artists have a whole museum to themselves:

rary art, but especially in its applied form, modern Danish art, crafts and design enjoy international recognition.

The public buildings and institutions such as libraries, schools and even factories which have been constructed over the past couple of decades all conform to the regime of good taste and simple lines, with furnishings and furniture designed to blend into the whole. In addition, each new public building includes works of art specially commissioned for the building; this is part of the legislation which requires 1 percent of the budget to be allocated to new works, thus enabling the current generation to produce monumental and

Asger Jorn in Silkeborg, Carl Henning Pedersen and Else Alfeldt in Herning.

In the less contemporary vein, the State Museum of Art houses a comprehensive international collection dating back to the 13th century, whereas the Hirschsprung Gallery concentrates on 19th-century artists of The Golden Age and the Skagen painters of the turn of the century (who have their own museum in Skagen). The classical sculptor Thorvaldsen has a museum of his own, built to his orders when he returned from Rome in 1838 after 40 years abroad.

Above, the Royal Life Guard on parade.

THE ROYAL DANISH BALLET

Danish male dancers have been influencing ballet throughout the world for the past 150 years. The New York Ballet is now led by Danish dancer and choreographer Peter Martins, and Peter Schaufuss moved from the London Festival Ballet to Berlin in 1990. They were both products of the Royal Danish Ballet School, with its great masters Harald Lander (1905–71) and August Bournonville (1805–79), who created what we know as "classical ballet", and whose methods still form the core of teaching today.

Despite his French name, Bournonville was born in Denmark, son of the balletmaster Antoine Bournonville, who had danced under Galeotti, the first balletmaster of the school. August studied in France but returned to Denmark and went on to lead Danish ballet for 50 years. He was a brilliant dancer and created many roles for himself in his early ballets. He created 50 full-length productions, of which *Napoli*, *The Dancing School* and, of course, *La Sylphide* are still regular items on every major ballet company's repertoire.

He commissioned the Danish romantic composers of the age to provide the music, and he trained his dancers according to a strict series of weekly programmes or "schools" – one for each day of the week. His Friday school is still in use and is shown on the stage in *The Dancing School*. The schools consisted of a long sequences of step compositions which could stand as entities. The exercises promoted the qualities he needed for his graceful and dramatically-based style, and the strength to perform the "new" techniques of pointwork for women and leaps for men. The *joie de vivre* and beauty which defined his ballet also provided its "Danishness".

New ideas and developments in the ballet came with the arrival of Harald Lander (1905–71) who was balletmaster from 1932 to 1951. Of his own ballets, the most successful have been *Étude* (1948) and *Quarrtsiluni* (1942), both with music by a Dane, Knudaage Riisager. But his main achieve-ment was the creation of a corps of dancers which, both at home and touring, brought the Danish Ballet much success in the immediate post-war years. Many of his pupils have gone on to become balletmasters and choreographers around the world.

The Lander School produced Poul Gnatt, who left Denmark in 1951 to play an important role in Australian ballet; Niels Bjørn Larsen was the most brilliant mime artist of his generation; Stanley Williams went to the New York City Ballet to teach, and Erik Bruhn joined the American Ballet Theatre. His most successful pupil was Flemming Flindt who has had a great international career.

Flindt was balletmaster in Copenhagen from 1966 to 1978, restaging a number of traditional ballets such as *The Nutcracker* and *Swan Lake* and creating memorable modern ballets such as *The Lesson*, based on a story by Ionesco, and *The Miraculous Mandarin*, to music by Bartok. In recent years Flindt has spent much time in the United States, and in 1990 he presented his ballet *The Overcoat*, specially created for, and performed by, Rudolf Nureyev with the Cleveland Ballet at the Edinburgh Festival.

During Flindt's reign in Copenhagen, new trends, mainly from American modern dance, were introduced into Danish ballet, and he took the ballet on extended world tours.

These traditions continued into the 1980s. The star of the 1960s, Henning Kronstam, became balletmaster, whilst two younger soloists, Peter Martins and Peter Schaufuss, began working overseas, directing and creating their own ballets. The current artistic director, Frank Andersen, invited Flemming Flindt to create a new ballet, *Karoline Mathilda*, based on a royal Danish love affair and set to music by Sir Peter Maxwell Davies. A traditional Bournonville favourite, *A Folk Tale*, has been restaged in a new production with decorations and costumes by Queen Margrethe II, an accomplished artist.

The home of the Royal Danish Ballet is the Royal Theatre, "Det Kongelige Teater", and the season runs from 15 August to 1 June. The summer is devoted to the overseas tours that continues to delight and to demonstrate to audiences that a nation of only 5 million people can produce some of the world's best dance.

Sleek mid-century Modern, the elegant, simple line that first became the Danish ideal in the middle of the 20th century, is fashionable again, and nowhere more so than in Denmark. The hottest items – streamlined chairs, glassware, even buildings – are drawing bids in the six-figure range from "antique" cognoscenti at major auctions. Signatures of the likes of Hans Wegner, Arne Jacobsen and Poul Kjaerholm drive prices up another 40 to 50 percent. Denmark's mid-century is now old enough to be "classic".

Danish Modern, be it authentic Danish, a Swedish copy or just ordinary "1950s Teak", is back with a vengeance and nowhere more appreciated than on home turf, where excellence of design is a fact of life. Sculptural teak chairs by the grand old man of Danish design, Hans Wegner, and clinically spare cocktail shakers in stainless steel by modernist Poul Kjaerholm are regular features in the auction catalogues of Bruun Rasmussen's in Copenhagen as well as Sotheby's and Christie's in London.

What's in demand: The earlier the piece, the greater its market value. Top dealers from Helsinki to Los Angeles, but especially in Copenhagen, comb Denmark's second-hand shops for finds. Then they ask collectors to pay small fortunes for original Arne Jacobsen bent wood and steel furnishings designed 40 years ago. Danish design, even when it is industrial, is suddenly on the move again and connoisseurs, the rich and the art-hungry are collecting the best of it. Like the Danes themselves, they intend to live with art and excellent quality.

The Danes have been doing that for centuries. Simplicity has always been in fashion. Previously, the spare look was the result of economic necessity. Gradually, it became the only acceptable taste for Danish barons, burghers and even farmers. But spare was not (nor is it today) equated with poor workmanship; quite the opposite.

Danes will not pay for "masses of fluff" but, according to Christian Jacobsen, director of the Applied Arts Museum in Copenhagen, will value "something that will last, is well put together from high-quality materials and is classic enough to keep its style for many years. That is real Danish design."

Jacobsen points to Hans Wegner as the archetypal Danish designer, citing his crafts and educational background. At 14, Wegner's career started in the local carpenter's shop where he nailed together coffins. Gradually he advanced to producing his own ideas for bedroom sets. He delivered these himself by dogcart in his native village, Tønder, on the German border. To improve his carving skills, he spent evenings copying in wood the delicate Royal Copenhagen porcelain figurines in the local heritage museum. Young lovers embracing was a favourite theme for the adolescent Wegner's knives.

Such practice made perfect when Wegner's first major design – a Jugendstil armoire inlaid with rare woods representing waterlilies, exotic fish, tadpoles and insects – was condemned as "impossible to produce" by the carpenters assigned the task. Indignant, Wegner himself took on the delicate, intricate job, using his pocket knife to prove them wrong. The armoire brought recognition and an invitation to study at Copenhagen's School of Applied Arts.

Within a few years, Wegner was scooped up by the country's leading design studio with an assignment to furnish the new town hall of Århus, Denmark's second city. This was an unbeatable opportunity to develop his own concepts and standards which subsequently laid the groundwork for a new taste in interior design, Danish Modern. The rest is history. Awards and one-man shows are still showering down on Hans Wegner.

Typically Danish in concept, Wegner's design principle dictates that furniture, architecture, flatware – all design – must suit the body and the eye, not vice versa. "A dining room chair or a desk chair must give correct back support. A lounge chair should be more relaxed," he says.

"The Round One", his first internationally acclaimed chair (1949), earned Wegner the prestigious Lunning Prize, a show in New York, and inclusion in the permanent collec-

Preceding pages: modern industry design display. **Left,** Danish "PH" lighting is world-famous. "PH" means designer Poul Henningsen.

tion of Manhattan's Museum of Modern Art. "We are working in our own special corner of the world, an inspiring corner," says Wegner. "To preserve that special feeling, materials must be Scandinavian. Usually I choose oak, beech, ash and some maple. An occasional piece of tropical teak will sneak by as a reminder of our seafaring background here in Denmark."

Trendsetter to classicist in just 30 years: that cannot be explained away as just a dash of mid-century nostalgia. For three decades, Scandinavia, led by Denmark, presented a consolidated design idiom wholly different from what was going on in the rest of the world. Extravagantly high-quality design

Scandinavian Modern was acclaimed the resounding success of Milan's august Triennale design fair that year. Simultaneously a three-year, 22-city tour of the United States dubbed "Design in Scandinavia" clinched the popularity of what the Nordic design organisations were doing, and created a huge new market. Denmark was credited with capturing in wood and steel the dynamic spirit of the streamline post-war period. "Something clean, free and vital," proclaimed the exhibition catalogue.

Critics and reviewers gushed. "Here is Functionalism that pleases aesthetically," wrote one. "Danish Modern is the visual expression of the socially just society," wrote

devoid of unnecessary decoration, superb workmanship and materials explain Danish Modern's enduring reputation and buyers' interest. It is perhaps the last style that confidently displays guild-quality workmanship.

Scandinavia's post-war political climate fostered the new taste. Popular social aesthetics such as the adage "More Beautiful Everyday Life!" helped to soften the hard edge of pre-war Functionalism. Pragmatically, the Danes refused to abandon their highly developed crafts traditions, thus adding superior woodwork and joinery to the new "look". By 1954, the "look" had been given a name.

another. Despite all that, the style was and remains definitely up-market, with its sophisticated lines and corresponding price tag. Still, a style had been born.

The most popular products were the most simple, often those with a geometric appearance. Arne Jacobsen took a giant egg form made of steel, scooped out the front of it, "as if I'd had it for breakfast," covered it in foam and leather, and balanced the results on one single stainless steel leg. He had created, naturally enough, his Egg Chair. "Sculpture to sit in!" was one reviewer's comment at the first appearance of the Egg at the opening of the SAS Royal Hotel in Copenhagen.

Disdaining all unnecessary elaboration, Danish designers displayed clearly and proudly their materials as the only permissible decorative element. Gratuitous ornament, especially nature motifs, is nearly unknown in Danish Modern design and was generally frowned upon by critics and designers.

Hans Wegner's "Cow Horns" chair fastens the two elements of massive walnut in its back support with a fully visible, flowing dovetail joint, lined with blond veneer in a virtuoso display of carpentry skills. Nothing unnecessary is included in a Cow Horns chair, materials are proudly displayed, as is superior workmanship and design that suits use, simple principles that have made Cow

the accent was on rare woods presented in their natural colours. Thanks to the Danish East India Company, there was plenty of high-quality Siamese teak and mahogany.

The smooth, curving forms of the Art Nouveau period at the turn of the century once again inspired Scandinavian artists. This so called "linear-organic" trend also took full advantage of the new materials appearing after World War II. Bakelite, plastics, wood laminates, spun steel and aluminium quickly became new avenues for design experiment. Silverware became stainless steel. Elegant stainless steel and brass pots and pans suddenly appeared on the dining-room table. Unfortunately, such materials led to

Horns the most imitated chair in the world.

In another interpretation of Danish Modern, technical solutions to design problems were made openly visible, even decorative, as in Poul Kjaerholm's scissor-action stools made of burnished, unglazed steel. Two distinct trends slowly developed: "organic funk" and "hard edge". The organic school drew heavily from traditional sources such as Denmark's cabinet-making schools where

Left, Bing & Grondahl's porcelain shop. Above, a characteristic display of Danish room design. Following pages: Flora Danica porcelain and Georg Jensen silver.

the flurry of cheap imitations that flourished in England, Italy and the United States – copies that lacked the spirit and finesse of Danish originals.

Hard-edge Scandinavian Modern might best be summed up by one of its major proponents, architect-designer Arne Jacobsen: "Industrial technique should satisfy all functional and aesthetic requirements." Needless to say, Jacobsen and his ilk were the spiritual children of Functionalist Le Corbusier and, like him, most had trained as architects. Their idiom of Danish Modern banked on technical solutions to the theme "aesthetical functionalism".

Steel was always a favoured material because of its flexibility and strength as well as the elegance of its burnished or pickled surfaces. Kjaerholm and Jacobsen were acknowledged the major trendsetters here. They strove for geometrically pure, elegantly minimal forms with what Kjaerholm liked to call "structural vigour".

Most of the hard-edge practitioners, openly influenced by their architectural tastes, gave acute attention to surface variety and contrasts of textures in their works. Poul Kjaerholm's "Hammock Chair 24" typifies the idiom's striking combination of materials. The tempered steel frame is dramatically pared down so that the flowing cane weave of the seat seemingly floats in the air, making the thinnest of silhouettes. Kjaerholm's individualistic departure from Denmark's traditions in wood earned him a Grand Prix at the 1957 Milan Triennials – and set off a new wave of imitations.

Kjaerholm, Wegner, Jacobsen and the other superstar designers of the Danish period set the standard for what Modern would look like for the past 40 years – until the advent of Memphis squiggles and coloured blotches. Critic Marika Hausen summed up the Danish Modern period best in a comment about a retrospective show: "For a short while during the Fifties, Scandinavia attained a sort of balance, when it seemed that the ideals and efforts of the utopian Thirties had been realised. There was still belief in consumer information, in good taste and quality."

Denmark retains much of that idealism. Copenhagen's largest department store, Illums Bolighus, regularly offers major design exhibitions that fill the store's first floor. The accent is on "good design that adds comfort and beauty to the home." Not surprisingly, many of these shows are retrospectives of Danish classics. Down the road, the Museum of Applied Arts proudly displays its complete collection of Mid-century Modern – pieces bought 40 years ago directly from the artists. Such farsightedness pays off today as the Danish Modern chambers draw the greatest number of visitors to the museum.

But every Danish home is a mini-exhibition of the style, as every Dane is a living conservator of the national idiom. Danish Modern was created to give Danes a taste of the good life and has become their way of life.

There is perhaps no better way to get a sense of Denmark's history than by visiting some of its churches. Danes are not, on the whole, faithful churchgoers, but the fabric of the church and the nation's cultural inheritance are fiercely guarded everywhere. Interesting old traditions remain, too: many Danish churches have a model ship hanging under the arch or from the ceiling as a reminder of the Danish maritime tradition and the sailors who work so far from home.

Christianity was introduced to Denmark in 826 by the French Benedictine monk Ansgar, but the small town of Jelling in eastern Jutland is presumed to be the site of the first officially-protected Christian church. In any case, the first historical statement of Denmark's conversion to Christianity appears on the Jelling Stones that King Harald Bluetooth raised to the memory of his parents, Gorm and Thyra (about 985).

Those stones stand today beside a small 11th-century church, below which the remains of two older, wooden structures have been found. The uppermost of these may have been built by Harald Bluetooth after his conversion. According to legend, this occurred after he witnessed an astonishing act of faith by a missionary monk named Poppo, who (in about AD 960) carried red-hot iron in his hands without apparent suffering or injury to his person.

By the year 1200, some 2,000 churches had been built around the country and those standing today tell the story of Denmark's heritage. Very little architecture survives from the Middle Ages apart from the churches, and their upkeep is evidence of social bonds and coherence through the centuries. They are often found on hills, and their towers afford sweeping views of the rolling landscape.

Most are from the Middle Ages, and many have characteristic shapes. There is usually a tower, dating from the 16th century, and their naves and apses are Romanesque in their foundations, built in the 10th, 11th and

12th centuries. In many cases the Gothic period (roughly 1250–1500) saw the churches enlarged and Gothic vaults erected on the earlier structures. To see purely Romanesque churches, one should visit west and north Jutland, while Gothic churches are abundant elsewhere in the country.

Like the Danes who worshipped there, the churches are not grandiose; Denmark has no churches on the scale and magnitude of the ecclesiastical architecture found elsewhere in Europe. Danish churches bear witness to

the pervasive and modest solidity of Danish culture and piety, and were built and decorated largely by peasant craftsmen. The churches in cities speak not of the nobility but of wealthy tradesmen, whose touchingly crude, carved and painted epitaphs mark the passing of daily life.

One uniquely Danish kind of church architecture is found in the round fortress-churches of Bornholm, Sealand, Funen and northern Germany. They were built in certain villages as refuges in times of war, and had wells and thick walls (resembling the curtain walls of medieval Europe), extremely narrow windows and battlements to withstand the sieges

Preceding pages: Føvling Kirke in Jutland. Left, a beautiful altar in Vor Frelsers Kirke in Copenhagen. Right, Maribo Domkirke.

which occurred, particularly in the Baltic. Østerlars Kirke on Bornholm is a particularly good example, while the church at Horne on Funen shows how some were altered by Gothic additions and extensions.

In Copenhagen, visitors should see Vor Frelsers Kirke (the Church of Our Saviour), which boasts a splendid spire with an external spiral staircase to the top. Unless you have a very good head for heights, forgo the climb, magnificent though the view is, and visit the interior of the 17th-century church, with its large windows and cheerful light. Christianskirke (also at Christianshavn) is amusing because the 17th-century burghers used their own boxes instead of pews. It was

Its current shape is from 1176, the year a fire destroyed its predecessor. It's a beautiful place; climb the stairs to visit the flat-topped bell tower for a wonderful view of the marsh and farmlands of southern Jutland. In common with other churches built around the same time, Ribe Domkirke originally lay outside the centre of the city – probably because its missionary activity wasn't completely accepted by the still-pagan Vikings of the nearby town.

While in the area, a visit to Christ Church in nearby Tønder is worth the time. It was built in 1591, and retains a tower from the late Middle Ages, but otherwise is notable for its use of space and light. Denmark's

like being in a private theatre but perhaps served a practical purpose, as Danish sermons in the 16th and 17th centuries could last for many hours. It could be restful to put the pulpit oratory at a peaceful distance for a while by closing the doors and windows.

Marmorkirken (the Marble Church) in the capital was finished in the 19th century. It speaks of Copenhagen's ambition to rival Rome and the Pantheon; although it's a sombre affair inside, the extension is splendid.

Ribe Domkirke, in Denmark's oldest town, (in the care of the Danish National Trust) is perhaps the best-preserved and certainly the largest Romanesque church in the country.

most beautiful Gothic churches are at the former Cistercian monasteries of Løgumkloster (just north of Tønder) and Sorø (on Sealand). Both were built during the second half of the 12th century, and are examples of the most important development in Danish architecture during the 12th century: the introduction of red brick as a building material.

From Viking times right through the Middle Ages, Roskilde was a great religious, cultural and political centre. There are 14 parish churches and five convents in the area as well as the magnificent cathedral, Roskilde Domkirke, the burial place for almost all

Danish Kings and Queens. Excavations have shown that building began around the year 1000 and chapels are still being added. The two most impressive are those of King Christian IV, in Dutch-Renaissance style from 1641, which has beautiful murals; the chapel of King Frederik V from 1770 was the masterwork of the architect, Harsdorff.

The whole cathedral has an enormous variety in architectural styles, both medieval and Renaissance, and has grown like a living organism over nearly 1,000 years. Haderslev Domkirke and Sct. Olai Kirke in Helsingør (both of which were rebuilt in the 1400s to fit more closely the ideal basilica type found in northern Germany) are other noteworthy

A great majority of churches, it is believed, were built on pagan cult sites. Quite often, a well is found in the crypt below the altar, and this is also true in Lund. Note also the granite-carved figures (especially above the doorways to the nave) which evoke the spiritual change required by the Catholic church as demons and ogres were replaced by Christian symbolism. Attention should be paid to the *kalk-malerier* (frescoes) carried out during the Middle Ages, which also help one distinguish between Romanesque and Gothic style. One notable example is Fanefjord Kirke on the island of Møn, where the vaults of the double nave display medieval man's lively experience of the impor-

churches. A trip to the university town of Lund, in southern Sweden, (once part of Denmark) and the cathedral there is also a memorable afternoon's excursion. The Archbishop of Lund was the primate of Denmark at the time of its construction and, though it has suffered a major fire and reconstruction since it was built, it remains an outstanding example of Romanesque architecture in southern Scandinavia.

Left, the round church at Østerlars, designed as a fortress for times of war. **Above**, Roskilde, the Bishop's residence and Cathedral. **Following pages**: Gisselfeldt Castle, and Rosenborg.

tant events of the Old and New Testaments. Unlike those of the Sistine Chapel, the paintings still show the artist's sense and use of space. They were all obliterated during and after the Reformation (1536), but careful restoration continues as conservators remove layers of whitewash to preserve these beautiful scenes.

The images, costumes and features of the people represented at Fanefjord Kirke are a unique means of understanding life in the Middle Ages. In common with many of the older churches, they give an insight into a past which has made the Danes the people they are today.

FORTRESSES, CASTLES AND MANOR HOUSES

The evolution of the Danish manor house can be traced to the early Middle Ages, when a wealthy property owner might surround his home and a cluster of smaller outbuildings within a wooden palisade and, sometimes, a moat or other defensive perimeter.

The first stone buildings began to appear around 1075, but from that time only the scant remains of a tower (from about 1100) can be found near Bastrup Sø (Bastrup Lake) on Sealand, a few kilometres west of Farum. The most interesting ruins in the Copenhagen area are those below Christiansborg Palace in the city itself, where visitors can see the foundations of the palace (from the late 1160s) built on top of the remains of the village of Havn.

Some other good choices will be the ruins of Korsør (about 1280), Kalø Slot (the foundations of which were laid in 1313) near Århus, and Gurre Slot (just southwest of Helsingør, from the late 1100s). The best preserved ruins in the country are either in the town of Vordingborg, on the southwestern coast of Sealand, where Gåsetårnet (the Goose Tower) from the early 1300s overlooks the remains of the fortress and the harbour below, and at Hammershus (from 1255) on Bornholm.

The Romanesque style, with its characteristic rounded arches and window openings, was gradually replaced in the 13th and 14th centuries by the Gothic, which had more intricate, pointed archways and subtle architectural detail. The best examples of Gothic architecture include Gjorslev (from about 1400), about 6 miles (10 km) south of Køge on Sealand, and Rygård (from 1525), between Nyborg and Svendborg on Funen.

Renaissance influence on Danish architecture began around 1550. Examples of the transition from Gothic to Renaissance style, as appearance became a more important design consideration than defence, include Gisselfeld and Borreby on Sealand, as well as Nakkebølle, Ørbæklunde, Hesselagergård and Egeskov, all on Funen and from the 1500s. The first public monument in Renaissance style is Kronborg castle in Helsingør, built by King Frederik II. The most obvious and numerous examples of Renaissance construction appeared during the reign of that voracious builder King Christian IV, who adopted Dutch Renaissance style and the architect Hans van Steenwinckel – and nearly bankrupted the nation in doing so.

Though there are no castles on the grand scale of Versailles in Denmark, a number of accessible and historically important ones are open to the public. The list includes Kronborg, Frederiksborg, Dragsholm, Gavnø Slot and Egeskov Slot. Amalienborg, on the harbour in Copenhagen, is the official residence of the Royal Family.

Be sure to visit Rosenborg Slot (dating from 1617) in Copenhagen, and its museum, which together with Kongens Have (the Royal Gardens) form a rare and complete whole. The little castle was built as the Royal summer house outside the city walls but today it is situated at the very centre of the city, near Norreport. The museum houses the private property of Denmark's royalty and the beautiful crown jewels. It is a small, intimate and lovely building.

The styles of many manor houses vary, but generally emphasise balanced proportion and scale. One does not encounter the gloomy fortress-like river castles of Germany. They are mostly open, friendly, and speak of the comfortable rural life of the aristocracy. Early examples are Hesselagergård on Funen, or Holmegaard near the city of Næstved in southwest Sealand. One might also look at Hvidkilde on Funen (from around 1550, with later additions). Gavnø, just south of Næstved, is from about 1400. Closer to Copenhagen is Søllerødgård from the late 17th century.

It is a characteristic of these manor houses that they are not grandiose – indeed, like so many things Danish, they are on a modest scale. Many, particularly on Funen, have been converted to unusual but homely hotels.

In the summer of 1988, for the first time, a thin layer of smog lingered over the streets of Copenhagen. It was nothing like the great palls in Los Angeles or Tokyo, but just enough to make breathing a little harder for people with allergies or asthma. The same summer saw an explosive growth in the number of yellow algae in the Kattegat between Jutland and Sweden, an incident which reportedly kept a large number of tourists away from the beaches that year. At the same time, Thorvaldsen's Museum in Copenhagen decided to remove a statue from the roof of the museum because acid rain had corroded it so badly that they were afraid it would break.

Denmark has its share of environmental problems. There are toxic waste dumps and dying lakes and too much garbage here, just as in most other countries. Yet the Danes are one step ahead in the way they regard the problems. Most believe the environment to be the single most important political issue, and for more than a decade, saving energy has been a top priority in Danish politics. Successive governments have kept oil and gas prices artificially high and have subsidised the research and implementation of alternative forms of energy.

Saving energy: The story began with the 1973 oil crisis. Denmark was then totally dependent on oil and coal from abroad, and the state banned all excessive use of energy. Driving was prohibited on Sundays, shops were left dark after closing time, and many trains, planes and buses were cancelled. Most accepted these measures as reasonable, even exciting, and, although they lasted for only a few months, many people formed permanent energy-saving habits.

Part of the reason was a hefty rise in the price of oil, gas and electricity, which brought a new awareness that natural resources were not unlimited, and a pattern of frugality emerged. The state mailed stickers to be posted on appropriate door frames: "Turn down the heat;" "Use the shower

instead of the bath;" "Turn off the light when you leave the room."

At one point in the 1970s, it was a sign of true public spirit to put meals in a haybox to shorten the time in the stove and to wear rush shoes instead of slippers in a cold living room. While the Danes locked off rooms during winter and insulated outer walls in homes all around the country, fashion introduced the eiderdown overcoat to make the winter bearable out of doors. For a couple of years, Denmark was submerged in plaids,

darkness and high principles, and bad consciences and guilt lurked whenever the craving for a little luxury peeped through.

The energy crisis created an interesting situation. On the one hand, the government tried to balance a tottering budget with high energy taxes. On the other hand a large group of people responded with enthusiasm and persistent interest in energy matters, and blamed the government for taking too little action. What evolved was a new perspective, not so much out of worry about the economy as out of concern for the environment. What if this were not just a temporary crisis? What about the pollution so obviously tied to the energy we expended? Through a combination of laws, taxes and voluntary renunciation, a whole new set of initiatives to reduce pollution and "energy gluttony" arose.

Some of the ideas gained recognition worldwide. The best known is probably the re-use of glass bottles. A system of standardised bottles with a fairly large redemption value (Dkr 1 per bottle) has persuaded people to return empty bottles to the shops, where the breweries pick them up; a beer bottle is re-used, on average, 30 to 35 times before it breaks and is remelted. The system, the most successful of its kind, has been blessed by the European Community, even though it imposes trade restrictions on for-

local power plant. State subsidies also made a windmill a profitable investment for many rural households.

At first, the mills were greeted with scepticism and worries that they would dominate the landscape. But, although windmills are a dominant feature of some landscapes today, the complaints have stopped; most people feel that they add a sculpture-like quality to the horizon. The worries are more about the durability of the mills. As a new product, they developed unexpected technical flaws and what promised to be a success, both locally and on foreign markets, has turned out to be a less than attractive investment. These first mistakes can be corrected, how-

eign breweries because canned beers may not be imported.

But re-use and recycling were only two of many strategies applied to reduce the energy problems. To inventors, the crisis turned out to be a challenge and they responded to it creatively. In western Jutland, windmills started purring and soon afterwards began to appear all over the country. Windmill parks were added to the landscape; one of the most spectacular can be found at a pier in Ebeltoft ferry harbour. In areas with good wind, a single windmill can produce enough electricity to cover all the needs of a farmer, and still enable him to share some of it with the

ever, and windmills may well return to the list of Danish export goods.

Another promising invention is an electrical car by the name of "Ellert" or *mini-el*. It is a small three-wheeled car, designed for short trips only. With an average of 25 mph (40 kph), it performs best in city traffic and has to be recharged for every 20 to 40 miles (35 to 60 km), depending on the weather and driving conditions. The energy used in a *mini-el* is a fraction of that used in a small car but, even more important, so is the pollution it creates. Nevertheless, shortly after the car was released in 1988, it ran into problems similar to those of the windmills and, after the first accident involving a *mini-el*, public confidence and sales dropped.

"All beginnings are difficult," a Danish proverb goes; but the most important result of the energy crisis is well established already, even though it will never be visible or tangible. Nothing would have changed if people's attitudes had not changed. Citizens take bottles with no redemption value to glass collection points, even though no-one thanks them for it; the sale of spray cans has gone down markedly since it was revealed that some of their ingredients break down the ozone layer; and many people will go an extra mile to buy organic groceries.

A study by Brugsen, the largest of the

vegetable lover, and some vegetarians would refuse to own a car at all; but, in the beginning, all these actions were taken in response to the same challenge – they are components of a new way of life that favours a sound soul in a sound body in a sound environment. The morning jog, the healthy food, the hair shampoo made entirely of natural ingredients, the windmills, and the low energy refrigerator all offer ways towards a cleaner, healthier life.

On a larger scale, one can also find community efforts to clean up the environment. Two vastly different examples are the free community of Christiania in Copenhagen and the city of Horsens in Jutland.

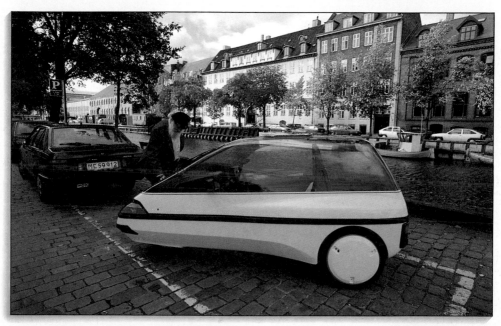

supermarket chains, shows that 15 percent of all carrots sold in its stores are organically grown and, because the increased demand calls for larger, more profitable crops, the price of chemical-free food is going down. The study proves that supply and demand now support each other, encouraging less polluted agricultural production.

Not everybody who owns an Ellert is a

Far left, staying fit is now a way of life. **Left**, compost bins and baskets come in many designs. **Above**, the "Ellert", an electric car designed and produced in Denmark. **Following pages**: the craze for cycling grows year by year.

From the beginning, Christiania has had an ecological perspective. Hens and horses compete with compost bins and heaps in creating a back-to-the-earth atmosphere. Shops on the premises carry a good selection of chemical-free food; aches and pains are cured in the Health House, often by unorthodox methods; and one of the big halls has been renovated for use as a recycling shop for building materials. The facilities for an ecologically sound life are there. But a move to Christiania also means saying goodbye to hot, running water, warm rooms on winter mornings, water closets, and, for most people, the luxury of one's own room. Whichever way one sees it, Christiania is an experiment that relies heavily on individual effort and conviction, and it will always have its own status as an exception. Nevertheless, many people have benefited from experience gained in Christiania and have moved on to apply it elsewhere.

Horsens has chosen a different path, approved not only by the state but also by the United Nations. The World Health Organisation (WHO) runs a scheme called *Healthy Cities Year 2000* in which 25 cities in Europe co-operate to improve the quality of urban living. Although WHO co-ordinates the project and assists with advice in technical matters, it is basically a local initiative, paid for by the city itself. An unusual feature is that the city didn't establish any goals for the project, other than to make people aware of health issues in a very broad sense.

A group of 13 people was selected from social institutions and councils in the city and supplemented by ordinary citizens with very different backgrounds: a bank executive, a welfare client, a school child and six other people who had shown an interest in making Horsens a better city to live in. Their first task was to make themselves heard and seen in Horsens. One early activity was a walking tour of the city, guided by a man who called in and proposed the idea as a fun way of exercising. But another high-priority project is of a much grander scale: to add a new residential quarter to Horsens, built to satisfy ecological principles.

It is still unclear, however, what these principles are: should the buildings recycle rainwater, use natural building materials only and leave room for the weeds; should each apartment have its own garden and chicken yard, or is a communal energy supply the essential feature? This is very much the current debate.

The new area, Torsted Vest, is scheduled to be finished in 1992, and then Horsens will have something to show visitors. But it seems that the real purpose of the project is education. The kind of democracy that encourages debate and gives the grassroots a say alongside politicians and experts is a truly Danish way of approaching the issue. Even though many more plans, ideas, and lofty schemes will be aired in Horsens than will ever be realised, the buildings will provide an outward and visible sign of the intent.

MORE BICYCLES THAN PEOPLE

For people who would disabuse themselves of the idea that Denmark is a flat little country, the best view is from the saddle of a bicycle. The highest point, Himmelbjerget (Sky Mountain) may not be much more than 500 ft (175 metres) but the narrow Danish road, rolling ahead like some minor switchback, can prove a tough test on the leg muscles.

Cycling is more than exercise in Denmark; it is a way of life, a blow struck for the environment. Every Danish town – Copenhagen more than any other – has its herds of cyclists speeding along the special cycle tracks (there are more than 3,500 miles/5,000 km of them), dismounting gently to cross the main road, where motor traffic must give way. Government Ministers, smart business suits, overalls, children riding pillion, bulging briefcases, and sandwich boxes strapped carefully on to luggage baskets are all part of the morning parade. In summer, shorts and long tanned legs predominate; in wet winter weather, the riders crouch like waterproof pyramids underneath their capes.

Outside the towns, cyclists stream towards the local station to tie up their bicycles at the station park, modern-day Wild Westerners hitching their horses before they set off for the working day.

Cycle tracks are strictly for bicycles. Woe betide the unwary foreigner who drives carelessly away from beach or lakeside along one of them. Bands of cyclists, unusually militant, leap off their cycles to wave and shout and behave in a very un-Danish manner because cycle tracks are sacrosanct. It is not just danger but outrage that motivates the protesters. When you realise the offence, the only recourse is to wind down the car window, point to foreign number plates and apologise in as obscure a foreign language as possible.

Cycling in Denmark has long moved from the days before World War II when it was simply a matter of being the cheapest way of getting around. Certainly, recent crises and Denmark's consequently high petrol prices gave a boost to this most pollution-free method of transport, which had begun to decline in favour of the motor car. But Danes also ride bicycles as part of their commitment to the Green movement and in order to get close to nature.

High though the standard of living is, per head Denmark has among the lowest private ownership of cars in Europe and the Danish Federation of Cyclists is a power, not so much in the land as on the road. Their annual Bicyclists' Day draws thousands to central Copenhagen. In Town Hall Square they meet old friends and swop cycling stories with all the zeal of anglers describing "the one that got away." Speakers from the Federation and other organisations extol the virtues of the bicycle and demand better road use by motorists.

Nevertheless, one result of this cycling enthusiasm is that Copenhagen, the first city to declare a street for pedestrians only, is normally much quieter and has less traffic noise and fewer fumes than any other European capital. Danish families also find cycling a good way of communing with nature, a preoccupation of all Scandinavians. As the schools close down in June, it is a common sight to see a family setting off with three or four bikes, toddler on the baby seat, heavily laden saddle bags and perhaps a small box trailer to carry all the heavier items.

For visitors, the passion for cycling brings benefits. The tourist industry did not take long to realise the potential of the Danish countryside for cycle holidays, particularly on the many islands around the coasts, which are quiet and carry fewer cars and lorries.

The view from a bike is the ideal way to see a country. You are part of the landscape. The rush of air against the face as well as the muscle pressure on the legs make a cyclist aware of every change in terrain and topography. It is surprising how often that bottom gear needs to come into play. By contrast in the cocoon of a car, it is easy to miss the detail of the thatched farm houses, the farm smells from the steadings, and the scent of wild flowers. Denmark in spring and summer is sweet with the small pink saucers of wild roses which bloom in hedges and bushes and right down to the edge of the beaches, as well as masses of blue and gold flowers that keep endless company with the road all over Denmark. You can jump off a bike to examine an interesting plant or stop at one of the white churches, and Danish farms are idyllic, sometimes thatched or with pantile roofs and white walls, cross-timbered with painted beams and window frames. They are so well kept that it would be a bold farm beast that sullied the farmyard. On a Danish island, it is simple just to lay down a bike in the grass and dip into the sea which, in the Great or Little Belts, Kattegat or Baltic, is calm and much warmer than the North Sea.

Today it is possible to hire bikes at most railway stations and in even modest-sized towns, with the added advantage of easy spares for a machine that goes wrong. Many tourist offices offer all-in holidays which cover hire of cycles, routes, accommodation and meals. Most are designed to cater for average cyclists, not those who regularly race or range from one end of a country to the other. The average daily mileage lies between 30 to 60 miles (45 to 90 km), and independent tours are also possible with routes, cycles and either camping or a book-ahead inn scheme on offer.

The Danish summer climate varies from between 60° F to 80° F (15° C to 25° C), with some rain, though rarely much more than recurring showers which makes the months of May, June, July, August and September good cycling weather. Though a cycle may expose you to wind and weather, and a perverse law ensures that the prevailing wind is always against the cyclist, a tip to remember is that in summer, the prevailing wind blows from the west. Plan the route carefully and you can at least hope to avoid its being personally prevailing.

One of the best areas for cycling is Funen and its islands of Ærø and Langeland, Tåssinge, and the rest. The southern part and the islands are particularly popular with Danes and the holiday period of mid-June to early August is best avoided. Funen is full of manor houses and castles and old villages with well-preserved houses. Ærøkøbing, the main town of Ærø, is particularly beautiful with cobbled streets, tiny painted houses, and doors marked California and Alemeda and the like – reminders that this was once an important sea-going town.

Tåssinge, with its popular yacht harbour, and Langeland are connected by bridge, but the boat trip to other islands is a welcome break and island ferries take bikes on board as a matter of course.

The island of Bornholm, in the Baltic off Denmark's eastern coast, is another favourite cycling island. It has country both flat and very hilly with beautiful beaches in the south, and many small fishing villages. Cycling on the island is easy with several cycle ways, some along old railway tracks. The 5 miles (8 km) between Klemensker and Rø is lovely, with one stretch squeezing through high rocks on both sides.

South of Sealand, Lolland, Falster and Mon have bridge connections including Denmark's longest bridge, the 2-mile (3-km) bridge over Storstrømen between the mainland and Falster. Even here, the traffic is separated from the cyclists. Møn has Denmark's most brilliant cliffs, made of gleaming white chalk from the glacier age.

But the most isolated areas in a country where distances are generally short and farms have tamed the landscape are in the northwest of Jutland, with a magnificent coast of sand dunes from Skagen in the north right down to Skallingen at Esbjerg. It is always best for a cyclist to avoid main roads, particularly in Jutland where cars head for beach and summer house at speed. The wise cyclist will stick to the long stretches of isolated beach road and small fishing villages. Though there are no true cycle ways here, the secondary road system does almost as well.

These are just four cycling suggestions in Denmark. There are many more and, for a distant start, Danish State Railways (DSB) carry bikes at modest cost, as do the alternative private railways though their network is not comprehensive. Country buses also carry bikes, space permitting. The best advice is to travel light, Danish hotels look grander than they are and the style of dress is very informal. Many people take to a bike for an extra week of a holiday and leave their main luggage in a hotel storeroom ready for the return.

A week on the road gives a good perspective on why the Danes love their cycles and, after all the health-giving exercise, it is an anti-climax to don more formal clothing and get back into a car.

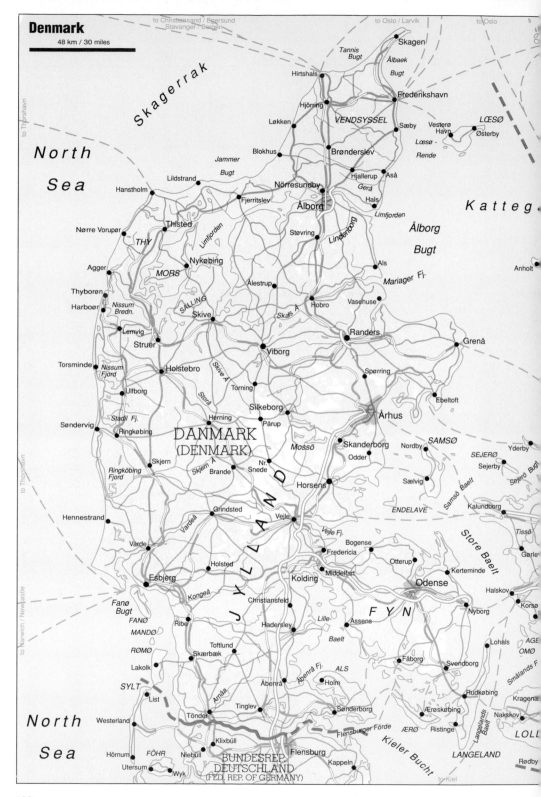

Denmark

48 km / 30 miles

Skagerrak

North Sea

to Thorshavn

to Christiansand / Egersund Stavanger / Bergen

to Oslo / Larvik

to Oslo

Skagen

Tannis Bugt

Hirtshals

Ålbaek Bugt

Hjørring

Frederikshavn

Løkken

VENDSYSSEL

Sæby

Vesterø Havn

LÆSØ

Østerby

Blokhus

Brønderslev

Løsø - Rende

Jammer Bugt

Lildstrand

Nørresundby

Hjallerup

Aså

Hanstholm

Fjerritslev

Gerå

Ålborg

Hals

Katteg

Limfjorden

Nørre Vorupør

Thisted

Støvring

Lindenborg

Ålborg Bugt

THY

Limfjorden

Nykøbing

Als

Anholt

Agger

MORS

Ålestrup

Mariager Fj.

Thyborøn

Harboør

Nissum Bredn.

SALLING

Skive

Skals Å

Hobro

Vasehuse

Lemvig

Randers

Grenå

Struer

Viborg

Torsminde

Nissum Fjord

Holstebro

Skive Å

Torning

Spørring

Ulfborg

Storå

Silkeborg

Ebeltoft

Søndervig

Stadil Fj.

Herning

Pårup

Århus

Ringkøbing

Skjern

DANMARK (DENMARK)

Mossø

Skanderborg

Nordby

SAMSØ

Yderby

Ringkøbing Fjord

Skjern Å

Brande

Nr. Snede

Odder

SEJERØ

Sejerby

Hennestrand

Varde

Vardeå

Grindsted

Vejle

Horsens

Sælvig

Sejerø Bugt

Vejle Fj.

Bogense

ENDELAVE

Kalundborg

Holsted

Fredericia

Otterup

Store Bælt

Tissø

Esbjerg

Kongeå

Kolding

Middelfart

Kerteminde

Gørlev

Fanø Bugt

Christiansfeld

FYN

Odense

Halskov

FANØ

MANDØ

Ribe

Hadersley

Lille Bælt

Assens

Nyborg

Korsø

RØMØ

Toftlund

Skærbæk

Fåborg

Svendborg

Lohals

AGE OMØ

Lakolk

Åbenrå Fj.

ALS

Holm

Smålands B

SYLT

List

Arnåa

Åbenrå

Rudkøbing

Kragenæ

Westerland

Tingley

Sønderborg

Ærøskøbing

Nakskov

LOLL

Hørnum

FÖHR

Tønder

Klixbüll

Flensburg

Flensburger Förde

ÆRØ

Ristinge

Langelands Bælt

LANGELAND

Rødby

Utersum

Wyk

Niebüll

BUNDESREP. DEUTSCHLAND (FED. REP. OF GERMANY)

Kappeln

Kieler Bucht

to Kiel

North Sea

to Thorshavn

to Nurwich / Newcastle

JYLLAND

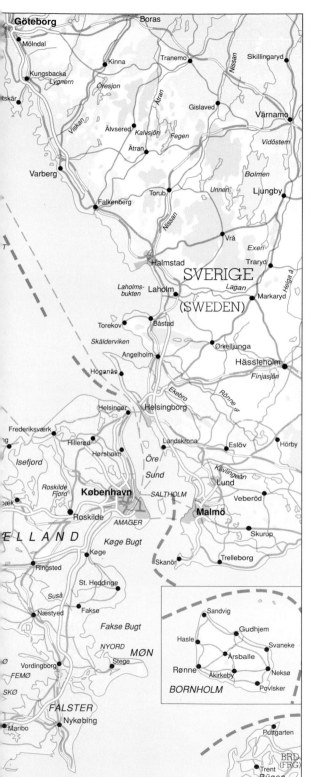

PLACES

Well-groomed farmland, white beaches, islands, gentle hills: this is Denmark. Unlike Norway and Sweden which, with Denmark, make up the Scandinavian trio, there are no mountains.

Denmark is neatly beautiful rather than grand. Encouraged by the mild climate, the fields are early spiked with green; a month or two later, the country-side glows with fruit blossom, and by summer the harvest fields are gold, contrasting with the sharper yellow of rape seed. Alongside every road, wild-flowers push pink, blue and yellow through the verges, best seen from a bicycle – a popular way to travel.

The sea is Denmark's second element. Ferries and bridges link the three main areas: Jutland, which has Denmark's only land border with mainland Europe; Funen, called the Garden of Denmark, with Odense, the birthplace of Denmark's most famous writer, Hans Christian Andersen; and Sealand, which holds the capital, Copenhagen, and Hamlet's castle, Kronborg at Helsingør (Elsinore), high above the narrow sleeve of water which leads to Sweden.

Nowhere is very far away. The long-est distances are in West Jutland where the coast roads follow the lines of ever-changing sand dunes. East Jutland has an intricate lake system, fine for canoe-ing and watersports, and also Århus, Denmark's second city, with an interna-tional arts festival in the autumn. Skagen in the north was a famous 19th-century artists' colony and painters still con-gregate here, attracted by the wonderful white light and the colours of the sea.

Denmark is a manageable country of only 5 million people, with few strains and stresses and lots of friendly people, eager to practise their English, and that all makes for one of the most comfort-able and civilised countries in the world.

Preceding pages: old houses in Odense; Copenhagen's famous Tivoli Gardens; Mount Rushmore Memorial at Legoland; Jutland's rich farmland.

139

COPENHAGEN

Few would dispute that Copenhagen is the liveliest of the Scandinavian capitals, with something going on almost any time of the day and night. When Denmark briefly ruled all of Scandinavia, the city was the capital of the three countries and the Danes like to regard Copenhagen as the region's most important and cosmopolitan city.

It is also a walking city, the first European capital to understand the pleasure of strolling through streets free of motor cars and exhaust fumes, and the casual pace of the crowds strolling in these walking streets suggests a carefree and relaxed way of life. Babies and toddlers in pushchairs, young people, old people, students and others who gather to enjoy a quiet beer, all seem content with their surroundings.

But the best way to get a first feel of Copenhagen is from the water. One is then surrounded by the city: wharfs and warehouses, some now converted to unusual hotels; Amalienborg, the Royal Palace set in a beautiful square where the Changing of the Guard is full of Royal pomp; quays with the ferries for Malmö in Sweden and Oslo; the Royal Danish Navy headquarters; Vor Frelsers Kirke (Our Saviour's Church) with its curious outside spiral staircase; and the Little Mermaid. Copenhagen still boasts its centuries-old nickname the "city of green spires". Copper plates, grown green in the salt air, cover the spires of castles and churches such as Vor Frelsers in the old city and tower over the medieval street network and 18th-century houses.

The city centre, as it is seen today, is mainly the result of two devastating fires and one bombardment. The fires, in 1728 and 1795, spread wildly among the timbered houses and wiped out large portions of the timber-built medieval town. Only a few solidly-built structures survived, such as **Helligaands Kirken** (the Church of the Holy Ghost), **Sankt Petri Kirke**, the tower of **Sankt Nikolai Kirke**, and a few other build-

ings. When Admiral Lord Nelson and the British Navy bombarded Copenhagen in 1807 (the first major blitz on a civilian population in modern history), the toll was heavy and destroyed, among other buildings, the old Cathedral of Copenhagen.

After these disastrous fires laws were passed which stipulated that houses erected on the burnt-out spaces should be made of brick or stone and have hard roofing; there were to be no more half-timbered houses with thatched roofs that flamed like torches. Because of this, most houses in the city centre today are baroque or neoclassical buildings, built over the old ruins.

The start: Before 1167 Copenhagen was just a small trading post and hamlet called Havn from which there was easy access to **Scania** (Skåne) across the **Øresund**. Scania is now part of Sweden but at that time southern Sweden was part of Denmark, and the village of Havn enjoyed a position in the middle of the kingdom. As wars, peace settlements and political unrest changed the

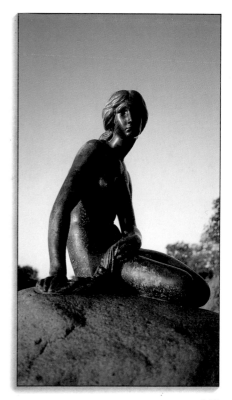

Preceding pages: wonderful, wonderful Copenhagen, with Christiansborg Castle. <u>Left</u>, red streamers flutter over Town Hall Square. <u>Right</u>, The Little Mermaid.

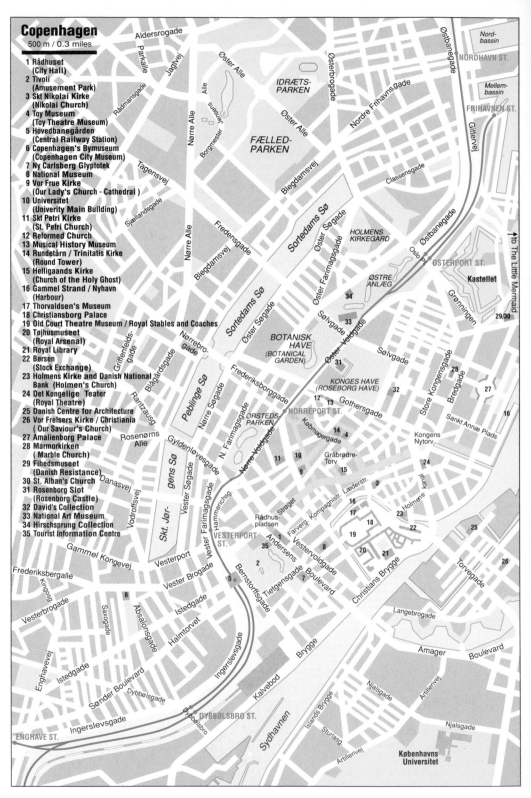

Copenhagen

500 m / 0.3 miles

1 Rådhuset
  (City Hall)
2 Tivoli
  (Amusement Park)
3 Skt Nikolai Kirke
  (Nikolai Church)
4 Toy Museum
  (Toy Theatre Museum)
5 Hovedbanegården
  (Central Railway Station)
6 Copenhagen's Bymuseum
  (Copenhagen City Museum)
7 Ny Carlsberg Glyptotek
8 National Museum
9 Vor Frue Kirke
  (Our Lady's Church - Cathedral)
10 Universitet
   (Univerity Main Building)
11 Skt Petri Kirke
   (St. Petri Church)
12 Reformed Church
13 Musical History Museum
14 Rundetårn / Trinitatis Kirke
   (Round Tower)
15 Helligaands Kirke
   (Church of the Holy Ghost)
16 Gammel Strand / Nyhavn
   (Harbour)
17 Thorvaldsen's Museum
18 Christiansborg Palace
19 Old Court Theatre Museum / Royal Stables and Coaches
20 Tøjhusmuseet
   (Royal Arsenal)
21 Royal Library
22 Børsen
   (Stock Exchange)
23 Holmens Kirke and Danish National Bank (Holmen's Church)
24 Det Kongelige Teater
   (Royal Theatre)
25 Danish Centre for Architecture
26 Vor Frelsers Kirke / Christiania
   (Our Saviour's Church)
27 Amalienborg Palace
28 Marmorkirken
   (Marble Church)
29 Fihedsmuseet
   (Danish Resistance)
30 St. Alban's Church
31 Rosenborg Slot
   (Rosenborg Castle)
32 David's Collection
33 National Art Museum
34 Hirschsprung Collection
35 Tourist Information Centre

geography of Denmark through the centuries, Copenhagen gradually moved from its central position to its present one – balancing on the easternmost tip of the country.

The process really began in 1167, when King Valdemar I ordered the local bishop, Absalon of Roskilde, to fortify Havn – or *Hafnia*, as it was called in Latin – to protect it against Wendic pirates. Absalon, whose statue stands at **Højbro Plads** (Højbro Square), built a fortress on the spot where **Christiansborg Castle** is today (just across the canal from Absalon's statue), thus beginning the rise of **København** (meaning the Merchants' Harbour) to its height as Denmark's biggest and most important town.

The fortress developed into Christiansborg, the king's castle. Centuries later, it remains the centre of Danish politics and today houses the **Folketing** (Parliament). Visitors can see part of the ruins of the original fortress in a sensible exhibition below ground level at Christiansborg Castle.

The Royal Guard at Amalienborg Palace.

During the long reign of Denmark's most famous king, **Christian IV**, from 1588 to 1648, Copenhagen strengthened its role as the country's leading town. This multi-talented monarch, an enthusiatic and visionary entrepreneur, was the inspiration behind Børsen, said to be the oldest Stock Exchange in Europe, a beautiful Renaissance structure with a distinctive spire made up of four dragons, steep roofs, tiny windows and gables galore. Christian was also responsible for the picturesque Nyboder residential area, which to this day remains reserved for officers of the Royal Danish Navy, and the Rundetårn (the Round Tower), planned by the king as an observatory. It is part of the church next door, which also merits a visit. Christian's palaces are Rosenborg Castle, which has many of his most precious objects and jewellery, and, to the north at Hillerød, Frederiksborg Castle, built between 1600 and 1620, with a magnificent chapel.

At various times throughout history, the Swedes, the British and the Germans have all tried to conquer Copenhagen. The Swedes came close to success in 1658. The Swedish army had taken almost the whole of Denmark by the time it reached Copenhagen, to be confronted by King Frederik III and the townsfolk standing side by side on the fortifications to defend their city. Men, women and children used every weapon and heavy object at their disposal, including boiling pitch, to scare off the Swedes. The kings's advisers suggested that he flee with the royal family but, at the sight of the brave Copenhageners on the battlements, he retorted: "I will die in my nest". He was not called on to do so; the Swedes recognised superior determination, if not superior force, and withdrew.

The Swedes never took Copenhagen – but to obtain peace (in 1660) the Danes had to cede **Scania** (Skåne), **Halland** and **Blekinge** on the Swedish mainland. Denmark was almost halved in size. For this blight on their national pride, the Danes have never quite forgiven their brothers across the water.

Copenhagen has many times outgrown the confined space within its medieval fortifications. The capital now houses almost a quarter of the Danish population – a ratio shared with only three or four other capitals in the world. It is one of the main reasons for Copenhagen's sovereign dominance in the country because no other Danish city matches Copenhagen's influence on political, economic, social, or cultural developments.

This self-importance, however, has not passed unnoticed, and Copenhageners are generally considered stand-offish by their countrymen in the provinces. To the outsider, the attitude of Copenhageners may seem cosmopolitan; but to provincial Danes the label "Copenhagenerisms" is used to characterise everything considered modern, incomprehensible, untraditional, abstract or radical.

Around the City Hall: Rådhuspladsen (City Hall Square) is the heart of Copenhagen. **Rådhuset** (the City Hall), on the southeastern side, is the administrative and political centre of the city, and the streets around the square constitute one of its most important traffic junctions. Here are connections to the airport, and major outlets from the city to the southern, western and northern suburbs. More than 16 bus lines gather in the square, and it is only a short walk to **Hovedbanegården** (the Central Railway Station). Rådhuspladsen is also the spot from which any signpost or milestone in the country measures its distance to the capital, and any street in the city has its lowest house numbers at the end closest to the square.

The square was not always the centre. Little more than 100 years ago, this site was actually outside the gates of the old town, one of which was at the beginning of **Strøget**, the main pedestrian street. Until the 1850s, the square was the haymarket, a function which had to be kept outside the narrow town streets because of the space it required, the fire hazard and the mess.

Rådhuspladsen was established as the site of the City Hall in 1900, and was designed with the shell-shaped piazza

Frederiksborg Castle, which houses the National History Museum.

of the Italian town of Siena as its model. Shortly after it was finished, however, the shell shape was sacrificed on the altar of rapidly developing traffic; the street cars in particular required space for their platforms and rails. Architects still grieve at the disappearance of the original square as well as at the traffic chaos which has efficiently destroyed the original charm of the most representative of Copenhagen squares.

Rådhuset, the City Hall itself, is one of the newer architectural pearls of Copenhagen. The building was designed by architect Martin Nyrup, built in traditional red brick, and finished in 1903. Constructed in the national romantic style, its inspiration was drawn from medieval Danish and Norwegian architecture with an interesting mixture of the *palazzo* style of northern Italy. The facade and the interior are full of quaint details from Nordic mythology, and above the main entrance is a relief depicting Bishop Absalon.

Inside the building the foyer holds the entrance to **Jens Olsen's world clock**, a unique and precise astronomical timepiece with 12 works. Among its numerous features, it shows time around the world, the postion of the planets and the Gregorian calendar. The foyer also sports a limestone relief of 25 men and above it a coloured fresco which portrays the first council.

For an elevated view of the entire city, the 346-ft (105-metre) **tower** is an ideal vantage point. During normal museum hours, an elevator takes visitors high above the city and into the tallest tower of Copenhagen. On a clear day there is a splendid view: some 30 miles (50 km) in all directions, across the sound to Sweden to the east and all the way to Helsingør in the north.

Outside the hall is a statue of Denmark's famed fairytale author and poet **Hans Christian Andersen**. The **dragon fountain** a little further out on the square was designed by Danish artist Joakim Skovgaard and erected in 1934. On the other (northwest) side of the square is a small statue of a Danish soldier, commemorating the 1864 war

The popular Café Kultorvet.

against Germany in which the Danes suffered major casualties and lost the southern part of the Jutland peninsula.

On **Vester Voldgade**, at the northeast corner of the square, is a pillar with a bronze statue of two Bronze Age *lur* players, whom the artist has confused with the Vikings. This statue is one of Denmark's most popular monuments.

Also on Vester Voldgade are two of Copenhagen's old traditional hotels. Closest to city hall is the **Palace Hotel**, one of the city's few buildings in the Jugendstil, and further north, past the square, is **Hotel Kong Frederik** with the stylish and expensive **Queen's Pub** restaurant.

Three of Denmark's major newspapers are housed on Rådhuspladsen: *Politiken* and its sister tabloid *Ekstra Bladet* in **Politikens Hus**, and next door is *Det Ny Aktuelt*. Copenhagen's largest **English-language bookstore** is on the street level of Politikens Hus, and the kiosks in the centre of the square sell magazines and daily newspapers in many languages.

On the opposite (southwest) side, on **H. C. Andersen Boulevard**, is a castle-like red brick building bearing the name **Little Rosenborg**. Here are the main offices of the Danish Tourist Board, open to travellers during office hours, to provide advice on activities, accommodation and places of interest, and brochures and information about Copenhagen or any other part of Denmark.

In the same building is the main entrance to **Tivoli Gardens**, as well as the entrances to the **Louis Tussaud Wax Museum** and the **Holography Museum**, Europe's largest museum for holographic art. Although considerably smaller than the renowned Madame Tussaud's in London, the wax museum has a fine exhibition, including all the kings of Denmark and many famous contemporary or older figures. Like its maternal model in London the museum also features a "Chamber of Horrors" in the basement.

For a quick lunch or a stylish dinner, the **Copenhagen Corner Restaurant** on the corner of H. C. Andersen's Boulevard and Vesterbrogade is an excellent choice. As you eat, the restaurant gives a good view of bustling Rådhuspladsen, and on the wall above the round table at one end of the restaurant hangs a masterpiece of Danish art, P. S. Krøyer's painting of two white-clad women walking along a beach at Skagen, on the northern tip of Jutland.

On the same side of the street, down past Tivoli, you come to the museum **Ny Carlsberg Glyptotek**. In a building designed by **Wilhelm Dahlerup**, the museum contains a fine collection of art begun by the brewer Carl Jacobsen and maintained by the Carlsberg Foundation. There are collections of ancient Egyptian, Greek, Roman and Etruscan art, as well as a number of French masterpieces. The conservatory houses displays of modern sculpture, and there are frequent performances of classical and modern music, some in the magnificent indoor winter garden.

Where business is done: The street that leads out of the southwestern side of Rådhuspladsen is **Vesterbrogade**, and that part of the street nearest to the

Tivoli Gardens: **Left**, balloons for all and, **right**, the bright lights of the main entrance.

square is Copenhagen's central business and entertainment district. Walk down the street away from the city hall and past another entrance to Tivoli, towards one of the city's few high-rise buildings, the 22-storey **SAS Royal Hotel**, designed by Danish architect **Arne Jacobsen**.

Directly across the street from the hotel is **Hovedbanegården** (Central Railway Station), which is also the terminal for the shuttle bus service to the airport. Built in 1912, the station was recently renovated and has one of the few service centres for young interrailers in Europe. Here they can rest, take a shower and store their backpacks safely while taking a look at town. Various other services are also available: there are two bank offices, a good newspaper and magazine kiosk, excellent stand-up and sit-down restaurants, a post office, and an information service. When people agree to meet "under the clock", that clock, unless otherwise specified, is the one just inside the main hall of the station.

Out in the middle of Vesterbrogade in front of the station, the obelisk commemorates the liberation of Denmark's peasants 200 years ago when the feudal system was abolished in favour of free, smallhold farmers. It was designed by the artist Nikolaj Abildgaard in 1792.

All the major international airlines and travel agencies are situated in this area, as are the cinemas. At **Axeltorv** is the **Palace Theatre** with nine different cinemas and a popular discothèque as well as several others nearby. Copenhagen cinemas show foreign films in their original-language versions, with Danish subtitles.

Right next to the Palace Theatre is the **Circus Dome**; one of the few stationary circus buildings in the world, it features high-quality family circus performances. The iron and brick sculpture on Axeltorv was designed in 1987 by sculptor Robert Jacobsen, and marked the square's transition to a pedestrian area. Across the street is **Scala**, a new multi-storey shopping mall and entertainment centre.

A rest during Copenhagen's riotous carnival.

150

Behind and to the southwest of Hovedbanegården is Vesterbro, one of Copenhagen's old residential areas. Closest is the **Istedgade** neighbourhood, Copenhagen's famed – or notorious – red-light district. With tourist hotels of varying standards scattered throughout the area, the streets abound with shops offering pornographic literature and movies, street prostitutes and massage parlours. Although as a whole Copenhagen is relatively safe to walk in at any time of night, this is one of the less recommended areas; after dark, its associations with the drug trade and related crime become clearer and a taxi may be recommended.

But, taking the wider area, Vesterbro is also a colourful residential district with thousands of southern European, Middle Eastern and Asian immigrants mixed into a Danish working-class population. Many students have also discovered the charms of this low-rent neighbourhood. Here is a quaint mixture of old-fashioned food and clothing stores and shops filled with exotic smells of unusual fruits, vegetables and spices, which are run by immigrants. The area offers a couple of very good ethnic restaurants as well.

København's Bymuseum (Copenhagen City Museum), at Vesterbrogade 59, has an historical and ethnological exhibition which includes the works of Denmark's famed existentialist philosopher Søren Kierkegaard. Just north of the museum, **Absalonsgade** has been established as a museum street and sports original cobblestone pavements and different kinds of old street furniture. Keep exploring before going back into the centre of town – there is always something going on here.

Tivoli's attractions: Other Scandinavian cities have tivolis but Copenhagen's 150-year-old Tivoli Gardens was the first and is somehow unique. It is a typical Scandinavian mixture of gardens, open-air dancing, restaurants, cafés, amusement park, theatre, open-air stage and concert hall, and the home of the Sjælland Symphony Orchestra, which attracts international artistes, so-

Copenhagen's night life ranges widely.

loists and ensembles throughout its summer season. The entrances are on Rådhuspladsen, Vesterbrogade and opposite Hovedbanegården. Tivoli is pretty at any time but best as daylight fades and the lights begin to glint among the trees.

The park site was once part of the fortification and demarcation area surrounding the city but in 1841 an enterprising journalist Georg Carstensen convinced King Christian VIII that if people were well entertained they were less likely to talk politics and sedition. The king gave him permission to establish a park "to provide the masses with suitable entertainment and fun," with the proviso that he also "remove anything ignoble and degrading." A quick glance at the happy faces watching the fireworks as they whizz across the lake on a Saturday midnight would seem to prove Carstensen correct in his political theories. That same lake and several of the walks are reminders of the old moats and fortifications.

Tivoli, and the youngsters who march

and play in the Tivoli Guard (a Royal Guard in miniature), have been favourites with both children and adults ever since it opened in 1843. With more than five million visitors each year, the park is more popular than any other Danish attraction. Open between 1 May and 15 September, from 9 a.m. to midnight, Tivoli is famed for its shady walks under proud old trees, its beautiful coloured nightlights and the abundance and diversity of the bedding plants, 140,000 of which are re-planted every summer.

For children and youngsters the greatest thrills come from the rides, the roller-coasters and merry-go-rounds. The Peacock outdoor theatre presents pantomimes and ballets every day, and the Concert Hall features daily promenade concerts as well as evening performances by touring world artistes.

Tivoli is also the place to enjoy a good meal, coffee and cake, or a drink. The park has more than 20 restaurants, of which the more stylish are among the most expensive in the city. The tall tubes in front of the "Moorish" palace close to the Vesterbrogade entrance, contain bubbling coloured water, to form an unusual sculpture designed by the Danish nuclear physicist Niels Bohr. Bohr was inspired to this creation by gazing at his aquarium.

Several nights a week, the gardens close with a giant fireworks display which can be seen and heard many miles away. Tivoli is highly recommended, but it's wise to take plenty of cash along: the place is not inexpensive.

The medieval city: If Rådhuspladsen is the heart of Copenhagen, then **Strøget**, the one-mile pedestrian shopping street, is the spine. It has endless shops, small as well as large, street vendors and buskers galore, and workshops, cellar galleries, and Illums Bolighus, the department store that concentrates on superb design and usually has a special exhibition on the ground floor. Strøget is where Copenhagers and visitors alike go to shop or just to promenade and look at window displays. All year round, street musicians play music from classical to rock, jazz and exotic folk

Tiger bus, part of an art project sponsored by the public transport system.

tunes, which attract crowds of listeners on selected corners. It has been a walking street since 1962, and was the first street in the world to be reserved for pedestrians only – an idea which has since spread like wildfire.

Starting at Rådhuspladsen, Strøget meanders through five streets and four squares before it runs into **Kongens Nytorv**, the largest square in the old town. Closest to Rådhuspladsen are **Frederiksberggade** and **Nygade**, the more lively part of Strøget, with many small clothing and record shops, and snack and burger bars. Nygade leads to a large open area made up of two squares, **Gammeltorv** and **Nytorv** (the Old and the New Square). Before the great fires of the 18th century, a block of houses separated the two, but new fire regulations required more space between buildings and the houses were never rebuilt.

Gammeltorv, Copenhagen's oldest marketplace, dates back to the Middle Ages, when it was the scene of jousting tournaments. Peep inside the gate of No. 14 to see a relief depicting the history of the square. The old village pond once lay where No. 10 stands today, and a plaque commemorates Havn, the original town.

The **Caritas Fountain** in the centre dates from 1608; it was donated to the town by **King Christian IV**, who thought it would make a proper contribution to the water supply, as well as the beauty of Copenhagen. On festive occasions golden apples placed on the jets dance on the water, much to the delight of the watching children.

Two of old Copenhagen's main streets lead from Gammeltorv: **Nørregade** goes north and, as its name suggests, **Vestergade** leads west. Vestergade was the village street in the Middle Ages, before Copenhagen began to grow. The rows of neoclassical houses in Vestergade remain the best example of the rebuilt city that followed the fire in 1795, and old merchants' houses stand behind several of the gates in Vestergade. Hans Christian Andersen lived in No. 19 when, as a young man,

Rådhus-pladsen, the City Hall Square.

he first arrived in Copenhagen from his native town of Odense.

The area behind Vestergade is one of the few remaining residential areas in the inner city. Living in the picturesque old houses is a mixture of old-time Copenhageners, artists and students, and it is here one finds the more exotic clothing shops. There are squares and side streets with quiet old courtyards made beautiful by plants and garden furniture to show that people love to sit outside when the evenings are long. Under the wide arms of the town trees, Copenhageners at pavement cafés talk, laugh and eat Danish pastries, washed down with coffee, beer and sometimes aquavit. **Sankt Petri Kirke**, on the corner of Nørregade and **Sankt Pederstræde** dates back to the time of the Hanseatic League and is the oldest church in Copenhagen.

The Chancelry towards Nørregade was built in 1450 in Gothic style. Though it was first used as a Catholic Church, it was converted into a cannon foundry when the Reformation came to Denmark in 1536. The church was reconsecrated in 1585, and today serves a German Lutheran congregation.

Walk back to Nytorv, where Copenhagen's first town hall was situated. In 1805 the present large brown building with columns replaced the old town hall which was destroyed in the fire 10 years earlier. Like most buildings on Nytorv, it was built in the neoclassical style prevalent during the rebuilding after the 1795 fire, and was designed by one of Denmark's finest architects, C. F. Hansen. The buildings behind and to its left were formerly used as a debtors' prison. When the present City Hall at Rådhuspladsen opened, the old structure became the seat of the Copenhagen City Court.

A mob of 10,000 citizens demonstrated against absolute monarchy in front of the town hall on Nytorv in 1848. King Frederik VII wisely saw the necessity for change, and his acceptance of a constitutional monarchy in the same year allowed Denmark to avoid the revolutionary bloodshed which

Colourful costumes for the travelling people.

most other European nations suffered.

Søren Kierkegaard, the 19th-century philosopher, lived in the house on the corner of Nytorv and Frederiksberggade. Walk along **Rådhusstræde** (leading to the southeast from Nytorv) to the little square, **Vandkunsten**, on the right-hand side and **Magstræde** with the youth centre **Huset**, a reminder of the 1960s, on the left.

At the end of that decade, hippies and squatters occupied Huset and demanded a place of their own for various activities. The city, which owned the run-down building, agreed to establish a culture centre, and Huset is still a gathering place for young people of all ages. It contains several bars with different kinds of music, from rock to jazz, a good and relatively inexpensive restaurant, a video art centre, a gallery and a cinema. In the same building, but around the corner from Magstræde, is **Use-It**, a publicly-run information centre for young travellers.

Farvergade, **Kompagnistræde** and **Læderstræde** (actually one uninterrupted street with the three names in sequence), just southwest of, and parallel to Strøget, are lined with shops dealing in oriental rugs, antique furniture, silverware and china. The prices aren't low, but on a good day it's still possible to find a fair deal. Apart from these three streets, the whole of this immediate neighbourhood is the place to find interesting gifts – whether art prints and posters or silver, pewter and china. Danish-made goods are almost always good value and you *can* find inexpensive gifts such as hand-made glass spheres which hang inside a window to reflect the light and catch a breeze, lovely table decorations and long-lasting candles, which Scandinavians light to welcome guests.

With their cobblestones and old houses, Magstræde and its extension, **Snaregade**, are among the most interesting in Copenhagen. Although most of the white-painted houses date back to the second fire at the end of the 18th century, Magstræde contains two original 16th-century Renaissance houses

Copenhagen shops compete to attract the passers-by in the thronged pedestrian streets.

(No. 17 and 19) which survived the flames. The Italian composer Giuseppe Sarti lived in No. 10 until he had to leave Denmark in 1775 because of overwhelming debts.

From Nytorv, continue along Strøget on **Vimmelskaftet** toward Amagertorv. On the left side of Vimmelskaftet is a narrow alleyway, **Yorcks Passage**, which leads to **Skindergade**, and **Fiolstræde**, another pedestrian street. **Amagertorv**, the widest part of Strøget, has lots of street musicians.

Helligaandskirken (the Church of the Holy Spirit), which stands on the left-hand (northwest) side, dates from the 14th century and was originally a monastery with hospital. The church and tower which still remain are from the late Renaissance and show a strong baroque influence. While the nave is almost unadorned – as required by the Reformation – the portal is sumptuously baroque. The oldest part, the wing towards **Valkendorfsgade**, which was the old hospital, is medieval. It is now used for exhibitions and charity arrangements. A monument to the Danes who died in concentration camps during World War II stands at the churchyard gate nearest Strøget; it was designed by Kaare Klint, the furniture designer.

For pipe smokers, Amagertorv 9 is one of those rare places you find where you least expect it: the **Tobacco Museum**, with its display of ancient pipes, tobaccos and smoking history. The opposite side of Amagertorv is occupied by the shops most often visited by tourists: **Illums Bolighus** (modern design), the **Royal Copenhagen** china shop and the **Bing and Grøndahl** shop.

It is possible to tour the displays and workshops of the Royal Copenhagen Porcelain Manufactory in the outer part of the city, which makes a fascinating half-day, and a chance to buy good pieces and seconds. (Other popular tours include the Tuborg and Carlsberg breweries, where you walk through the whole process of brewing and end with a glass of the best.)

The **Stork Fountain** in the middle of the square is the most popular fountain

Christian IV's Round Tower and Observatory, built for the astronomer Tycho Brahe.

in Copenhagen, and the place where hippies gathered in the early 1970s. Before 1850, Amagertorv was the main traffic junction where streets from the city's four gates met. To the north is **Købmagergade** – yet another pedestrian street – and to the south **Højbro Plads** with the equestrian statue of Copenhagen's founder, Bishop Absalon. Look past Absalon and his horse and see the canal which surrounds **Slotsholmen** and **Christiansborg**, the seat of the Danish Parliament.

In the opposite direction, the area north of Vimmelskaftet and Amagertorv is the old **Latin Quarter** where the University of Copenhagen has its main building. The Latin Quarter is bordered on its other sides by **Nørregade**, **Nørre Voldgade** and Købmagergade, and is the place to go for a cosy dinner and a drink on a night out.

Although the University has outgrown its limited space in the city centre and moved the Faculties of Medicine, Science and Humanities to the other side of town, the Law School and a few other departments are still scattered around the area.

Centrally placed in the Quarter is **Gråbrødre Torv** (Greyfriar's Square), which can be reached from Strøget by walking past the west side of Helligåndskirken and through the picturesque narrow passage at the corner where Valkendorfsgade turns to the right. The Square, which is free of traffic, is one of the most beautiful in town and a popular place to enjoy a summer evening meal or drink at the outdoor tables of one of the many restaurants. The buildings surrounding the cobblestoned square are baroque houses in bright colours, built after the first fire of 1728. Some 40 percent of the town was destroyed in that fire, with 74 streets and more than 1670 houses being ruined.

Leave Gråbrødre Torv by way of **Lille Kannikestræde** and turn left at **Store Kannikestræde** (Little and Big Canon Streets) to see **Københavns Domkirke** (Copenhagen Cathedral) on the left. The original cathedral was destroyed in the 1728 fire and, as if that

You are never far from the waterside in Copenhagen.

weren't enough, its replacement was hit by an English incendiary bomb during the siege and bombardment of 1807. The current structure is from 1829, designed by **C. F. Hansen** in neoclassical style and inspired by the Basilica in Rome. Inside the church are statues by the sculptor **Bertel Thorvaldsen**.

Old university: Immediately north of the cathedral is the main building of the University of Copenhagen, founded in 1479. The seat of the University Board, beside Nørregade, dates from 1420 and is the oldest building in Copenhagen, while the Commons building (**Kommunitetet**), also on Nørregade, was at one time used as a dormitory for students and professors and dates from 1731. On the other side of the University, alongside Fiolstræde, is the University Library. In an exhibition on the first floor, one can see the book *Defensor Pacis* (Defence for Peace), pierced by a cannon ball in 1807.

Fiolstræde is known for its antiquarian bookshops, and **Krystalgade** is the site of Copenhagen's synagogue. Continue northeast along Krystalgade to reach Købmagergade again. On the corner of Krystalgade and Købmagergade is **Regensen**, the oldest and best known of the student dormitories.

Regensen was founded in 1623 by King Christian IV, but only the wing facing Store Kannikestræde is original. The rest dates from 1731, having been rebuilt after the fire of 1728, while the arcade in Købmagergade was established in 1909. Until 1895 the students at Regensen were able to earn a little extra income as undertakers.

Across from Regensen is one of Copenhagen's most fascinating buildings: **Rundetårnet** (the Round Tower) was built in 1642 as an observatory for Denmark's world-renowned astronomer Tycho Brahe. It still has a viewing platform on the top which is open for visitors on clear nights. During the day there is access for visitors to the platform on the roof of the 111-ft (36-metre) tower. To reach the roof one walks up a 620-ft (200-metre) spiral ramp – not as hard as it sounds. The

Street band during the Jazz Festival.

ramp won international fame in 1716 when Czar Peter the Great rode a horse all the way up; the Czarina Catharina was driven up in a carriage. One of the city's latest novelties, the **Tycho Brahe Planetarium** also commemorates the astronomer. Near Sankt Jørgen's Lake in the city centre, its space theatre has "omnimax" film performances which put the audience into reclining seats and fill the huge dome with pictures so that they travel through the stars or move deep under water.

While Rundetårnet is mainly an observatory, it also serves as a tower for the attached **Trinitatis Kirke**. Built in Nordic Gothic style in 1656 for students, the church has an exquisite baroque altarpiece, made in 1731 by **Friedrich Ehbisch**, as well as a fine 1757 Rococco clock above the pulpit.

Another 230 ft (70 metres) up Købmagergade away from Strøget is **Kultorvet** (Coal Square), with Copenhagen's main municipal library. The small street **Åbenrå**, with its restored 18th-century houses, is just behind the

library. No. 30 houses the **Museum for Music History** and its collection of European musical instruments from as early as the 11th century.

Return to Rundetårnet and on the way back towards Amagertorv visit the world's only museum for puppet theatres, **Prior Dukketeater** at Købmagergade 52, on the second floor. Opposite the museum, in Store Kannikestræde, is one of Copenhagen's finest old houses. **Admiral Gjeddes Gård** at No. 10 has retained its half-timbered oak walls (for which the trees were felled on the site in 1567). No. 12 is another old students' dormitory, **Borchs Kollegium**, and No. 11 with a picturesque yard and garden was a professor's residence from 1750.

On the corner of Købmagergade and Valkendorfsgade is one of the city's main post offices, housed in a fine baroque palace from 1730. There's a small postal museum in Valkendorfsgade and at No. 13 a **Toy Museum** with old toys and children's films.

The last section of Strøget (from Købmagergade to Kongens Nytorv) is

Carnival revels go on day and night.

the home of the exclusive and expensive. Fashion shops, furriers, the **Georg Jensen** silversmith shop and Copenhagen's two main department stores, **Illum**, at the corner of Købmagergade and Strøget, and **Magasin du Nord**, across the small square on **Bremerholm**. **Østergade**'s reputation as the street with the best shops for ladies' wear dates back several centuries, and the street was also the first in the country to feature "panorama" shop windows, around 1828.

Behind Østergade, on the right-hand side, is the **Church of Saint Nikolaj**, the patron saint of sailors. The tower from 1591 is in Dutch Renaissance style while the church itself was built in 1917. It is no longer consecrated as a church, but is owned by the City of Copenhagen and used as an art gallery for various exhibitions. The area behind Nikolaj which borders on the canal has quiet cobblestoned streets and well-preserved houses from the end of the 18th century. **Holmens Kirke**, beside the Danish National Bank on Holmens Kanal, was built in 1619 and is the Royal Chapel and Naval Church. The National Bank, covered with marble from Greenland, was designed by Arne Jacobsen and erected in the 1970s.

The area on the other side of Østergade has been restored over the past 30 years and is now a small, exclusive shopping area and the place to find the city's popular cafés. Passing through picturesque **Pistolstræde**, with its restored old houses, one comes out at **Grønnegade**, which has several pre-18th-century houses, at one time the slum of Copenhagen, now refurbished and comfortable once more. **Gothersgade**, at the end of Grønnegade, constitutes the boundary of Copenhagen's medieval area and was developed in 1647 when the town was extended towards the north with the area which is still known as **New Copenhagen**.

The Reformed Church at No. 111 is a fine baroque building, built in 1688 with red brick from Holland. It was consecrated to serve a Calvinist congregation from Germany, France and Hol-

Kongens Have, a peaceful spot in the busy city.

land and, even today, has services in French and German.

Across from the Church, **Kongens Have** (The King's Garden) has been a favourite with Copenhageners for centuries. With its tall, old trees, statues, shadowy walks and grassy lawns, the park constitutes an important "breathing space" in the densely packed city. It's a fine place to go for a picnic, or to relax away from the noise of town.

Rosenborg Castle, in the eastern corner of the park, is also one of Copenhagen's most attractive sights. **King Christian IV's** exquisite palace in Dutch Renaissance style is now a museum, and contains three centuries worth of Royal treasures as well as the Crown Jewels.

Power centre: Slotsholmen (Castle Island), surrounded by canals, is the seat of the Danish government and administration. The imposing **Christiansborg Palace**, built on the same spot as the original old castle of Copenhagen, contains Parliament, the Prime Minister's office, the Supreme Court

and the Royal Reception Chambers. Bishop Absalon built a fortress on this little islet in 1167, and from 1416 it was the home of the Danish king.

Absalon's fortress was replaced by a new castle in 1367 and, in the 1730s, King Christian VI, Denmark's first absolute monarch, ordered a new, more suitable palace. This one, a magnificent baroque building, burned in 1794 and was replaced yet again with a new palace which, ill-fated as it was, also burned down in 1884. The present version of Christiansborg is less than 100 years old, built between 1907 and 1928. The granite facade was made from stones gathered in every parish in the country. The equestrian statue, erected on the Palace Square in 1876, depicts King Frederik VII (1843–1863) and was erected in 1876.

When the foundations for the present Christiansborg were dug in 1906, Denmark's National Museum excavated the remnants of the oldest buildings on the site, and the ruins of Absalon's old fortress and the medieval

Copenhagen's canals are home to hundreds of pleasure craft.

castle are now accessible to visitors. **Parliament** and the **Royal Reception Chambers** are also open to visitors.

Southeast of Christiansborg is another of Copenhagen's best-known buildings, **Børsen** (The Stock Exchange), built in 1619 in Dutch Renaissance style by King Christian IV, with the prominent spire which is formed by the entwined tails of three dragons (representing Denmark, Sweden and Norway). Continue towards the harbour with Børsen on the left and ministerial buildings on the right, and a right turn on to the harbour front leads to the entrance to the garden of the Royal Library.

Open to all interested users, the **Royal Library** is the largest library in Scandinavia with 2.5 million volumes, 4 million charts and pictures, and more than 55,000 manuscripts, including some by famous Danes such as Hans Christian Andersen, Søren Kierkegaard and Karen Blixen (Isak Dinesen). Of special international interest is the library's famous Judaist Department.

The area where the Library Garden now stands was once a naval harbour, and one can still see mooring rings on the walls of the old buildings along the side. With its statue of Kierkegaard and a goldfish pond in the centre, the beautiful garden has a peaceful atmosphere which makes it a welcome refuge in the middle of the busy city. The building to the right contains Denmark's **Geodetic Institute**, while the long building on the left, built in 1598, houses **Tøjhusmuseet** (The Arsenal Museum) and its unique collection of old weapons.

The arcade of the building opposite the library, which houses the National Archives, leads back to Christiansborg and the entrance to Folketinget (The House of Parliament). Turn left and continue across the canal; to the right on Frederiksholms Kanal is Denmark's **National Museum**, commendable for its collections of ancient "bog" finds from the Stone, Bronze and Iron Ages. The museum also has unique historical and ethnographical collections.

Four and four make eight – sailors at the harbour...

Cross back over the canal to Slotsholmen on the old Marble Bridge to see the large, well-preserved riding grounds from the 1740s. They are bordered by the only surviving buildings from the first Christiansborg, destroyed by fire in 1794.

In the wing on the right side is the **Museum of Royal Stables and Coaches**, and adjacent to that the old **Court Theatre** and **Theatre Collection**. It is one of the oldest court theatres in the world, designed in 1766 by the French architect Nicolas-Henri Jardin. French acting troupes and Italian opera singers performed here for royalty and the court in the early years of its existence and there were often masquerades. The equestrian statue on the riding grounds depicts King Christian IX, who died in 1906.

Continue through the main entrance to Christiansborg, go back to the palace square and turn left to arrive at the Palace Chapel (erected in 1826). With the Pantheon of Rome as its ideal, the church is formed as a small temple with a row of classical columns in front.

Behind the Chapel is **Thorvaldsen's Museum**, which contains the works of Denmark's great sculptor Bertel Thorvaldsen (1770–1844), who lived and worked in Rome for 40 years. Thorvaldsen lies buried at the centre of the museum, which opened in 1848, only four years after his death. On the outside walls a coloured frieze with life-size figures depicts Thorvaldsen's triumphant homecoming from Italy in 1838.

Christianshavn's culture: Cross the harbour via the bridge **Knippelsbro** to get to **Christianshavn**, one of Copenhagen's oldest and most colourful residential areas. Christianshavn was built on an island in 1617 by King Christian IV and is surrounded by the original (and still nearly intact) star-shaped ramparts. Christianshavn is worth a visit for its special environment, marked by its proximity to the water. Apart from the harbour, the island is surrounded by tree-lined moats and has a central canal.

To the left on the Christianshavn side

...and cherubs in the church.

CHRISTIANIA: ANATOMY OF A FREE STATE

In 1971, a group of hippies founded Christiania, to launch what they claimed would be an alternative society. Although "peace and love" and "flower power" have long gone out of fashion, the hippie playground in the heart of the city has somehow managed to survive as one of the more exotic features of Copenhagen.

You will find the area in Christianshavn in what in 1971 was a recently abandoned 19th-century military barracks. Since then, the Christianites (as they call themselves) have converted barrack blocks, workshops and powder magazines into dwelling houses, workshops, restaurants (the best known is Spiseloppen) and shops, where they can live and work, not always in great comfort. The exteriors may be colourful with imaginative murals but inside many of the buildings need a lot of repair and some have neither water, gas nor electricity. The whole 84-acre (41-hectare) site is surrounded by the original fortified walls, built in a star-shape 300 years ago.

Since the beginning, Christiania has been at the centre of worldwide public and media interest but, despite political disputes and police raids, the 1,000 inhabitants continue to live their unconventional lives. Many Danes are fiercely opposed to the existence of this unusual "suburb" and arguments rage on the need to justify or eliminate the "Free State". However, neither politicians nor police have taken any real steps to close the area. On the contrary, in 1981 Christiania was given official status as a social experiment. As its fame spread, it became a favourite laboratory for researchers.

The main problem for the old core of true Christianites, who have faithfully continued the idealistic fight, has been Christiania's magnetic attraction for criminals and drug dealers. Many Danes maintain that the "Free State" has become a hard-edged haven of thugs and drugs, and residents have found themselves wrestling not only with established society but with criminals of all sorts who use the area as a hideout. Many in Copenhagen feel some sympathy with people who sought only an alternative to established Danish society and now find their lives made unsafe by motor-cycle gangs and the widespread drugs trade that has moved in uninvited.

Among Christiania's harshest critics have been the governments of Sweden, Norway and Finland, who look on the area as a regional centre of the drug trade and claim, probably correctly, that Christiania has become a haven for countless runaway teenagers.

As part of their belief in their way of life, the Christianites refuse to condemn the open sale of hashish and marijuana; but, in recent years, they have successfully campaigned against hard drugs. The area's suggestively named "Pusher Street" was once thickly lined with drug dealers of all kinds but now the trade in hard drugs has moved to other parts of Copenhagen, and hashish and alcohol are still Christiania's favoured stimulants.

In 1989, when the drug dealers had become too numerous even for Christianites, the main entrance was blocked and the pushers lost a good deal of market space and most of their exposure.

The dark side of the "Free State" has also created another big problem: Christiania's disastrous relationship with the Copenhagen police. The only police to enter the area are riot squads, who have made as many as 40 raids on the community in one year. For their part, the police claim that, when they do patrol Christiania in the normal way, they are threatened by the inhabitants and risk having bottles, stones, and firebombs hurled at them by angry residents.

Despite all the stains that have come to tarnish the original bright ideals, Christiania survives. The real reason may be practical: political anxiety on the part of politicians in general and the Copenhagen authorities in particular. As it is, the Christianites, unwilling to move and opposed to the idea of their lives being directed by the Establishment outside, are conveniently gathered in one place. To scatter them around Copenhagen, where there is already a critical housing shortage, could simply create a new set of problems. Visitors who want to see for themselves can take the number 8 bus to Prinsessegade.

of Knippelsbro is the Danish Foreign Ministry, housed in the big grey buildings which were completed in 1980. Further along the harbour wall are two old warehouses placed at right angles to it. Both have been meticulously restored. The first one, **Eigtveds Pakhus**, is closed to the public, but the second one, **Gammel Dok**, houses the **Centre for Danish Architecture**, which features various public exhibitions.

Until recently a run-down working-class neighbourhood and the site of Denmark's largest shipyard, Christianshavn has changed its appearance greatly in the past 10 years. Thanks to its central location, it has become fashionable and now features a quaint mixture of smartly renovated 18th-century city houses, big apartment blocks, old and new industry and commerce, and a good deal of the state's administration. On a summer day, the canal attracts all kinds of people, who enjoy a beer and the leisurely pace at the wharf.

Take a stroll down the streets of Christianshavn and glance into the courtyards of some of the old houses. **Strandgade 12**, an old merchant's house, has a beautifully restored courtyard as well as a fine baroque wrought-iron gate. Other interesting courtyards can be found at **Strandgade 6** and **44**, which housed the old Strandgade barracks. **Amagergade 11**, at the other end of Christianshavn, is said to have the finest courtyard in town and is surrounded by old galleries.

Christianshavn is also the home of **Christiania**, the "free state" whose colourful inhabitants have set their mark on the whole area (*see facing page*). Two of Copenhagen's more notable churches are also in the area.

Vor Frelsers Kirke (The Church of Our Saviour) in **Prinsessegade** attracts the most attention. Built in red brick in 1694, its tall copper-clad tower (from 1750) is a Copenhagen landmark. For a magnificent view over Copenhagen, the tower is open for visitors who dare and care to climb the 150 gilded steps on the *outside* of the spire – not a trip for windy weather. **Christianskirken** in

Left, painted murals are a colourful aspect of Christiania. Below, inside and outside as dusk begins to darken Nyhavn.

Strandgade is a Rococco building from 1754 with an unusual interior. It has been built as a theatre, with three of the walls covered by boxes, including one for the royal family.

"**New Copenhagen**": One leaves the narrow eastern end of Strøget and enters the spacious openness of **Kongens Nytorv** (the King's New Square), another of Copenhagen's most cherished spots. The **Hotel D'Angleterre**, on the corner of Østergade and Kongens Nytorv, is the grand old hotel of the city, offering first-class suites to the rich and famous and a very good restaurant.

The square, one of the largest in the city, was laid out in 1660 to follow the French model of a *place royale* with an equestrian statue in the middle. The original statue of **King Frederik V** contained too much lead, however, and collapsed quietly over the centuries; in 1946 it had to be re-cast. The small garden with the statue and surrounding shady trees is called **Krinsen**; in late June every year the new high school graduates dance around it to celebrate the end of their final examinations.

Although the quiet charm of Kongens Nytorv is disturbed by traffic, it is still one of the most stately places in Copenhagen. Dominating it is **Det Kongelige Teater** (The Royal Theatre) which borders the square to the south. The theatre is the national stage for ballet and opera as well as drama. August Bournonville, the influencial French-born choreographer, created a number of repertory pieces for Denmark's world famous Royal Ballet in the first half of the 19th century. Company members are still the world's leading performers of the Bournonville School, and companies everywhere are eager to recruit Danish ballet dancers. The present theatre was designed in the 1870s with the Parisian Opera as its ideal. Another prominent building on the square is **Charlottenborg**, which since 1754 has been the home of the **Royal Academy of Fine Arts**, where painters, sculptors and architects get their formal training.

Go through the front gate at Char-

The characteristic sign of the Danish Royal Mail.

lottenborg, and into the back courtyard to find the **Charlottenborg Kunstudstilling** (Charlottenborg Exhibition) and varying exhibitions of the works of Danish artists. Charlottenborg's neighbour, **Kongens Nytorv 1–3**, is also a part of the Academy of Fine Arts, and was built in 1740 by C. F. Harsdorff, Denmark's great classical architect. The building also served in the middle and the end of the 18th century as a model for new construction in Copenhagen. **Thotts Palace**, at Kongens Nytorv No. 4, was built in 1680 and today houses the French Embassy.

The narrow waterway of **Nyhavn** was dug by soldiers in 1673 and is another famous Copenhagen landmark. Old wooden schooners line the quay and the north side is a charming combination of sailors' bars and new restaurants. The south side was always "the nice side" but the north side used to be "the naughty side" where sailors on shore leave would spend their liberty drinking, whoring, and being tattooed. Tattoo Ole and Tattoo Jack still offer

their services. While there are still a few of the old bars left, Nyhavn is now a perfectly safe place for an evening.

Hans Christian Andersen also recognised the charms of Nyhavn and lived in no less than three places here: a plaque commemorates his residence during the 1860s at No. 67, and for shorter periods he lived in numbers 18 and 20.

Kongens Nytorv and Nyhavn are the southern borders of **Frederiksstaden**, an area built in the 18th century by the noble and well-to-do who wanted stately homes close to the centre of town. In contrast to the winding streets of medieval Copenhagen, Frederiksstaden is marked by wide, straight streets laid out in a regular pattern.

Walk up one of the streets leading north from Nyhavn, to reach **Sankt Annæ Plads**, a long tree-lined square with an equestrian statue of King Christian X, the father of Margrethe II, the present queen. Christian X reigned during the German occupation between 1940 and 1945 and his daily rides around the city on horseback became an

Tato Bob's one of Nyhavn's best-known tattoo shops.

important symbol of liberty for the population during those years. Legend has it that, in proud contempt of German regulations that Danish Jews wear a yellow Star of David to identify themselves, the King rode the streets wearing a star on his own sleeve.

Bredgade, at the northwest end of the square, and **Amaliegade**, which leads north from the centre of the square, were the main residential streets of the area and both are lined with large houses which today are primarily used as offices. Note **Odd Fellow Palæ** at Bredgade 28, one of Copenhagen's finest rococo palaces, which is the home of a leading concert hall. Bredgade and its parallel twin, **Store Kongensgade**, are the main shopping streets of Fredrikstaden.

At Bredgade 68 is **Kunstindustrimuseet** (the Museum of Decorative and Applied Arts) with historical European and Oriental works as well as a library. The building dates from 1757 and was originally a hospital for 300 patients. In one of the wings (Bredgade 62) is the **Medicinsk-historisk Museum** (Museum of Medical History), which is still reminiscent of the old hospital. On the other side of Bredgade, across from the museum, three domes tower over **Alexander Nevski Russian Orthodox Church**, which was built in 1881 by the Russian government and contains a number of fine icons.

Frederikskirken, popularly known as **Marmorkirken** (the Marble Church), hovers practically next door, at the western end of **Frederiksgade**. Marmorkirken was meant to be a grand monument at the end of the street, but the king ran out of money during its construction and the church was not completed until the 1870s. When the project was resumed it was built not in marble, but in limestone. From the dome, which is accessible to visitors, there is a splendid view over town and across the sound to Sweden. The statues outside the church represent important Danish churchmen and theologians.

Amalienborg Palace, directly across Bredgade toward the harbour, is

Amalienborg Palace with the statue of Frederik V on horseback.

the residence of the Royal Family, one of Europe's less assuming royal domiciles. Nevertheless, the Royal Guard are always on duty, and the changing of the guard at noon every day is a sure attraction for both children and adults.

Amalienborg's four separate palaces were originally planned as the centerpiece of the grand plan for Frederikstaden, but King Frederik V did not want to assume the expense of building the palaces himself. Instead, he offered a 40-year tax holiday for those who would foot the bill. Nikolaj Eigtved designed the four Rococo palaces which were completed in the middle of the 18th century. Only in 1794, when Christiansborg Palace was destroyed by fire, did the Royal Family finally move in.

The exquisite equestrian statue in the middle of the square represents Frederik V and was made by the French sculptor Jacques Saly. **Det Østasiatiske Kompagni** (The East Asiatic Company), one of Denmark's most prosperous trading companies of the day, promised to finance the statue, but there was disagreement between the artist and his backers and it took 20 years to complete the work. In 1771 Saly returned to France a sick man, bitter about the miserly fees he had received, while the stockholders of the East Asiatic Company complained equally bitterly about the enormous amounts they had had to spend.

The other end of the east-west axis through the plaza ends in **Amaliehaven**, a newly established park donated to the city by the A. P. Møller shipping company in 1983. The park was given a somewhat mixed reception by Copenhagen residents. Although the location is popular among strollers, the park is often referred to by locals as the "Deep-Freeze Mausoleum". Behind the park are three 18th-century warehouses, the Blue, (which is actually red), the Yellow and the West Indian.

Walk west, past Marmorkirken, and turn right on to **Store Kongensgade** to visit Denmark's oldest housing development, **Nyboder**. The long rows of

Unexpected music greets visitors to the Royal Danish porcelain building.

yellow houses were built in 1638 as quarters for naval staff and the 616 apartments are still used for staff and retired officers.

Harbour, parks and lakes: In contrast to the busy streets, the natural areas around Copenhagen add a welcome openness to the city. The harbour which cuts through the city on the eastern side, a string of parks on the western side and the outer belt of artificial lakes mean that there is never any great distance to travel to reach green places and water. They provide residents and visitors with much-needed breathing space, and the trees help to clean polluted air. The five parks, including Tivoli, lie in a semi-circle around the inner city like a string of pearls; they were established in the middle of the 19th century when the fortifications were abandoned, a far-sighted piece of city planning.

Ørstedsparken, named after Denmark's famous 19th-century physicist Hans Christian Ørsted (known for his discovery of the principles of electromagnetism), is marked by its winding lake and large shadowy trees. Adjoining it on the north side is **Israels Plads**, a large square which houses one of the city's fruit and vegetable markets and, in the summer months, an antique market on Saturdays. Israels Plads is five minutes' walk from **Nørreport Station**, the busiest subway station.

Just north of Israels Plads and Nørreport Station is **Botanisk Have** (the Botanical Garden), at the corner of **Gothersgade** and **Øster Voldgade**. Visit the rosarium, the perennials and a huge conservatory with tropical and subtropical plants. Adjacent to the Botanical Garden lies **Østre Anlæg**, with lovely shadowy lawns, a large playground which is popular with children, and two important museums.

At the southeast corner of the park, near **Sølvgade** and **Øster Voldgade**, is **Statens Museum for Kunst** (the National Art Museum), which exhibits Danish and European works, including a large Matisse collection; on the west side of the park (with an entrance from **Øster Farimagsgade**) is **Den Hirsch-**

The Nyboder district, built in 1638 as naval officers' quarters, and still used for naval staff.

sprungske Samling (the Hirschsprung Collection), a commendable private collection of 19th-century Danish paintings.

Kastellet, the most northerly of the parks, is the only one to have kept its old ramparts intact. Part of the area is still military property; the headquarters of Copenhagen's Defence Forces and the Danish NATO headquarters are here too.

Churchill Parken, a tiny park just beside Kastellet, provides a home for **Frihedsmuseet** (Danish Resistance Museum) which commemorates the Danish underground fighters of World War II. The museum exhibits objects, pictures, books and publications to recognise and explain the attitudes and reactions of the Danes to Occupation. From passive resistance and civil disobedience to active sabotage and fighting, the achievements of the resistance movement and its co-operation with the Allies are described.

Nearby is **St Alban's**, Copenhagen's only Anglican church. Services are conducted in English, and the congregation includes both residents and English-speaking visitors.

Immediately beside the church is the city's largest monument, the Gefion Fountain, dedicated to the Nordic goddess Gefion, who had four great sons fathered by a giant from the Jotunheim massif (the home of the giants) in Norway. When Odin, king of the Gods, decided that the heavenly kingdom needed more land, he sent Gefion and her four sons to try her arts of persuasion on King Gylfe of Sweden. The king was sufficiently charmed to tell the goddess she could take as much land as she could plough in one day. Quickly transforming her sons into oxen, Gefion set to the task and by nightfall she had ploughed a huge area of central Sweden. That is how, so the story goes, Denmark got the island of Sealand, while Sweden gained its largest lake as the beautiful waters filled the empty space to form Lake Vänern.

North of Langelinie, renovations at **Frihavnen** (the Free Harbour) have been taking place along the lines estab-

The Gefion Fountain near St Alban's Anglican Church. Following pages: work and leisure at Nyhavn.

lished in London and several other major European cities whose harbours have stood decayed and virtually deserted since the late 1960s. The most architecturally interesting of the new buildings is **Paustians Hus** (Paustian's House), designed by Jørn Utzon, who also designed the Opera House in Sydney. Paustian is one of Copenhagen's finest furniture stores; the building also houses a good restaurant.

On the west side of the inner city is another distinctive body of water. Three artificial lakes stretch about 1½ miles (2.5 km) from **Østerbrogade** in the north to **Gammel Kongevej** in the south. With their regular shapes the three linked lakes, **Sortedams Sø**, **Peblinge Sø** and **Sankt Jørgens Sø**, resemble a river and provide the city with a peaceful place to go for a walk, as well as a home for flocks of birds. The lakes were dug to add to the city's western defensive perimeter and also served as a fresh water supply. On display at Christiansborg Palace are the remains of the wooden pipes used to provide water underneath the palace.

Food and fun: Danes are confident that they provide the best food in Scandinavia, and few who have stood at a lavish Cold Table, *Det Store Kolde Bord*, in a Copenhagen restaurant will disagree. This magnificent spread of herring, fish, meat, pâté, salads and desserts usually also includes warm dishes, and there is an earlier more modest *kolde bord* in most hotels for breakfast. At night, Copenhagen is lively with dozens of restaurants where the food is again excellent. Danes love jazz and bands and you find music clubs, piano and jazz bars, and cafés open late all over the city. At weekends from Tivoli Gardens comes the sound of military music, played by the Tivoli Guard, all dressed up as a youthful replica of the Royal Copenhagen Guard as they parade and play along the paths, and the evening ends with the whoosh of fireworks.

On summer evenings like this, when darkness is short, gardens, squares and pavement cafés are full until well into the night and Copenhagen feels like a city that enjoys itself around the clock.

NORTH SEALAND

Unless they prefer city life, people who work in Copenhagen look to the north as the most desirable and impressive place to live. It also makes a classic tour for visitors, with its green and undulating countryside, beech forests, lakes and good beaches (particularly on the extreme north coast) as well as numerous castles, manor houses, royal hunting lodges, art galleries and museums, all within an easy drive of the capital.

The coast road from Copenhagen to Helsingør is officially called **Strandvejen**, but is also known as "The Danish Riviera" for its stylish houses and fine views across the Øresund to Sweden. The drive along here is delightful at any time of year – spectacular in summer with the infinite varieties of blue that make up the clear Scandinavian sea-and-skyscapes, and hauntingly dramatic in the occasional hard winter when the Sound is frozen into Arctic scenes which glisten in the winter sun.

Small protected boat harbours punctuate the road, to shelter working fishing boats and millionaires' yachts alike, and several converted marine buildings now house fresh fish restaurants, which range from plain and simple to those offering true gourmet food. The annual "Round Sealand" yacht race in mid-June, one of the world's largest sailing events, often attracts up to 2,000 entries. It also offers very exciting spectator-sport from Strandvejen.

Midsummer: If you are in this area on Midsummer's eve you will have an unforgettable and enchanting experience. Revellers crowd around the bonfires on the beaches, firework displays light the skies and a procession of ships passes through the Sound, blasting their horns to celebrate the peak of the short, intense Danish summer and the best-loved Scandinavian night of the year.

While it is true that the essence of North Sealand can be glimpsed in a day, it really warrants more time, either by an overnight stop at one of the charming Danish *kros* (inns) or by taking several day tours from Copenhagen. A car gives flexibility for touring but there are good bus and train services from Copenhagen to Helsingør and other towns in this area, many of which are covered by the excellent value Copenhagen Card (see Getting Around section of *Travel Tips*).

Starting from Copenhagen, you drive north, through Hellerup, past the mighty Tuborg breweries. Continue through the fashionable suburb of Charlottenlund to **Klampenborg**, where, less than 30 minutes' drive from the city centre, there is an ancient 2,500-acre (1,000-hectare) royal deer park, first mentioned in official documents as early as 1231. You can leave your car here and take a horse and carriage drive through the enchanting woods and parkland. Too often this form of transport is just a catch-penny tourist attraction but here, although they can be expensive (it is essential to agree a price before you set off), they are the ideal way to see the park, and much used by Danes. Forest walks are indicated by yellow spots painted on trees.

In another part of the deer park lies what is claimed to be the world's oldest fun fair, **Bakken**, a forerunner of the far more sophisticated Tivoli. Bakken heralds the start of the Danish spring every year when it opens its famous red gates on 1 April. **Peter Lieps'** rustic restaurant in the forest is the place where the locals go to drink hot chocolate after winter walks and for a romantic summer rendezvous.

Art lovers will enjoy the quiet elegance of the nearby **Ordrupgaard Art Gallery** in Vilvordevej, in a charming house so little changed since it was built in 1918 that it gives an insight into the lifestyle of wealthy Copenhagen citizens of that time. It has a permanent collection of Danish and French paintings which include major works by Matisse, Corot, Manet, Renoir, Sisley and Gauguin. Gourmets should also know that one of Denmark's best restaurants is to be found in the conservatory of the **Skovshoved Hotel**, just a few minutes' walk from the small fishing harbour, on the old Strandvejen, which runs one block inland from the sea in Klampenborg.

Out of Africa: Less than half an hour's leisurely drive north brings you to **Rungsted**, famous now for "Rungstedlund", the family home of Karen Blixen, the Danish writer who sprang to worldwide fame when her book *Out Of Africa* was filmed. Karen Blixen died here in 1962 and, in accordance with her wishes, was buried in the grounds which are open to visitors. Plans are under way to turn the house into a museum devoted to her life and work.

At Humlebæk you could easily spend an entire day at the **Louisana Museum of Modern Art**. This was opened in 1958 with a collection of modern Danish art, aiming "to show the interplay between art, architecture and landscape." New galleries have since been added and frequent international exhibitions are held in a breath-taking setting. The rich permanent collection includes sculptures set in the surrounding gardens and there are also film, concert and theatre programmes.

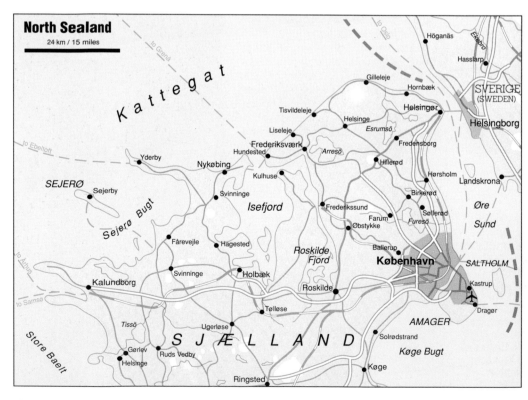

North Sealand

24 km / 15 miles

Helsingør is perhaps best known as the main ferry crossing to Sweden (which takes just 25 minutes) but it is also famous for its massive Renaissance-style **Kronborg Slot**, Hamlet's Castle of Elsinore. Originally built by King Eric of Pomerania when he introduced the "Sound Dues" – fees to be paid to the Danish crown by all ships passing through to the Baltic – Kronborg has been rebuilt several times, and it has provided a fabulous backdrop for many international productions of Shakespeare's play. Even today, its atmosphere is eerie and smells of intrigue and royal plots.

The castle also holds the statue of Holger Danske, a Danish Viking chief who, according to legend, will fill Danes with his fighting spirit when the country is in danger. His name was used as a codeword by the Danish Resistance during World War II.

Helsingør is one of Denmark's most historic towns, with entire streets of well-preserved, colour-washed buildings. The 15th-century **St Mariæ Church** and the **Carmelite Monastery** are among the best preserved Gothic buildings in the world. Hans Christian Andersen, who lived in Helsingør for a time, described it as "one of the most beautiful spots in Denmark, close to the Sound, which is one mile wide and looks like a blue stream swelling between Denmark and Sweden."

Escape route: The coast road leads on to **Gilleleje**, the most northern town of Sealand, a fascinating, small working fishing port, which has a fish auction each morning. Gilleleje played a heroic role in World War II. From here many Jews escaped to neutral Sweden through the efforts of the Danish underground and local fishermen. "**Hos Karen og Marie**", housed in an unpretentious green-painted wooden building, is one of the best simple fish restaurants anywhere. Ask to sit upstairs facing the harbour.

If the weather is good, you could return via the sun-worshippers' beaches of **Tisvilde** or **Liseleje**, or carry on to **Solager**, taking the short ferry to

Stag and hind, two of Dyrehaven's large herd. Following pages: one of North Sealand's most peaceful stretches of water.

Kulhuse and drive through a forest of ancient oak trees to **Jaegerspris Castle** (open April–October), where the rooms occupied by King Frederik VII are left unchanged. At the end of June, authentic Viking plays are staged at **Frederikssund**, 4 miles (6 km) away, with audience participation and traditional feasts.

Turning inland for the return to Copenhagen, **Frederiksborg Castle**, built between 1605 and 1621, is on the outskirts of Hillerød, 22 miles (36 km) from Copenhagen on the E47. Apart from the chapel, most of the castle was destroyed by fire in 1859 but rebuilt to the original plan within six years. The interiors were finished with large grants from the brewery king, J. C. Jacobson.

Under the Carlsberg Foundation, Frederiksborg has been Denmark's **National History Museum** ever since. The most notable rooms are the Council Hall, Knights' Hall, where the walls are hung with shields presented by many famous visitors, and the chapel with its original Compenius organ, built in 1610. It makes a fine setting for concerts held in July and August. North of the lake is one of the best-preserved baroque gardens in Northern Europe, and to the west there is a large English garden with a small Renaissance château built in 1581, which King Frederik II used as a bath house. In summer, the lake offers boat trips.

Just 5 miles (9 km) from Hillerød, **Fredensborg** is known for its royal palace and its famous 19th-century inn, the **Store Kro**. The palace was built in Italian style in 1722, and is now used as a residence for the Danish Royal Family in spring and autumn, to provide an exquisite setting for royal entertaining. Part of the castle is open to the public in July only. There is a formal French marble garden west of the palace and the park which leads to a delightful lake called Esrum Sø, has a distinctive collection of sculptures.

The ancient thatched **Sollerød Kro** in an idyllic village near Birkerød on the northern outskirts of Copenhagen is one of the best in Denmark – an expensive but enjoyable way to end a tour.

SOUTH AND WEST SEALAND

As a visitor to Denmark, you can hardly fail to find yourself in South Sealand, as it includes Copenhagen airport as well as the main road, rail and ferry routes across the country and south to Germany. Although the northern part of the area also contains the suburbs and industrial estates south of Copenhagen, South Sealand is a peaceful place, full of history, where every one of the numerous castles and manor houses has its own story.

Over the centuries, this part of Sealand was the scene of invasions and strife, and the Viking influence was also strong; there are remains of a 1,000-year-old Viking fortress at Trelleborg in the south. Roskilde to the west was an important trading centre in Viking times and today its museum holds five magnificent Viking ships. It was also once the seat of the reigning monarch and, after the Danes were converted to Christianity, the town became one of the most important religious centres in Northern Europe.

Roaming geese: In the 19th century, more peaceful "invasions" of artisans came to South Sealand to teach their skills and some of their rituals now form part of local festivals. In spite of the presence of the international airport on Amager island, the old fishing village of **Dragør** has streets of half-timbered houses, geese still roam the streets and the descendants of the Dutch immigrants who brought their knowledge of horticulture to Denmark celebrate their traditional Shrove-tide customs. With a barrel suspended over the course, the men dress up in fancy costumes and ride their horses at full tilt, lances outstretched to spear and splinter the barrel in half. It certainly enlivens a bleak Danish winter.

Serious shoppers have been known to re-route their cars to take in the special attractions of the airport itself where the shopping centre is based on Copenhagen's Tivoli Gardens. There are masses of flowers and old-fashioned signs hanging outside ultra-modern shops which sell the best of Scandinavian goods. Sometimes, craftsmen demonstrate the making of luxury items such as chocolates, cigars and fur coats; and regular promotions of treats such as oysters and champagne make this one airport where you might even enjoy a flight delay.

The international motorway to Germany runs from Dragør to Køge, passing popular bathing beaches, crowded with sun-loving Danes, and summer camp sites. Its inhabitants claim that **Køge** has more half-timbered houses than any other town in Denmark, which is saying something, and the oldest, dated 1527, stands at 20 Kirkestræde. Also visit Skt. Nikolai Kirke, which has one of Denmark's most beautiful town church interiors. Not far from the busy market place is **Hugo's Vinkælder**, (wine shop) which has one of the oldest inns in Denmark serving good old-fashioned draught porter.

Just south of Køge is **Vallø**, a beautiful Renaissance castle surrounded by a

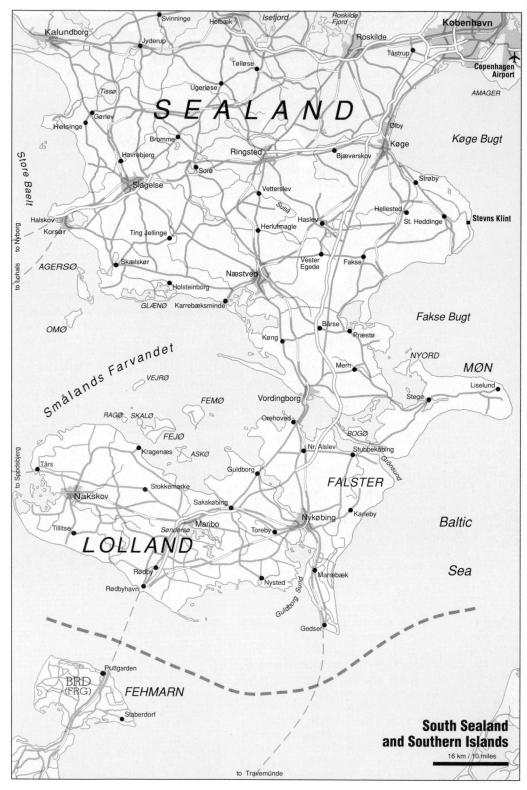

Kalundborg
Svinninge
Holbæk
Isefjord
Roskilde Fjord
København
Roskilde
Jyderup
Tåstrup
Copenhagen
Airport
Tølløse
AMAGER
Ugerløse
Tissø
S E A L A N D
Helsinge
Gørlev
Ølby
Køge Bugt
Bromme
Køge
Havrebjerg
Ringsted
Bjæverskov
Sorø
Strøby
Slagelse
Vetterslev
Hellested
St. Heddinge
Stevns Klint
Halskov
Suså
Hasley
Korsør
Herlufmagle
Ting Jellinge
AGERSØ
Skælskør
Vester
Egede
Fakse
Næstved
Holsteinborg
Fakse Bugt
GLÆNØ
Karrebæksminde
Bårse
NYORD
OMØ
Køng
Præstø
MØN
Smålands Farvandet
Mern
Liselund
VEJRØ
Stege
FEMØ
Vordingborg
RAGØ *SKALØ*
Orehoved
BOGØ
FEJØ
Baltic
Kragenæs
ASKØ
Nr. Alslev
Stubbekøbing
Tårs
Grönsund
Guldborg
FALSTER
Stokkemarke
Sakskøbing
Nakskov
Nykøbing
Karleby
Maribo
Baltic
Tillitse
Søndersø
Toreby
LOLLAND
Rødby
Marrebæk
Sea
Rødbyhavn
Nysted
Guldborg Sund
Gedser
Puttgarden
BRD
(FRG)
FEHMARN
Staberdorf
Store Baelt
to Nyborg
to Lohals
to Spodsbjerg
to Travemünde

**South Sealand
and Southern Islands**

16 km / 10 miles

188

moat and wide parkland. Its two massive towers are unmistakable. Since 1737, the castle has been owned by a charitable trust, set up to provide a dignified setting for the unmarried daughters of noblemen in their later years. A few of these ladies still live in the castle but are unlikely to patronise the Vallø Slotskro opposite the castle, an old inn which specialises in traditional Danish food.

Bay of battles: Køge Bay was the scene of two great naval battles between Denmark and Sweden, and the Danish National Anthem celebrates the first of these with the words: "King Christian stood by the lofty mast" – though some claim that the King actually watched from Skt. Nikolai Kirke.

On the way to the Stevns Klint chalk cliffs, the grounds of **Gjorslev Manor**, situated between Magleby and Holtug, are open to the public. The manor has a crucifix-shaped ground plan and was built in 1400 for the then Bishop of Roskilde. **Stevns Klint** on the south headland of the bay may not be quite as dramatic as the chalk cliffs on the island of Møn further south but they are very impressive when the sun lights them to brilliant white. How long this will last, however, no-one knows because the waves pound ceaselessly, eating into the chalk below, and the 13th-century **Højerup Kirke** at the top is only precariously intact in its fight with the sea. In 1928, the sea won a partial victory when some of the building crashed down the 130-ft (40-metre) cliffs and, in the end, it seems inevitable that the old church will tumble into the sea.

Further south, **Fakse** has a nice beach near Vemmetofte Manor, and is also the home of a very successful brewery, one of the few not associated with the giants of Tuborg and Carlsberg. Fakse Breweries claim that all their beers are brewed with "coral water" because the town lies on what was once a prehistoric coral reef.

On the inland side of the main road (E4), 3 miles (5 km) from the ancient town of Haslev, Hans Christian Andersen is said to have found inspiration for what is perhaps his most famous story, *The Ugly Duckling*, in **Gisselfeld Slot**, built in 1554. (To an observant visitor, it is astonishing how many castles and towns in Denmark claim connections, sometimes conflicting, with one or other of Andersen's stories.) Nearby is **Bregentved Slot**, with its copper spire, which is Sealand's largest private estate. It is open Wednesday, Sunday and public holidays. In spring there is also the intoxicating sight of the vast cherry orchards around **Dalby** which supply the Cherry Heering Distillery there.

The **Holmegaard Danish Glassworks** at Fensmark were founded in 1825, when glassmakers were brought from Norway and Bohemia. This is a popular target for tours from Copenhagen, and visitors can watch glass being blown, and marvel at the highly-skilled glass blowing required for the special artistic pieces created by the company designers. The Glass Museum has a fine collection which reflects the history of this famous company, and "seconds", often with almost indiscernible flaws,

The islands are a delight of sand and sea.

are superb bargains. If you are in luck, you may be able to hear music played by the company's famous glass band The band uses instruments made of glass which are remarkably tuneful. It is best to enquire in advance.

Although so well-geared to social equality – the Danes are nothing if not democratic – **Herlufsholm Manor** in nearby **Næstved** is one of Denmark's most prestigious private boarding schools, which retains many unique customs and traditions. It was founded in 1565 by nobleman Herluf Trolle and his wife, who were childless, and the public are admitted to the courtyard, park, and chapel at limited times. The tombs of Herluf Trolle and his wife lie together behind the altar, below an altar crucifix that is one of the art treasures of Europe, and unique in Denmark. Carved from a single elephant tusk, it is believed to have originated in southern France in the middle of the 13th century, and arrived in Herlufsholm no one knows how.

Næstved has been an important trading town for most of its history and has an attractive city centre, The Gothic **Skt Peder Kirke** has a richly carved pulpit from 1671 and **Skt Mortens Kirke**, built around 1300, has a lavishly decorated altarpiece. An interesting museum of local history is housed in **Helligåndshuset** (House of the Holy Spirit), built in 1492, and is well worth a visit.

Gavnø Manor, on a tiny island linked by road, 4 miles (6 km) south-west of Næstved, is open May to August. By the 13th century this was already used as a pirates' castle but, in 1398, Queen Margrethe bought Gavnø and turned it into a convent. It became a private manor house in 1584. In spite of the sale of paintings worth 4.2 million Dkr. in 1976, Gavnø still has Scandinavia's largest privately owned picture collection.

Cliffs and orchids: The island of **Møn** ("The Maid"), linked to Sealand by road bridges, forms the extreme southeast of Denmark. According to legend, its spectacular stretches of luminous white

Riding festivals are regular summer events all over Denmark. Amager's is the most famous.

chalk cliffs, topped with beech woods and studded with fossils, became a refuge for Odin, father of the gods, when Christianity made him homeless. This now-peaceful place has also been invaded, it is said, by "every Northern tribe" and has Bronze-Age tombs, 13th-century churches with medieval frescoes, and primeval forests with more varieties of wild orchids than anywhere else in Denmark. Marked paths lead down to the beach, a place to find coral fossils and sea urchins. Over the past 200 years, most of the "invaders" of Møn have been writers and painters, lured there by the inspiration of its beauty and drama.

Liselund "Castle" is actually a thatched mini-château, built in 1796, which has been called the "Danish Petit Trianon". This miniature palace has a thatched roof, and there is a cottage with a Norwegian exterior and Pompeiian interior. The ubiquitous Hans Christian Andersen wrote his tales *The Tinder Box* and *The Little Match Girl* in a summer house known as the "Swiss Cottage" on this estate. At one time, Liselund had several more buildings but they have long disappeared into the sea as part of the cliff collapsed. South of the cliffs, the fishing port of **Klintholm Havn** has a good hotel and seafood restaurant, Ålekroen, which specialises in smoked, fried, or stewed eel.

Møn's churches are famous for their frescoes, particularly those at **Keldby**, **Elmelund** and **Fanefjord**, the last standing in a beautiful setting of an isolated hill which overlooks the narrows of Grønsund. Beside the church is the longest barrow grave in Denmark, **Grønjægers Høj**. The island's main town of Stege has a unique town gate and medieval ramparts.

The Farø bridges, completed in 1985, connect Sealand to the island of Falster, and the ferry routes to Germany. The main town of the island is **Nykøbing**, famous for the **Czar's House**, where Peter the Great stayed in 1716 (the year of his famous horse-riding exploit up the steep 620-ft/200-metre ramp in Rundetårnet, in Copenhagen). It is a

Strange formations on the cliffs of Møn.

museum. The area around **Marielyst** has some 12 miles (20 km) of fine white sand dunes where local families take traditional beach holidays, and Bøtø has a well-known nudist beach over a mile long. **Stubbekøbing** is a market town with ferry connections to Bøgø and Møn, and it has the largest veteran motorcycle museum in northern Europe, with old radios and loudspeakers also on display.

There is a choice of road bridges from Falster to Lolland, to reach one of the island's main attractions, **Ålholm Slot**, near the old seaport of Nysted. The castle dates from the 12th century, was once known as the robber's castle, and has a massive collection of vintage cars owned by the present Ålholm Baron. It is one of the world's finest collections of rare cars with all sorts of oddities and also the special train carriage which the Baron's father, then Foreign Secretary, used on his travels.

From Ålholm, the road north and west runs past the beautiful lakes to **Maribo** and on to **Knuthenborg Safari Park**, where exotic animals live in open grounds. In the far west, the Tars-Spodsbjerg crossing connects the island with Langeland and Funen.

To continue the tour, drive back north and over the bridge from Orehoved in Falster to **Vordingborg**, Sealand's southernmost town. This has the **Goose Tower**, which dates from 1370, and the ruins of a fortress that was once the second largest in Scandinavia and now forms Denmark's best-preserved medieval buildings. Further north is **Ringsted** in the heart of Sealand, with **St Bendts Kirke**, dedicated to all Danish kings who bear the name of Valdemar. Inside the church, the tombs and coats-of-arms are a tribute to the time when this modest country town was one of the most important in Denmark.

Heading west, either along the E66 (the main route from Copenhagen across Denmark) or on one of the smaller roads that pre-dated it, the next stop is Sorø and **Sorø Kirke**, part of the oldest abbey in Denmark. Behind the altar is the tomb of Bishop Absalon of

The Viking ship hall in Roskilde Museum.

Roskilde, founder of Copenhagen. The former abbey building is now a boarding school, Sorø Academy, set beside a lake which makes a beautiful setting for a peaceful walk.

The road continues west to Slagelse where, 3 miles (5 km) from the centre, is **Trelleborg**, an abandoned Viking fortress some 1,000 years old. It was once a huge fortified camp that housed as many as 1,000. Trelleborg today has reconstructed one of the houses outside the circular walls and on a cold spring day it is easy to understand how tough the life here must have been hardy though the Vikings were.

Past Slagelse, on Sealand's west coast, travellers on Denmark's main east-west route board the ferry for Funen, but Sealand explorers turn north for the extreme west of the island where **Kalundborg** is also a ferry port for Jutland, via the island of **Samsø**, famous for the cheese it exports all over the world. Despite a turbulent history, Kalundborg is now a quiet place known chiefly for its magnificent five-towered church, built in 1170 by Esbern Snare, brother to Bishop Absalon. It is surrounded by ancient buildings in **Lindegaarden**, one of which holds the town museum.

Lerchborg Manor nearby (open June to August) has a Music Week in August, and a road leading from its courtyard to the **Rosnæs peninsula** where there is a windmill and lighthouse. **Dragsholm Slot** at Fårevejle was the prison of the Earl of Bothwell, the ambitious but ill-fated husband of Mary Queen of Scots, who in 1567 fled to Denmark in a vain hope of sanctuary after her downfall. Chained to the dismal walls, the Earl waited long for death. His cell is open to the public, and Dragsholm itself has become a hotel and restaurant.

Viking town: Perhaps the main highlight of the whole of Sealand is the town of **Roskilde**. Considered by some to be in the north of the island, others in the south and west but, in fact, lying along the neck of land which joins the two, it is usually visited as a tour in its own

Ready for dinner in the dining room at Ålholm Castle.

right from Copenhagen. The train journey is little more than 20 minutes from the capital. Roskilde is Sealand's second largest town and its **Domkirke** (cathedral), built in 1170, is the burial place of generations of Danish monarchs. Their elaborate tombs lie in side chapels to the main cathedral. The most impressive chapels are those of King Christian IV, built in 1641 in Dutch Renaissance style with magnificent murals, and the chapel of King Frederik V from 1770, the masterwork of the architect Harsdorff.

Modern excavations at the Domkirke have revealed that building began around AD 1000 and was probably not completed until 1410. Even today, chapels are still added and the cathedral has a sense of being alive and growing. There are many treasures, not least the gold triptych altarpiece built in Antwerp in 1560 and the much loved St George and the Dragon clock, which chimes on the hour.

Roskilde's **Viking Ship Museum**, down beside the water, is one of the great delights of Denmark and rivals the similar exhibition in Oslo. Its five ships were found in 1962 at the mouth of the Roskildefjord. The ships had lain there since the 11th-century defenders of Roskilde had sunk them to block the entrance of the fjord against enemy ships. The restored ships include a warship of the type portrayed in the Bayeux Tapestry and an awe-inspiring longship, the dreaded Viking man o' war, immensely seaworthy and used for long-range raiding. It was easily large enough for a crew of 40 or 50 men.

Although other Viking craft have been discovered, this longship is the only one of its kind ever found. The ships are superbly displayed in a way which makes them seem to sail on the fjord once more, and they illustrate the outstanding shipbuilding skills of the Vikings. A film tells the story of the complicated excavations which recovered the Viking ships.

To end the day with a truly Viking flavour, turn into the museum restaurant for a draught of the favourite brew of these hardy sailors, *mjød* or mead.

BORNHOLM

The enchanting island of **Bornholm** stands in the middle of the Baltic Sea between Sweden and Poland. Although the island seems remote, Copenhagen is only seven hours away by ferry, and 30 minutes by plane. The ferry trip to southern Sweden takes about two and a half hours. It is a peaceful place; an area of 227 sq. miles (588 sq. km) is home to about 48,000 Bornholmers and the island has a wealth of natural history. There are no large towns and almost no industry; visitors have a perfect opportunity to relax.

It is an island of contrasts. Rugged, rocky shores, and miles of long, sandy beaches alternate along the coast. There are small picturesque fishing villages and pleasant market towns; peaceful forests and working farm fields lie side by side. All of Denmark's natural variety is packed into this one small area of Bornholm.

Living history: The past is everywhere on the island. Passage graves from the Bronze Age and monoliths from both the Bronze and Iron Ages are numerous. Stone carvings, most likely built in praise of the gods and maybe to induce them to provide good weather, are found in many fertile agricultural areas.

Bornholm was a maritime centre in the Baltic Sea during the Iron Age. Jewellery, coins, and relics from as far away as Rome and the Near East have been discovered and two old forts, both known as **Gamleborg**, found in **Paradisbakkerne** (The Hills of Paradise) and at **Almindingen Skov**, date from the Viking period. It is generally believed that Bornholm became a part of the Kingdom of Denmark at around that time. On stormy days a thousand years later, one is reminded of the strategic importance of the island, as fishing boats, freighters, and yachts take shelter from heavy seas.

Hammershus was built in the Middle Ages to defend the island against attack, and is today Scandinavia's largest fortified castle. It stands on a huge,

rocky knoll on the northwest corner of the island, and the ruins are impressive. At the time the castle was built (around 1250), Bornholm was owned by the Archbishop of Lund (in what is now southern Sweden, though then part of Denmark); he was openly at war with the Kings of Denmark. In a brief period of its history, Hammershus was occupied by soldiers from Lübeck (1520), and the Swedes (1645 and 1658), and it was regularly plundered until 1822, when it was placed under the protection of the National Museum. Restoration continues on what is today the most magnificent relic of the history of Bornholm.

There are amazing examples of medieval architecture in the four round churches: **Østerlars**, **Nylars**, **Nyker**, and **Olsker**. When the Slavic Wends ravaged the island, they were occasionally used as places of refuge, and stand as further reminders of the historic importance of the island. During the 14th, 15th, and 16th centuries Hanseatic merchants from northern

Preceding pages: Christiansø, north of Bornholm; weekend at the harbour. **Left and right,** everything grows and flows on Bornholm, including the seven-stemmed tree and leafy waterfall.

Germany would move in during the herring season (May to September), and then sail on to other sites in Denmark and Sweden.

In the middle of the 17th century the island was occupied by the Swedes during one of the numerous wars with Denmark. The Swedish commandant, Colonel Printzenskjöld, was murdered in a conspiracy in 1658, and the islanders drove the rest of the Swedish forces from the island two years later. By popular consent, the islanders then gave themselves and the island to King Frederik III (1648–70). Their allegiance to the kingdom has had a notable effect ever since.

Almost 300 years of peace followed, until the last occupation of Bornholm during World War II. When Germany capitulated to Allied forces on 4 May 1945, the German commandant on the island refused to surrender. After warning the local population to evacuate, the Russians then bombed the two largest towns (**Rønne** and **Nexø**), and brought about the German surrender on 9 May 1945. Several hundred Russian soldiers remained as a garrison on the island until March 1946.

Strong separatist feelings still exist among Bornholmers, some of whom wish for independence from outside rule for the island. Their banner is a Danish flag with a green cross instead of the familiar white one.

Abundant flora: The variety of plant life on Bornholm is almost overwhelming. No other part of Denmark has more hours of sunshine. The long summer and mild autumn weather encourages plants which are otherwise only found in France and Italy. The northern part of the island is extremely rocky and, by radiating heat picked up from the sun, the rocks keep the surface warm enough for figs, grapes, mulberry trees and other plants from southern Europe to grow well.

About 20 percent of Bornholm is woodland, making it Denmark's most densely wooded county. **Almindingen**, in the centre of the island, is Denmark's third largest forest. **Paradisbakkerne**

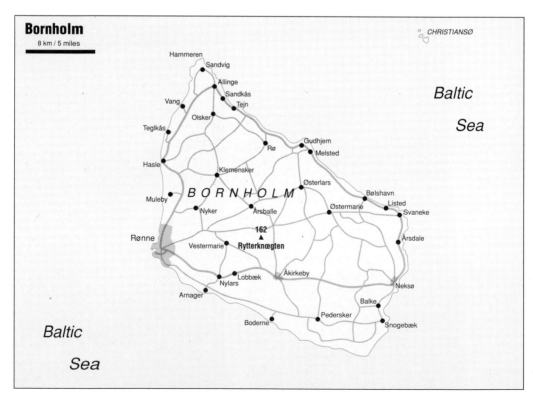

is a unique place, with more and wilder vegetation than Almindingen; it is best enjoyed on foot. In many parts of the island there are moors with unique river valleys. The underlying soil is extremely fertile, and botanists especially enjoy the area.

There are sweet cherry trees all over, which blossom in June, giving a colourful show. Their berries ripen in late July and August. Red orchids are common on the banks in the river valleys and thousands of woodland flowers, especially blue, yellow, and white anemones, cover large areas.

Numerous geological faults make the island's surface a mosaic of rocks of varying age and type. Impressive formations remain from the Mesozoic, Paleozoic, and Pre-Cambrian periods, and professional geologists return frequently to study them. The sea has battered the steep coasts during the 12,000 years since the last Ice Age, creating especially beautiful cliffs in the north and west.

The ruins of Hammershus.

Attitudes today: There is little industry, but Rønne and Nexø are important fishing ports, and the harbours are full of life. Small farms are scattered all over the island: the average farm is 50 acres (20 hectares) or less. Unlike their counterparts elsewhere in Denmark, farmers on Bornholm were never indentured to wealthy landowners – the most important result of the islanders' loyalty to the Danish throne – and the result today is that really big estates do not exist. When the 200th anniversary of the end of indentured labour was celebrated in the rest of Denmark in 1988, the event was hardly mentioned on Bornholm, where independence is considered an obvious human right.

Climate, natural history and the sea all influence the mentality of Bornholmers. One may get the impression that they are reserved; but history has taught the islanders to be restrained in making new friendships. Most visitors are attracted by their quiet and friendly ways and also find interest in the unspoilt nature.

From early July until the end of Au-

gust is holiday time when the beaches may become overcrowded. During this period the population of Bornholm is four times greater than during the rest of the year. The good news is that for the other 10 months a year one rarely meets a visitor. Though most of the residents are unmoved by tourists, a tiny minority still dreams of profits from casinos and tower-block hotels to rival the Costa Brava but such dreams are unlikely to come true.

The conservation lobby: A few years ago local politicians, concerned about potential damage to their island's unique environment, initiated what was known as the "Green Island Project". This effort to preserve the natural beauty of Bornholm and to raise the environmental conciousness of its inhabitants, as well as those of the rest of Denmark, has borne fruit. The project has received financial support from the European Fund for Regional Development. The confined area and isolated positon of Bornholm provide an ideal laboratory in which to study changes in

the environment, and the project is followed with great interest from the outside. Recycling and alternative energy projects have developed all over the island, with the hope that the example of Bornholm will lead to greater consciousness of, and personal responsibility toward, the natural world.

Rønne, with 15,000 inhabitants, is the largest town on Bornholm, and its harbour is one of the largest provincial ports in Denmark. Ferries depart daily for Copenhagen and **Ystad**, in southern Sweden, and in the high season one can also catch a boat to Germany or Poland. Buses from the harbour provide connections to all parts of the island nearly every hour. The area around the main square is the centre of town.

Some parts of the town have been beautifully preserved, especially in the area just east of **Skt Nikolai Kirke**. The beautiful **Kastellet** (Citadel) is on the east side of town; today a military museum. The ceramics and pottery works are open to the public and, together with **Bornholms Museum** and its collection of paintings and hand-crafted items (Skt Mortensgade 29), is worth visiting. **Rønne Theatre** (Østergade 7) is the oldest private theatre still operating in Denmark. Bornholm has inspired many Danish painters, as well as having produced a few of its own: Oluf Høst is probably the best known.

Nexø, with a population of 3,000, is an old fishing and sailors' town on the east coast. The population still depends on the fishing industry for survival, but increasing pollution in the Baltic Sea forces some local fishermen to sail as far as the Indian Ocean and the coasts of Africa in order to maintain their standard of living. **Åkirkeby** (around 1,400 residents) is the main town on the southern part of Bornholm, and the only one of the larger towns situated inland. The name of the town can be roughly translated as "the town of the church-by-the-stream."

The church was built around 1150 as a chapter house in the Archbishopric of Lund. The large tower was extended around 1200, and at the same time it was fortified with walls even heavier than

Bornholm's little towns are ideal for safe cycling. This is Svaneke.

those of either Hammershus or the round churches. It is especially well known for its sandstone baptismal font, imported from Gotland (southern Sweden) in around 1200. The font depicts the life of Christ in 11 relief carvings; the figures are explained in runic script, and end with the signature of the stonecutter, "Sighraf, master".

Town preservation: The easternmost town in Denmark, **Svaneke**, has a population of about 1100. In 1975 it was awarded the European Gold Medal for Town Preservation. For centuries, the success of shipping captains has fuelled its prosperity. The largest buildings were originally merchants' houses; north of the town is an old Dutch mill, and nearby an untraditional water tower, built by the architect Jørn Utzon in 1951.

Bicycling downhill is forbidden in **Gudhjem** (which translates as "good home"), a very pretty place, built on steep rocky slopes down to the water. The huge windmills around the town once provided electricity. The former railway station has been converted into a museum and provides an excellent way of exploring local history. There is an agricultural museum just southeast of Gudhjem, at **Melstedgård**, a settlement which first gained prominence as an important trading centre during the Middle Ages.

From **Gudhjem Harbour** one can sail to the group of islands collectively known as **Ertholmene.** The largest of these are **Christiansø** and **Frederiksø**, about 13 miles (20 km) to the northeast. With a total population of about 130 between them, they are interesting places to visit, if not to live. A naval base was constructed there in about 1864, but today only fishermen and their families live on this "fortress in the sea". The islands are rocky, with old castle towers, batteries, and cannon serving as reminders of the past.

To the northwest is the uninhabited island of **Græsholmen,** protected as a sanctuary for seabirds. The top of the lighthouse provides a good view of the entire island group, which once housed

Energetic sea-angling from the Bornholm rocks.

political prisoners, and is worth a visit.

Østerlars Kirke (consecrated to St Laurentius), just over 2 miles (4 km) from Gudhjem, is the largest of the four famous "round churches" of Bornholm. The enormous support pillars create the impression of a fortress, which was the second purpose of the structure. Inside the church (built around 1150), the vault is painted with fine frescoes of biblical scenes. On the north wall of the oval-shaped choir, stone steps lead to the second storey, where the hollow central pillar has two entrances. The outer wall has a watchman's gallery 5 ft (1.5 metres) wide. The double altar piece was painted by the local artist Poul Høm. The dual-purpose of church and fortification is rare except in Denmark. One can find other interesting places on the island, but those mentioned here are important in local history. Tourist offices can provide more information on particular subjects, and the public library in Rønne is an excellent source of greater detail.

Entertainment: Scandinavia offers numerous classical music festivals, and one of the most important is held on Bornholm. From the middle of July until the beginning of September, many visitors come only to hear the music. In the winter season professional Danish theatre companies visit. **Rønne Theatre** provides an excellent and intimate stage for their work; local amateur theatre groups also perform.

The contrast between the busy summer season and the quiet life of the rest of the year is obvious. Some like it, some do not. Almost all the residents are members of one club or another; pigeons, stamps, mushroom picking and various sports all have their own fans, and every conceivable hobby has a club of its own.

During the summer months, freshly landed herrings are delivered to the smokehouses. Here they are turned from their original silver colour into the "golden Bornholmers" dearly loved by Danes. Elderwood gives them their special taste. One can eat them warm from the oven or put them on black

Bornholm's famous herrings are smoked in houses like this.

bread, sprinkle them with salt, chopped chives, radishes and an egg yolk on top.

Baltic salmon is said to be the finest edible fish in the world, and is normally available here. Pickled herrings were once served for breakfast, but now they're a lunchtime speciality. The best spiced herrings are produced on Christiansø. Farm products are of high quality, and one can often find a good bargain at roadside stands.

Of course, one *can* rent a car or take a bus, but still the best way to travel around Bornholm, like the rest of Denmark, is by bicycle. You hire a bike for a couple of days to escape the noise, smells and hassle of traffic, and an extensive network of bicycle paths has been established on former railway rights-of-way. It is easy to find houses, hotels, and campsites, but remember to book lodgings in advance in the summer season. Use the tourist offices to solve problems or answer questions.

Residents often rent rooms or houses to visitors – at various prices. Bear in mind that there are many tourists on the island during the summer season, and that most are drawn to the southeast part of the island and to its wonderful beaches, **Dueodde** and **Balka**.

Future dilemmas: During the late 19th and early 20th centuries the island attracted immigrants from the impoverished districts of southern Sweden who came to look for prosperity on Bornholm. For a closer look at that phase of the island's history, read the novel *Pelle Eroberen* (Pelle the Conqueror), by the Danish novelist Martin Anderson Nexø, or see the Oscar-winning film. In those days the immigrant Swedes earned their living on the farms and in the granite quarries; today the situation is reversed, as young Bornholmers seek work in the high-technology factories of heavy industry in southern Sweden.

Will Bornholm survive because of, or in spite of, the tourist industry? Its status as a "Green Island" necessarily competes with the practical need to develop industry and keep its younger people. Yet the importance of tourism to the local economy cannot be ignored.

Long beaches and waves are good for water sports.

FUNEN

The island of **Funen** has a comfortable atmosphere that visitors like. Nothing threatens in this gentle landscape and there are few unknowns. These qualities and the lushness of fields and orchards inspired Hans Christian Andersen, Denmark's most famous writer of children's fairy tales, to call Funen "the Garden of Denmark." The title is apt for an island that is a mixture of winding roads, neat fields, well-trimmed hedges and old village farmhouses, often with thatched roofs, lilac trees, and spikes of pink hollyhock against their white walls.

Funen's 1,335 sq. miles (3,458 sq. km.) snuggle neatly into a rolling landscape with no hill higher than 450 ft (130 metres), and everything tucked into a convenient circle. It might have been designed to provide two or three days or even a week of comfortable touring by car or, even better, by bike.

Shelter and soil: There are two main towns. Odense in the north is the birthplace of Hans Christian Andersen and is devoted to his memory; Svendborg to the south is the gateway to the islands of the Funen archipelago, which come in many odd shapes. Some are no more than a rocky speck but, where nature has been kind in providing shelter and soil, everything grows.

Funen is also an island of manors and country houses. Until 1788, the peasants were tied to a particular landowner and worked as feudal tenants. Danes regard the abolition of villeinage, due to the efforts of men such as Johan Ludvig Reventlow of Brahetrolleborg, as one of the major events in Danish history. It was the start of Denmark's system of social rights, which makes the country one of the most liberal in the world. Today, the manor houses seem benevolent, even protective, and many are hotels and restaurants, where you can enjoy a drink or eat outside in the long Scandinavian twilight.

The Garden of Denmark provides much of the country's horticultural produce and corn, and tomatoes and cucumbers sprout in the ubiquitous greenhouses. Funen also provides the house plants which grace Danish windowsills and, as well, exports them all over Europe.

When coming from Copenhagen, the usual way to reach Funen is by train or car, including an hour-long ferry journey from **Korsør** across the Great Belt to **Nyborg** on the east coast. (Coming from the west across Central Jutland, you can drive or arrive by train straight on to the island at **Middelfart**). The choice then is between circling the islands from Nyborg or Middelfart and basing yourself either in Odense or Svendborg to make excursions.

Distances in Funen and its islands are short, as they are in most of Denmark, but this comparatively small island has a lot to offer and is well worth two or three days at least. Driving is easy but the most satisfying way to see Funen is to cycle. The perspective is quite different. You are close to the villages you cycle through and can stop at a gate to

Preceding pages: murals at Hans Christian Andersen's House in Odense. Left, drystone wall, typical of Funen. Right, two wheels are often better than four.

look at a prize sheep or lean your bike beside one of the little white-washed churches to take a look inside.

Above all, you do not miss the clusters of wild flowers that lie on either side of the roads below the wild rose hedges. Soon it may feel as though Denmark is not as flat as supposed, but the effect of the fresh air and exercise is marvellous. Most of the older towns started as ports and fishing and trading centres and there is a long tradition of seamanship, particularly in south Funen and the islands. Since the days when Funen ships plied the seas of the world, the shipping trade has shrunk in size and importance but these calm waters and the smaller ports have become havens for eager leisure sailors who flock in from all over northern Europe.

Before heading north out of Nyborg for Kerteminde and the Hindsholm Peninsula, take a look at **Nyborg Slot** (Nyborg Castle), one of the oldest of Denmark's royal castles, which dates from 1170. It was built to defend the country from the Wends of North Ger-many and, during the Middle Ages, was the meeting place for the three ruling powers of monarch, nobility, and clergy. But fashions change; Copenhagen became the seat of power and, in 1722, much of Nyborg Slot was demolished to provide building materials for Odense Castle. Today, part of the original ramparts and moat remain to give a magnificent view, and the castle has a fine interior of great echoing, empty rooms, with a 100-ft (30-metre) banqueting hall.

North from Nyborg, a short detour just southwest of Kerteminde takes you to the underground remains of a Viking chieftain's burial ship at **Ladby**. With him in his 72-ft (22-metre) Viking ship, the chief took what he prized most: his weapons, hunting dogs, and 11 horses.

Kerteminde is the island's foremost fishing village, with old half-timbered houses in Langegade, and a couple of museums. Most towns in Funen have little workshops and craft workers of many different skills, and Kerteminde offers stoneware and pottery at local

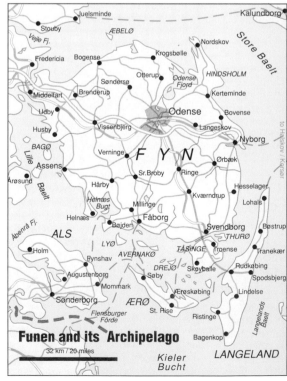

Funen and its Archipelago

32 km / 20 miles

workshops. Many of the island's traditional manor houses are today put to new and often original uses and, not far from Kerteminde, is one of the most beautiful, **Ulriksholm**, which has become a lovely manor-house hotel. At Ulriksholm, visitors seem to share in a more gracious past, with an obligatory ghost and four-poster beds in many of the rooms.

Kerteminde leads north to the peninsula of **Hindsholm**, which pushes out into the Kattegat and has a more dramatic landscape than the rest of Funen, and some excavated barrows to indicate long habitation.

Back southwest from Kerteminde, **Odense** is one of Denmark's best-known cities, and celebrated its 1,000th anniversary in 1988. But before you reach it, stop at **Munkebo,** where a potter demonstrates and sells wares at Bjørnholt Keramik.

Odense never forgets its most famous son, Hans Christian Andersen. To keep to the chronology of his life, the first place to go is **H. C. Andersens Barn-**domshjem (Andersen's childhood home), a simple cottage where his family lived in one room. It holds many childhood mementoes and also letters from the novelist Charles Dickens and the "Swedish Nightingale," the singer Jenny Lind, long admired by Andersen. This small homely museum is a contrast to the main **Hans Christian Andersen Museum**, a large collection devoted to the writer's life, with pictures, letters, manuscripts, and personal belongings. One room is a re-creation of his later study in Copenhagen. It is very evocative and gives the feeling that he could have sat there the night before. There is even a clue to the height of this tall man from the size of his long, narrow boots, tossed aside into a corner as though he had been glad to ease his feet out of them at the end of a hard day.

Eight miles south at **Nørre Lyndelse**, the reminders are of music rather than literature. It was the childhood home of Denmark's foremost composer, Carl Nielsen, and a few rooms are converted into a memorial to the composer, who

Smoked cheese is a favourite Funen delicacy.

wrote about his childhood in the book *My Childhood in Funen*. Another more recent and formal museum, **Carl Nielsen Museet** in Odense itself, newly expanded, is devoted to the composer and his wife, Anne Marie Nielsen, who was a sculptor of no mean talent.

Odense's **Funen Village** gives a feeling of the whole of Funen. It has around 20 farm buildings from different areas, with an old vicarage, workshops, and a windmill and watermill. Many of the buildings are still in working order and the Funen Village is a delightful spot, where the blackbirds whistle in competing chorus on a summer afternoon. Odense also has a **Tivoli,** a smaller version of Copenhagen's park, a 13th-century church, **Skt Knuds Kirke**, named after King Canute who met his death on this spot, and river and canal cruises.

Odense merits an overnight stop. Before taking the route direct to Fåborg the next morning, detour southwest to the Tommerup and Vissenbjerg area, home of **Frydenlund Fugle-og Blom-** sterpark, literally a bird and flower park, with 2,000 species in idyllic surroundings. Then it's back to the main road and south to Fåborg.

Fåborg is a lovely little town, with **Klokketårnet** (the Belfry), which four times a day plays a hymn tune. This is the largest carillon in Europe and the town's main landmark. Places to visit include **Den Gamle Gård** (the Old Merchant's House), built in 1725 and established as a museum in 1932.

But if you could chose only one place to visit in Fåborg, the choice must fall on **Fåborg Museum for Fynsk Malerkunst**, the art gallery, which has a wonderful collection by the "Funen artists", mainly from the period 1880–1920. This 1915 gallery, now restored, shows the typical style of the Funen painters, renowned for their use of light which so often illuminates Scandinavian art and is displayed here in the pictures of painters such as Peter Hansen, Fritz Syberg and Johannes Larsen. There are also works by the sculptor Kai Nielsen, who has provided

Left, thatched roofs and white walls are typical of Funen.

CARL NIELSEN

At the height of his fame at the banquet for his 60th birthday, the composer Carl Nielsen told the audience that his mother had always said to him: "Don't forget that Hans Christian Andersen was poor like you." There may have been something about the 19th-century air of the island of Funen which inspired poor boys to rise to fame but it is more likely that Nielsen was inspired by this most famous of Danes, 60 years Nielsen's senior. Their circumstances were similar. Both came from humble homes. Both left Odense to seek fortune in Copenhagen. Both were successful.

Carl Nielsen was born in 1865 in a small house in the village of Nørre Lyndelse, 7 miles (10 km) south of Odense. His father was a tradesman, working mostly as a house painter – his nickname was Niels the Painter – but he was also a folk musician, the local fiddler, in great demand for his traditional dance tunes at parties, weddings and christenings. Playing the violin was relaxation for Niels as well as a source of additional income but his principal instrument was the cornet which he played with the local music society.

From musical society and peasant gatherings, young Carl, who often joined his father to entertain the peasant farmers, gained an education in, and love of, the music of Haydn and Mozart as well as the traditional airs of Funen. The latter's flavour, along with the island's lighthearted humour, he incorporated in his *Springtime in Funen*, written in his fifties.

His father must certainly also have influenced Carl Nielsen when, at only 14, he became a trombonist in the Regimental Band of Odense, winning a competition for the place. He was also an accomplished violinist and had begun to play the piano and compose. His earliest compositions, at the age of eight, were two dance tunes – and all this while working as a grocer's apprentice. Like Andersen, Nielsen also wrote a memoir, *My Childhood*, which indicates that, as Andersen's musical abilities were apparent in his singing, Nielsen was no mean writer.

Like Andersen, Nielsen took himself to Copenhagen when he was 18 and managed to influence the influential into giving him an education. He introduced himself to the composer Niels W. Gade, and to J.P.E. Hartmann, not only the greatest name in Danish Romantic music but, even more important, director of the Copenhagen Conservatoire. At this stage, Neilsen's main instrument was the violin but his aim was to compose. The sweeping style of the great Finn, Jean Sibelius was also a strong influence.

At the Royal Theatre Orchestra, where he became second violinist, he found another patron in the Norwegian conductor and composer, Johan Svendsen. In 1908 Nielsen had graduated to First Conductor when Svendsen retired and, in the meantime, Svendsen had encouraged Nielsen to compose. Nielsen worked right across the range of composition from the symphonies and other orchestral and chamber music, through concertos, organ and piano works, to opera and choral music, and songs.

At 25, he won a prestigious fellowship which allowed him to travel, and went straight to Dresden to steep himself in Wagner's ideas and to Berlin to hear *Die Meistersinger*. To his diary, Nielsen confided: "The plot is the trunk, words or sentences are fruits and leaves but, if the trunk is not strong and healthy, it is no use that the fruits looks beautiful." Wagner, it would seem, lacked "trunk".

Nielsen composed two operas: the dark drama of *Saul og David* and *Maskarade* (Masquerade), a comic opera with much in common with Mozart's *The Marriage of Figaro*. Both operas are popular in Denmark, along with many of his great choral works, such as *Hymnus Amoris*, written in his thirties.

On his 60th birthday in 1925, the celebrations were magnificent, on a par with earlier festivities for Hans Christian Andersen. The King dubbed Nielsen Knight Commander of the Order of the Dannebrog, and the day culminated in a gala concert in the Tivoli Gardens and a great banquet. Surrounded by the famous, Nielsen's speech nevertheless recalled his childhood. Looking down from the seat of honour, perhaps the mind's eye of the poor boy from Funen suddenly saw earlier and more robust celebrations among the peasants of his own island.

213

a more controversial example of his style in **Ymerbrønden** (Ymer Well), also in Fåborg.

From Fåborg, the next major town to the east is **Svendborg** and the area between the two places can well claim to be the most beautiful in Funen. Its hilly terrain is the result of the last Ice Age, 12,000 years ago, and the heather-covered **Svanninge Bakker**, about 6 miles (10 km) north of Fåborg is a national park. Svendborg is the opposite pole to Odense in the north, a market town and a good centre for touring, with interesting manors and country houses nearby. Along with Fåborg, it is the gateway to the southern islands.

A few miles north of Svendborg is **Egeskov Castle**, one of Denmark's most famous. Egeskov means oak forest, and the oaks were felled around 1540 to form the piles the castle stands on. It is now Europe's best-preserved island castle, with gardens that range from Renaissance and baroque to English and French designs elegant enough to gain admiration even from the pro-

fessionals. There is also a **Veteran Motor Museum** with a fine collection of old cars, aircraft, motor cycles, and horse-drawn carriages. Egeskov's restored banqueting hall, used as a concert hall, is open to the public.

Egeskov's most recent restoration (opened 1990) is a reconstruction of its 200-year-old maze. The new "labyrinth", as it is now called, has just under a mile of paths screened by 2,200 bamboo shoots, now 10 ft (3 metres) high and still growing.

By 1985, the ancient maze was in near-ruins when Egeskor's owner asked a remarkable Dane to redesign it. He is Piet Hein, architect, writer, scientist who first saw the old maze in 1938. His restored labyrinth is claimed to be the biggest "island" maze in the world. As a last resort, the terminally lost can use one of the strategically-placed emergency exits.

From Egeskov, turn again southeast towards Fåborg, and drive past **Brahetrolleborg,** once a Cistercian abbey, and later a baronial castle. Here,

Two views of Funen's best-known castle, Egeskov: the exterior...

at the end of villeinage, Johan Ludvig Reventlow allowed his peasants to burn a wooden horse to symbolise his granting of their freedom.

From Fåborg, turn northwest for the island's west coast. Almost immediately, on the right are the impressive gates of **Steensgårds Herregård**, a three-winged manor house hotel, a lovely place to stay, with period style bedrooms (but with modern facilities) and the ideal spot for a meal in the garden. At Millinge is Grete Hjort Design's studio-shop, with hats, clothes and handbags. Just south of Assens, it is hard to miss **De 7 Haver**, the Seven Gardens, outstanding gardens created by Tove and Gunner Sylvest.

In the town of **Assens** are the **Willemoes Mindestuer** (Memorial Rooms), the birthplace of Peter Willemoes, the Danish hero who commanded a battery during the bombardment of Copenhagen with such bravery that even Nelson is said to have complimented him. It is a museum of cultural history, largely marine subjects.

North from Assens on the road to **Middelfart**, a broad west-facing bay at **Tybring Vig** is a site for underwater archaeology, and gradually this northwest area becomes flatter as one nears the coast. The exception lies just north of Middelfart, where the landscape ends in steep dramatic cliffs down to the sea. Off the little town of **Bogense**, at low tide you can walk to the island of **Æbelø**, an unspoilt landscape rich in undisturbed wildlife. A few miles east of Bogense is the castle of **Gyldensteen**, late-Renaissance with an impressive gatehouse. Here, Karen Blixen (Isak Dinesen) author of *Out of Africa*, wrote some of her books during the German Occupation of Denmark during World War II. Nearby is the early seat of the Blixen-Finecke family, **Dallund Manor House**.

From Middelfart, you can complete the Funen circle by touring along the north coast back to the Hindsholm Peninsula and Kerteminde. But most turn west, to Jutland to explore another and completely different part of Denmark.

...and the hunters' room.

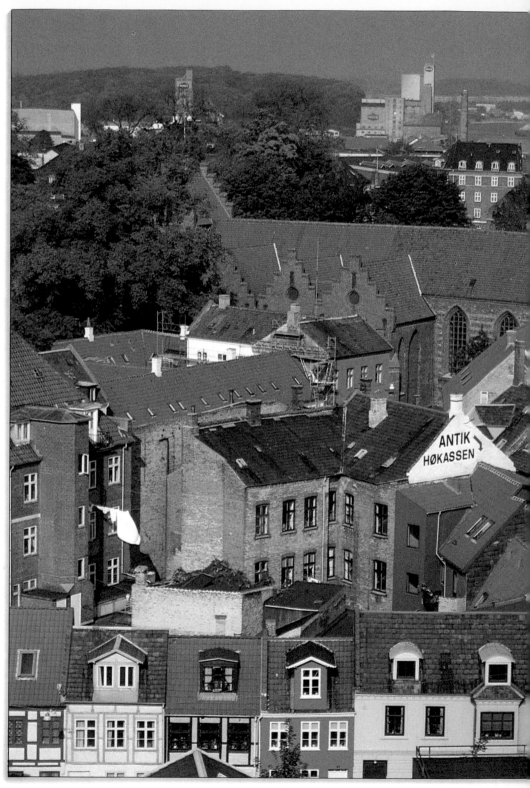

ANTIK
HØKASSEN

ODENSE

The first official reference to the city of Odense is found in a document from 988, signed and sealed by the German Emperor Otto III, in which he grants certain tax privileges to its church community. But Odense, situated conveniently for commercial traffic in the estuary of the most important river on the island of **Funen**, had been in existence for a long time before it achieved the status of a cathedral city in 1020. The name "Odense" is the modern form of an Old Norse name which combines the wise and mighty chief god (*Woden*), with the word for "sanctuary" (*vi*). Thus the place was considered important enough to be worthy of the god's protection before the Christianisation of Denmark.

Barely 100 years after Emperor Otto's charter, King Knud II was murdered by some of his rebellious subjects in the no longer existing wooden **Skt Albani Kirke**. They were dissatisfied with the exorbitant rate of taxation imposed by the king to support raids against England. The Pope responded by canonising the King as St Knud, and the martyred king's grave was transferred to the stone church he had built just a year before his death.

In 1139 this church was reconsecrated as **Skt Knuds Domkirke** (cathedral) and the shrine soon became a popular goal for pilgrims. King Knud's stone cathedral was a three-aisled cruciform church, which was badly damaged by two terrible fires during the following two centuries. In about 1300, with only some of the original crypt intact, it gave way to the construction of a still more impressive church in the High Gothic style, which has been added to on several occasions, resulting in the cathedral we know today.

Recent excavations around the cathedral show that Odense was dominated by the institutions of ecclesiastical life throughout the Middle Ages. With six monasteries and three large churches dating from the early

12th century, Odense profited from the fact that the medieval cathedral cities were the nerve centres in the far-flung Church of Rome, and prospered commercially, politically and culturally, as well as religiously.

Royal patronage: The first Danish history – about St Knud and his ancestors – was written just after 1100 by the English monk Ælnoth, who had either been persuaded or forced by the Vikings to come to the country. In 1482 the first Danish books were commissioned by the bishop of Odense and produced by printers brought from Germany for the purpose.

Perhaps the most impressive testimony of these fertile years, when the rulers could afford to buy the services of skilled foreign specialists to beautify their religious buildings, is the exquisitely carved altarpiece from the now demolished Franciscan church. It was the work of a German wood cutter Claus Berg at the command of Queen Christine, wife of King Hans, 1481–1513, who held court in Odense in the early 16th century. The finely detailed and gilded altarpiece has not been lost however, and is now in the cathedral.

The Reformation, which came to Denmark in 1536, meant the end of an era as a primarily ecclesiastical centre for Odense. But the commerce which had been a natural activity in such a well-situated city and which thrived in the wake of church business did not slacken until the city became a victim in Denmark's bitter and continuous struggle with Sweden. Taxes were needed to finance the ambitious wars fought by King Christian IV and Frederik III, and the relative prosperity of Odense was a welcome source of extra revenue. Denmark fared badly in the wars, and the whole island was looted by the occupying Swedish army of King Karl X Gustav in the middle of the 17th century.

It was hard for the city to rise again to its former glory after these years of severe taxation and plunder, and it did not have the drive or resources to take advantage of the growing industrialisa-

Preceding pages: old windmill at Skovsgård; the old and the new in Odense.

tion which was to form the basis of modern life. Among the more curious plans to revitalise the economy was an effort to convert the local prison and paupers' home into an industrial enterprise. The initiative failed, but the building still exists and is now used as part of Odense's social administration. The manufacture of gloves flourished during the late 18th century, but the industry could not be sustained.

Not until the beginning of the 19th century did new prospects open up. Contemporary commerce and industry required easy facilities for the exchange of goods and manufacture, and Odense once again took advantage of its fortunate geographical position. The city, which had until then been confined to the north side of the river, began to expand southward with the building of new bridges.

From the middle of the 19th century, Odense shared in, and contributed greatly to, the gradual transformation of the nation from a largely rural community to a modern industrialised state, as the Danes moved into the growing urban areas. Between 1900 and 1950 the population tripled, and today Odense is the third-largest Danish city, with about 170,000 residents.

Modern Odense: The most striking feature of today's Odense is the way it presents itself to visitors accustomed to the frequently ugly, drab townscapes of provincial cities. Odense is largely a garden city, with green foliage as characteristic as the red of brick and tile. From the slightly elevated vantage point of the highway just west of Odense, the skyline of the city is broken only by the cathedral tower in the very centre, the high-rise university hospital, the chimneys of the power station (which provides the whole of Funen with electricity and all of Odense with heat), the Thrige-Titan engine factory, and the harbour cranes.

In few other cities will one find a river in the centre of town that is clean enough to offer amateur fishermen both sea trout and eel, and urban anglers are a familiar sight. The quarter around the

An old Danish farmhouse at Odense's Funen Open-Air Museum.

old factory buildings has become very popular, especially with the young people of Odense. In the summertime the place is teeming with life, especially during performances of live music. Perhaps the most spectacular conversion has been the transformation of the old city slaughterhouse into the headquarters of Denmark's second state-owned television channel. The former textile mill **Brandt's Klædefabrik** in the city is now a spacious multi-purpose building for permanent and travelling exhibitions, concerts and shows.

For modern design and architecture visit the **Blangstedgård** area to the southeast of the city, where architects and construction firms have presented the latest ideas on different kinds of housing and town planning. The postmodern wave in architecture has combined with traditional Danish craftsmanship in many of the buildings here, a combination at which the Danes excel. After an initial period of exhibition, it is now a residential area.

The **University of Odense** was de-

signed with daring architectural vision in concrete and rusted iron, built in the prosperous 1960s, and is a relatively recent addition to the city. But its four faculties (medicine, natural sciences, humanities, and political science with business studies) have already gained considerable recognition in the international scientific community.

Both Hans Christian Andersen and composer Carl Nielsen spent their early years in the city. The part of the city where Andersen was born and spent his early childhood in the early 18th century has been renovated, but it doesn't stand as an abandoned ghost town.

The houses are inhabited, and can be bought and sold like any others. With twice-weekly markets and everyday activities, there is an atmosphere of business-as-usual. The **Hans Christian Andersen Museum** is unobtrusively placed in the centre of the quarter.

Although he isn't as well known as Andersen, Carl Nielsen (*see page 213*) is nonetheless associated with such other modern musicians as Schönberg and Stravinsky. Not only did Nielsen compose music which is now on the international concert repertoire, but he enriched the Danish song tradition with a number of new tunes inspired by the local folk traditions, the best known being his *Springtime in Funen*.

The city supports a variety of theatres in addition to a new concert hall at the edge of the Hans Christian Andersen quarter. It houses the city's symphony orchestra as well as visiting orchestras, and ensures that the living tradition for stagecraft and music is not only maintained but encouraged to new levels of achievement. It was taken as a sign of particularly well-timed encouragement by Fate that the score of an unknown symphony by Mozart was found in the city archives in 1982. It is now officially known as the *Odense Symphony*.

The shift from drab provincial town to lively city is relatively recent, which helps to explain Odense's restless energy. There is no doubt that Odense today again enjoys the material and cultural prosperity that it did in the Middle Ages.

Danny Kaye played the writer in the film *Hans Christian Andersen*.

Hans Christian Andersen

Although his fairy tales had been read by generations, Hans Christian Andersen himself was not widely known internationally until Hollywood made a sentimentalised film of his life in 1952. Portraying him, Danny Kaye immortalised the song *Wonderful, Wonderful Copenhagen* and, arguably, the film, the song, and the Little Mermaid (a character from one of Andersen's stories) have done more for tourism in Denmark than all its natural delights put together. One of Andersen's maxims was: "To travel is to live," which forever endears him to the travel industry.

His own life story, *The Fairy Tale of My Life*, written in 1855, is as fascinating as any of his well-loved tales. A shoemaker's son, born in poverty, he achieved international acclaim in his lifetime, travelled the world, and was a guest of the rich and famous.

Hans Christian Andersen was born in 1805 in Odense, on the island of Funen, a town which is now firmly connected with this event. The H.C. Andersen Barndomshjem (Childhood Home) is a small half-timbered house in Munkemøllestræde where, from 1807 to 1817, he lived with his parents. This house was converted to a museum in 1930 and is today a part of of the main Hans Christian Andersen Museum in Hans Jensens Stræde, where local tradition claims the writer was born only two months after the marriage of his parents.

Founded in 1905 on the centenary of his birth, the museum has since been extended twice. In 1930 a large domed hall was added, with frescoes depicting scenes from *The Fairy Tale of My Life*, and in 1976 it was re-built to twice its original size. The museum contains many of his pictures, letters, manuscripts and books, as well as editions of his works in more than 100 languages. Its reconstruction of his Copenhagen study contains his desk and working tools. Andersen's day boots are thrown carelessly aside, and it is easy to see from their length how tall he must have been.

Quite apart from his skill as a writer, Andersen had a good singing voice and gifts as an artist. After his father's death when he was 11, the writer owed much of his upbringing to his paternal grandmother. At the age of 14, he set off from Odense for Copenhagen to attend the Royal Theatre School and "become famous". Though his only success there was a walk-on part as a troll, the Theatre Board was perceptive enough to realise his gifts and found him a place at a state grammar school in Helsingør.

His travels began early with a visit to Germany, and ranged widely. In all, Andersen made 29 journeys in Europe (never without a rope to save his life in case of fire). Later, he stayed in the castles and manor houses of his many patrons but Copenhagen remained his permanent home for 50 years. Andersen never married, nor did he run a house of his own, preferring to live in furnished rooms or in a hotel.

Though he is now best known for children's fairy tales, Andersen wrote other books. His first, in 1831, *Shadow Picture of a Journey to the Harz Mountains and Saxony*, was the result of his early travels, and is a vivid account of his first journey. Through his life, he continued to write poems, novels and plays and, in fact, his earliest taste of fame came not from his fairytales but from an obviously autobiographical novel, *The Improvisatore*, which described the rise to fortune of a poor Italian boy. It was translated into both German and English and became very popular.

His early fairytales, including *The Tinder Box* and *The Princess and the Pea*, were published in 1835 and brought him immortality. But his diaries record unrequited love, extreme loneliness and constant awareness that he was "ugly", which has given rise to many scholarly articles on the dark side of his psyche. In 1840, he met the Swedish singer Jenny Lind, known as "The Swedish Nightingale," and fell deeply in love with her, though she always called him "brother". One of his fairytales, *The Nightingale*, was inspired by her.

When told he was to be made an honorary citizen of Odense in 1867, Andersen replied that it was "an honour greater than I had ever dreamt of." When he died at the age of 70 on 4 August 1875, one newspaper obituary wrote: "Andersen knew how to strike chords that reverberated in every human heart," and this is still true today.

FUNEN ARCHIPELAGO

You could spend a lifetime trying to visit all the magic islands of the Funen Archipelago, and still miss a few. Only 19 are inhabited permanently and you would need not just time but also a boat to visit many where only the birds form huge but solitary populations. Even the largest islands hold no more than a few thousand people, and others just a couple of families. But whatever the difficulties of getting there, these islands, with their untouched landscape and contented yellow beaches, make a marvellous holiday. By contrast, all summer long, the harbours of the main islands are full of boats from Denmark, the rest of Scandinavia, Germany and as far away as Britain.

The Funen islands are a cradle of Denmark, dotted with prehistoric monuments which indicate that primitive people lived here thousands of years ago. As the Viking era ebbed, pirates saw the value of the islands for plunder and devastated the communities. In turn, many of the islanders became wary and savage and took wicked revenge on shipwrecked mariners. But prosperity returned and, by the middle of the 19th century, the south Funen archipelago was the second largest naval centre in Denmark.

Today, past glories of the sea are long gone and there is unemployment and depopulation on the more distant islands, as young people are forced to leave to make a living in the cities. The traditional industries of fishing and farming have declined and, though many of the larger islands have been able to turn to tourism in a small way and to providing facilities for leisure sailing, distance is always a problem. The remoteness of this old-time way of life may seem "quaint" and appealing to the short-term visitor but many islanders are bitter at what they see as central government neglect.

The irony is that only in the depth of a cold winter can some of the islanders forget their isolation, when the ice is thick enough to carry a car – just as it once carried an invading Swedish army. Though many of the ferries are old, power supplies are inadequate and large-scale modern farming methods unsuitable on these small farms, one encouraging sign is that 27 of the smaller islands have formed an association to plan development projects.

Fåborg and Svendborg, with regular ferry services, provide the best jumping-off points from Funen. From the former, it is just a short trip to the most beautiful island of all, Ærø. Take the car ferry to **Søby** at the north of the island and, before you set off, visit its 12th-century church, **Store Rise**. At **Tingstedet** nearby, there is also a 4,000-year-old "barrow". Even if you have chosen to drive around Funen, to get the full flavour of the lovely island of Ærø, leave the car at Fåborg and hire a bike for the short cycle run from Søby to **Ærøskøbing,** the main town, and the old naval town of **Marstal** to the southeast. Cycling is easy and the roads wend through fertile fields and past pic-

Preceding pages: cabbages and kings. <u>Left</u>, a long row to hoe in the beetroot fields. <u>Right</u>, fishermen set lobster pots at Røskøbing.

turesque thatched farmhouses, medieval churches and windmills.

Living film set: The American author Temple Fielding said that Ærøskøbing was one of the five places that one should see in the world. And certainly the cobbled streets, with their brightly coloured houses, almost seem like a film set. The oldest house, rosy-coloured and half-timbered, dates back to 1645, and the citizens of this perfect small town pay for their privileges by accepting rigid controls on what they may do and not do to their houses. Look particularly at the doors of the little houses, all painted differently in unique designs, with two in Vestergade claiming to be the most beautiful.

Ærøskøbing also has a "ship-in-a-bottle" collection of around 750 models, which is well worth seeing, and a similar collection of more than 520 sailors' pipes from all over the world. **Det Gamle Posthus** (The Old Post Office) is Denmark's oldest.

Marstal was once one of Denmark's greatest ports, which might have held

up to 300 wooden sailing ships in its harbour. The tradition of wooden ships continues today because the town has one of the few Danish shipyards which still builds in wood and attracts customers from many lands. Marstal is also famous for its huge collection of model ships, and both towns have interesting maritime museums.

From Fåborg, ferries also run to the nearer but smaller islands of **Avernakø** and **Lyø,** both of which have good, cheap inns. Lyø's main village is beautiful, with 11 ponds lining the main street, and no trace of the strife of 1223, when King Valdemar and his son were captured by German warriors. These and other smaller islands are paradise for ornithologists but, though nature is the main attraction, in May you can see the ceremony of raising the 100-ft (30-metre) **Majstang** (Maypole). As late as the beginning of this century, the islanders believed that crops would not grow without this ancient fertility rite.

Svendborg is the best gateway to the southern islands. The first, reached by a narrow bridge, is **Tåsinge**, with some 5,000 inhabitants. This idyllic island was the setting for the tragic love affair between the Swedish Count Sixten Sparre and a Danish tightrope artiste, Elvira Madigan. Their sad story, which ended in suicide in 1899, was immortalised by the Swedish film director Bo Widerberg in a 1967 film; the couple lie in the graveyard of **Landet Kirke.**

Candlelit church: Next, you come to **Valdemars Slot**, one of Denmark's oldest privately owned castles, with a wonderful view over Svendborgsund. It was built in 1640 by King Christian IV (responsible for much Danish architecture) for one of his sons, Prince Valdemar Christian. Most interesting is the castle church, with a restaurant underneath which serves excellent food. The church itself is lit only by candlelight and is quite beautiful. The **Tea Pavilion**, mirrored in its own lake like the Taj Mahal, is now a café and looks over **Lunkebugten Bay.**

The loveliest village on Tåsinge is **Troense,** which the Danes pronounce with cooing, dove-like sounds that

A lighthouse warns of shallow waters in this popular sailing area.

228

match its gentle charm. Troense was once the home port for many sailing ships. To sit on a summer evening on the verandah of the Troense Inn is one of the pleasures of a Funen summer, as the pencil-slim masts of the sailing boats gather in the harbour against a darkening sea, and their wind-burnt owners carry their gear up to the inn.

The most famous son of the next island, **Langeland** (connected to Tåsinge by a causeway-bridge), is H. C. Ørsted, born in the main town of **Rudkøbing.** He discovered electromagnetism. Another famous Dane, N.F.S. Grundtvig, a clergyman and founder of Danish education, spent three years on Langeland as tutor to the young son of the manor house of Egeløkke. Grundtvig was one of the first to preach the ideas he had thought out on Langeland, of "popular enlightenment" and the value of folk high schools, which are now an important part of the Danish education system. The result was that in 1851, the village of **Ryslinge** in eastern Funen found itself with one of the first Danish folk high schools, followed by a free primary school in Dalby, both formed by Grundtvig's supporter, Christen Kold. Funen has continued as a centre for the free-education movement.

On the same road to the north of Langeland is the dramatic height of the 13th-century **Tranekær Castle**, with gardens and parkland open to the public. To the south, Ristinge and Bagenkop both have good bathing beaches but nowhere along the coast of Funen and its islands are you ever far from good places to swim and sail.

In all this tranquillity and beauty which means peace and recreation to visitors, it is sad to think that the real islanders are too often forced to leave to find work. Tourism can help to bring some prosperity, but the families that live on the small farms are hoping that new means of agriculture and the great movement towards "natural" organic food may bring a stable prosperity to these islands and enable the past to live on in the possibilites for the future.

Most Danes aim to spend their summers in or on the sea.

The magic of East Jutland is not just in the air but in the water, the trees, and the ground as well. This outdoor area, which faces east to the Kattegat, includes the Lake District around Silkeborg, and Himmelbjerget (Sky Mountain), at 482 ft (147 metres) a mere hill in comparison with the peaks of next door Norway but Denmark's highest "mountain". The Gudenå, Denmark's longest river, runs north through East Jutland towards Randers on the Randers Fjord, and the Djursland peninsula juts out into the Kattegat. The largest town is Århus, Denmark's second city, also on the east coast and famous for its early autumn arts festival which includes everything from ballet to beer-tent jazz.

Since prehistoric times, the Lake District has been inhabited by people who may have practised ancient religions and held mystical powers of healing and, in recent years, these lakes and hills between Silkeborg and Horsens have attracted modern healers and therapists and their devotees. Despite this modern invasion, however, eastern Jutland is not all history, mystery and meditation. More secular souls also find the landscape beautiful and an active holiday therapeutic.

Long history: Further south, East Jutland stretches as far as the towns of Vejle and Fredericia. Vejle has a commanding position at the head of the Vejle Fjord, and behind it lies the picturesque valley of Grejsdalen, 5 miles (8 km) long. Here too are many relics of a long history. Fredericia, further east on a promontory that forms the bridgehead to the island of Funen, was yet another of the towns planned by Denmark's brilliant king, Christian IV, though it was built in 1650 by his son Frederik III, whose name it bears.

Far the strongest motivation for a holiday in eastern Jutland is a love of nature, outdoor life, and active pursuits. The rivers that criss-cross the country make it the perfect place for botanists and birdwatchers, fishing or canoeing, and walking and cycling tours, but the popularity of the area means that you are rarely far away from other nature lovers. Lately, to protect the landscape, the Danes have limited the numbers of canoes on the upper part of **Gudenåen** at the start of its journey to the sea. Gudenåen is a marvellous river for leisure pursuits and a Danish favourite but it is certainly not the setting to choose for a survival training programme.

Peaceful and quiet paddling comes closer to the truth and children are welcome. It is possible to canoe all the way from the spring of Gudenåen in Tørring, through lakes **Mossø** and **Julsø** to Silkeborg, and further on through **Tange Sø** to Randers. The trip takes at least four days, six to seven with children in the boat, and local tourist offices can reserve canoes.

On land, walkers will take just as much pleasure in the hills and forests that surround the lakes. "We were not created to live where the mountain winds blow; we thrive best where the hills are low," wrote the founder of the Danish folk high schools, N.F.S. Grundtvig, in 1820. Nevertheless, the last Ice Age left parts of eastern Jutland at a height uncharacteristic of Danish landscape, a fact reflected in many place names.

But even if **Himmelbjerget** is a mere hill in comparison with other mountains, the view from the top is as good as any and it is far easier to get there. One flank of Himmelbjerget runs straight into Julsø lake, the starting point for the paddle-steamer *MS Hjejlen* (Heron) which carries passengers to Silkeborg. It is the world's oldest paddle-steamer still in use and provides a relaxing way to see the peaceful Lake District.

Himmelbjerget has its own hotel and there are also camping sites, youth hostels, inns and hotels in the towns of Ry, Gammel Rye, Skanderborg and Silkeborg, all comparatively close. Others lie along Gudenåen. The lakes give a special character to these communities, and a network of small roads and paths lies through the trees on either side to connect the small communities.

Where the Gudenå links Lakes Julsø and Birksø, the vegetation is lush enough to give a feeling that is almost sub-tropical.

Skanderborg lies at the southeast end of the lake chain, the area's oldest community, with a charter granted more than 400 years ago and a 12th century royal palace, built on a lake promontory. The chapel, Slotskirken, and a round tower are all that remains of this once strategic fortress.

Ry is the town closest to Himmelbjerget, not large but full of life particularly during the summer when campers, canoeists, walkers and bicycles jostle with students from the town's Folk High School. All over this popular holiday area, it is a good idea in summer to make reservations ahead or to bring a tent (note that camping is prohibited outside the established camping sites). For holidaymakers on a tight budget, youth hostels mean sharing a room with other travellers but compensate by having fine waterside locations just outside the towns.

Preceding pages: swans and young are a common sight in Jutland; Himmelbjerget (Sky Mountain), at 482 ft, is the country's highest point.

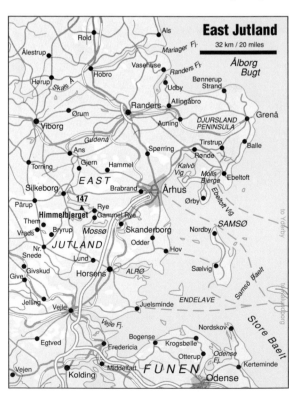

East Jutland
32 km / 20 miles

The **Them** district, further west than Ry, is in the heart of woodland that forms some of Denmark's most untouched nature. Lakes snuggle between the trees, some with their waters protected against pollution, such as Tingdalsøerne (lakes) where the waters are the only habitat for a few rare plants. This is the "edge" of Jutland; to the east are gentle vistas of water and trees, while towards the west, wide stretches of moor lead to West Jutland. An unusual way of getting around is by the old steam railway from **Byrup** to **Vrads**, which runs past lakes, over dams and heather moors and through the forest. The old station restaurant at Vrads is still active and offers meals and drinks between journeys.

While **Gammel Rye**, just south of Ry and Himmelbjerget, is the Lake District's smallest and oldest town, **Silkeborg**, at the northwest end, is the new and modern city. Gammel Rye, nevertheless, was a cultural centre in the Middle Ages and as a result has several churches and **Skt. Søren**, a notable holy spring. Silkeborg resembles most other provincial towns in Denmark with a couple of pedestrian streets and large residential areas. This is a young town, founded in the 1840s by paper manufacturer Michael Drewsen, who is now commemorated in a statue in Torvet, the main square.

But if the town is young, the **Silkeborg Museum** has some of the oldest relics in the country, the artefacts of more than 2,000 years of habitation. The remarkable centrepiece is the Tollund Man, who was hanged and thrown into a bog 2,200 years ago. His surprisingly well-preserved body was discovered, by two local farmers in 1950 who rushed to report their discovery to the police and, at first, most believed he was the victim of a modern crime. The museum displays the corpse as it lay when discovered but only the head is genuine; the rest of the body is preserved for research while that seen by the public is a well-made copy.

Best beer: The recent **Silkeborg Kunstmuseum** (Museum of Art) is

Fruits of the forest – mushrooms in early autumn.

built around the work of the painter Asger Jorn, who was born in Silkeborg. His paintings are surrounded by those of 20th-century artists such as Dubuffet, Arp, Alechinsky, and others from the COBRA (**C**openhagen, **Brus**sels, **A**msterdam) group. The privately-owned Galerie Moderne supplements this collection with changing exhibitions of painters and sculptors from the same period. While in Silkeborg, no-one should miss the chance to sample Neptun, the local brew which, according to a panel of tasters in Paris in 1986, is the world's best beer.

Northwest of Silkeborg, the Gudenå winds through the hills of **Gjern Bakker**. Along the river banks are an old road from Viborg to Skanderborg, once reserved for kings and nobility, and the towpath used by bargees to pull their barges back to Skanderborg from the fjord port of Randers. Nowadays, the towpath has a less arduous role as one of Denmark's foremost nature trails. There are several protected areas around the town of Gjern, also the ruins

of abbeys at Tvilum (where the church still stands). Further ruins by Alling Sø (lake) were built by monks some 700 years ago. The town itself is home to Jutland's Car Museum.

The river meanders northeast to **Randers**, which claims it has the most beautiful girls in Denmark, and certainly has a fjord ideal for sailing, fishing, swimming, or sunning. Here too is a vintage railway which runs throughout July from Randers to Mariager, the northernmost town of the area, known as the town of roses, with its cobbled streets and half-timbered houses. Castles and manor houses flourish in this part of Jutland, one of the best being Gammel Estrup. The old house still has 18th-century furniture, and an excellent agricultural museum traces the history of farming life from 1788 to the present day. A complementary exhibition of country kitchens from 1788, 1888, and 1988 helps to give a good impression of life both outside and inside the farmhouse.

The Djursland peninsula (*djur* means

February frost.

animal or beast) has wide, white beaches in the north, forests with deer and other animals, and the Mols Bjerge (hills) on their own smaller peninsula in the south, part of a beautiful nature reserve. Djursland is a summer playground for Danes, with good fishing, walking and cycling, though the Mols Berge, shaped by the receding ice, test out the cyclist and prove that Denmark is not as flat as its reputation. Djursland is easily reached from either Århus or Randers. To get a good view of the Mols Bjerge from the south, stop at the ruins of Kalø Slot, built in the Middle Ages on the edge of Kalø Vig, the bay just north of Århus.

Mols Bjerge are not just a challenge on a cycle; even a car needs care, for many of the roads may not be paved and lead through deep woods. One of the most spectacular is from Agri to Tinghulen, an 80-ft (25-metre) ravine. This great crevasse was caused by a huge lump of ice trapped below the surface as the ice above retreated. Gradually, it melted and the ground above collapsed into the gap. Tinghulen was used by the court until late into the 17th century, though the history of Mols dates back much longer, with cairns and grave mounds from prehistoric times scattered over the hills. The most impressive relic, the Posekjær Stonehouse, lies along the road from Knebel and Agri to Grønfeld.

Only 200 years ago, this isolated area was still largely cut off from the rest of Jutland, and the peasants spoke their own dialect. When they made one of their rare visits to Århus by boat, the townspeople looked on them as rustics and began to tell "*molbo* stories" which detailed their supposed stupidity. When the peasants decided to save their church bell from invaders, so one story goes, they rowed out and sank it in the sea. Then came the realisation that, unless they marked the spot, they would never find the bell again. Solemnly, the peasants cut a notch in the side of the boat at the place where the bell lay and, congratulating themselves on their cleverness, rowed home once more!

Gammel Estrup Manor House.

LEGOLAND

Around a million visitors a year come to the Legoland Park in the small town of Billund in the centre of Jutland. They come to marvel at the wonderful "Lilliputian" world created from over 35 million of the famous eight-stud plastic bricks which have taken the world by as much storm as the Vikings did long ago.

The word Lego is a contraction of two Danish words, *Leg Godt*, which mean "Play well" and also, by a fascinating coincidence, "I put together" in Latin. The name was coined by Ole Kirk Christiansen, a Danish carpenter who began making wooden toys when he was unemployed during the 1930s Depression. His inspiration, so it is said, came from a miniature model of a ladder he built to save wood by using this small-scale version rather than a large construction model.

Christiansen's philosophy was: "Only the best is good enough. The world of the child is as infinite as its imagination. Give free reins to its creativity and it shall build a world richer and more imaginative than any adult can conceive."

By 1947, wood had changed to plastic when the company installed Denmark's first plastic injection moulding machinery for toy-making and, by 1949, the plastic bricks were part of the Lego product range. During the

1950s they were developed to become the basic components of the then-revolutionary "Lego System of Play."

This concept was developed by the son of the founder, Godtfred Kirk Christiansen, who became a part-time apprentice in his father's workshop at the age of 12. After his father's death in 1958, he took over the running of the company and, by the mid-1960s, he had the idea of creating a permanent open-air exhibition of Lego buildings and other models. This led to the opening of Legoland Park in 1968.

Since then, the Park has developed into a miniature world with houses and statues from many places. The business remains in the family and the founder's grandson, Kjeld Kirk Kristiansen – the disparity in spelling of the surname was apparently an error by the registrar! – became managing director some years ago.

The park's "Miniland" is a tiny mirror of the real thing – the Statue of Liberty, castles on the Rhine, a temple from Bangkok, a Norwegian village, and much more, including traditional Danish scenes such as the Amalienborg Royal Palace in Copenhagen, Peter Liep's House, the well-known rustic inn set in the royal deer park north of the capital, Klampenborg railway station, and Copenhagen's port. In almost all cases, the principle is that the park buildings are made only from Lego bricks that can be bought anywhere. Only occasionally have the designers had to manufacture special colours to add authenticity. Above all, everything works, trains run when signals tell them to, church organs play music, and ships sail.

The Lego train tours the park, and a safari ride is flanked by exotic Lego animals. Because Lego's motto is to "learn through play," successful pupils in the motoring school get a Legoland Driver's Licence, based on safety, road positioning and the real Highway Code. The amazing Legotop, a rotating panoramic lift, provides an overview of the whole fantasy area.

Although the Legoland Park season is from 1 May to the third Sunday of September only, the varied and interesting indoor exhibits are open all year round. The Doll Collection has 400 dolls and doll's houses from 1580 to 1900 and, among the most fascinating, the exquisite miniature Titania's Palace, which has 18 halls filled with 3,000 tiny models of inlaid furniture, paintings, sculpture and linens decorated with gold, silver and precious stones. There is even a tiny book in one room, which those with perfect vision claim contains perfect type.

Built at the turn of the century for his daughter, by Sir Neville Wilkinson, an English eccentric, the palace includes items given by Queen Mary (grandmother to Britain's Queen Elizabeth II) inscribed "From the Queen of England to the Queen of Fairyland." Titania's Palace was purchased by Legoland from Christie's of London for £135,000 in 1978.

The park does not just fascinate children. Seven out of 10 visitors are adults and, of these, 17 percent come without children. ●

Wind power: Just below the Mols Bjerge on the Ebeltoft Vig is the small, immaculate town of **Ebeltoft**, with the bright flowers of Raadhusgaarden echoing the tiles of the Gamle Rådhus, the old town hall built in 1789 and the smallest, unaltered town hall in Denmark. There are old houses, cobbled streets and even a night watch, to see that all is well. A new interest is the longest wooden ship in the world, the frigate *Jylland*, the last of a line of famous wooden battleships. The *Jylland* is still being restored but tours can be arranged at any time. Ebeltoft harbour's Wind Power Mill Park is a modern rarity, with 16 wind-powered generators of 55 Kw and one of 100 Kw. They produce enough electricity for around 600 families and, once again, this small town can claim "the biggest" – the biggest marine-based windmill park in the world.

From Randers, the road to the port of **Grenå** (as far east as you can go unless you chose to visit the small island of **Anholt** some three hours away in the Kattegat) needs but a short detour to visit Djurs Sommerland, an amusement park built at the beginning of the 1980s. Its main attraction is Waterland for water fun of all sorts, as well as Cowboy Land, pony riding, and a science centre, some 50 activities in all. Djurs Sommerland is aimed at families and children and the advantage is that, once you have paid its relatively low entrance fee, everything is free.

(For children and youthfully-minded adults, a day at Legoland, Denmark's best known summer attraction, at **Billund** in the extreme southwest of the area, is also an imperative because the word Lego has gone into children's vocabulary in many different languages (*see page 238*).

Lions at large: On the road south from Århus, also on the coast, is **Horsens**, today a modern, industrial city but one with a long history. Part of Horsens Abbey Church dates back to 1200. From Silkeborg, the route south can take in one of the many smaller inland roads that provide interesting diversions. On road 18 (from Herning to

Vejle) is the popular **Lion Safari Park** at **Givskud**. Lions, elephants, zebras, giraffes, monkeys, and many more animals walk freely in the park, which tries to reproduce their natural environment as far as the climate of a Northern European country permits. Visitors view from the safety of their cars. In setting up the park, the aim of the owner, Jacob Hansen, was both to share his enthusiasm for wildlife and to give people a chance to see for themselves species that are now endangered and so perhaps to acquire a greater understanding of the needs of conservation.

One of **Vejle**'s greatest charms is its spectacular setting with the tree-clad hills behind it, facing the Kattegat which separates Jutland and Funen. An old monastery clock continues to chime, though it has long lost its monastery which once stood where you find the 19th-century Rådhus (Town Hall). Another old building, the 1799 Smidske Gård, is now the tourist office and has an exhibition based on Vejle's history.

After giving his name to **Fredericia**,

The Valiant Soldier at Fredericia. Following pages: two Vægtere (night watchmen) make their rounds at Ebeltoft.

to the southeast, Frederik III also conferred a special constitution and town "president". The constitution granted right of asylum for religious refugees, debtors and also, according to the less charitable, to "foreign murderers and malefactors." The privilege remained until 1820, when freedom of worship made it no longer necessary, and though many had moved there "in case", only around one person a year ever claimed asylum. Until religious freedom was established in Denmark, Fredericia was the only place where many religious sects could practise their religion. Not only was there a Jewish synagogue, refugees from other countries also arrived, including Huguenots, sorely persecuted in France, who brought a knowledge of cultivating potatoes and tobacco, and established a cigar-making industry. Until 1982, Fredericia had one remaining cigar manufacturer and, even today, you may find cigar-makers who roll cigars by hand, and the telephone book still contains French-sounding names.

Despite much strife, first with Sweden when Fredericia was barely completed, and between 1848 and 1864 in the wars between Germany and Denmark, the town inside its ramparts remains all that a planned town should be. But it has not forgotten its robust past. Every year, Fredericia celebrates the evening of 5 July, with a memorial service on the following morning, to commemorate a victory in 1849 when the Danes poured out to rout their German besiegers.

Closer to Vejle is a much older memorial on the road through Gresdalen. The **Jelling runic stones** lie beside the church between two huge burial mounds. King Harald Blåtand (Harald Bluetooth) carved the stones 1,000 years ago to proclaim his conversion to Christianity and in memory of his parents, King Gorm the Old and Queen Thyra Danebod, who were buried in the mounds. Jelling Kirke has the oldest frescoes in Denmark, to make Jelling one of the most historic sites in an area which holds a great deal of Denmark's early history.

ÅRHUS

Århus, Denmark's second largest city, started life around AD 948 as a Viking settlement on the mouth of the river which now bears its name. With a population of around 250,000, Århus is now one of the busiest ports in Scandinavia. To the north and south of the town are both woods and beaches (among the best Denmark has to offer), and some of the country's most beautiful landscape is not far to the west.

The cultural life of the city reflects a very large student population. Apart from the modern University of Århus to the north of the city, there is also a conservatory, a commercial college, and **Journalisthøjskolen** (the Danish State School of Journalism). In addition, the city hosts an arts festival in September each year which attracts visitors from far and wide.

Visitors coming from Copenhagen will immediately notice the more relaxed atmosphere of Århus, where people seem to have more time to stand and stare. Many find that this city provides a fine impression of urban Denmark at its best, as it is in many ways like a larger version of the typical Danish provincial town.

Seaman's saint: Begin with a visit to the **Domkirke** (the Cathedral of Saint Clemens), which manages to dominate not just its immediate surroundings but the whole city as well. The nave of the church is unusually long, a full 316 ft (93 metres), longer than any other in Denmark. The first stage in the construction of the cathedral (which was consecrated to the patron saint of seafarers and is the third church on its site) was begun at the end of the 12th century and continued well into the next century. The cathedral was substantially rebuilt during the 15th century, and underwent restoration from 1877 until 1882 and again in 1907.

It is well worth spending some time exploring some of the treasures inside the cathedral. The altar screen dates from 1479 and represents the flogging of Christ. In addition, Saint Clemens has the largest collection of epitaphs and commemorative tablets in Jutland; a beautiful stone tablet is dedicated to the zealous builder of the church, **Bishop Jens Iversen Lange**.

The area around the cathedral was a cemetery until 1813, but has been rearranged on numerous occasions. Nearby buildings, including the bishop's palace and the old city hall, have been removed. A bustling open-air market is held on the square in front of the cathedral on Wednesdays and Saturdays, and the **Århus Theatre** stands on the opposite side. The theatre occasionally performs Shakespeare (in Danish), as well as a representative cross-section of Danish plays.

While in the area of the square, pay a visit to the cellar of the **Andelsbank**, also opposite the cathedral, where there is a small Viking museum. It houses finds made during one of Denmark's first large-scale urban excavations in 1962–63, when the bank was being constructed, and the display reveals a

Left, the foyer of Århus Concert Hall, a popular meeting place for informal concerts. **Right**, exhibitions of modern art feature in the festival.

good deal about the way in which the Århusians lived between the 10th and 14th centuries.

Behind a large glass panel is an excavated cross-section of refuse heaps which had accumulated some 10 ft (3 metres) below the present street level. As no further layers of rubbish are evident after the mid-15th century, the 4,000-odd descendants of the Vikings seem to have become more conscious of their environment. The museum also contains a reconstruction of a small house from Viking Århus, one of six which were found. It is not known whether larger dwellings existed in the area at that time.

Another church of interest is 900-year-old **Vor Frue Kirke** (the Church of Our Lady), which is only a few minutes' walk from the cathedral. A crypt was discovered, almost by chance, beneath the choir of the present church and is the oldest vaulted room known in Scandinavia.

The **Rådhus** (City Hall), completed in 1941, is unmistakable in its coat of Norwegian marble; the exterior at first glance resembles well-built scaffolding but visitors can go up the 200-ft (60-metre) high tower, which provides a superb view of the city and the bay below. The local tourist information bureau is at the foot of the tower.

Up behind Rådhuset is the splendid **Musikhuset** (municipal concert hall), home of the **Århus Symphony Orchestra**, the **Danish National Opera** and the **Århus Festival**. The building was designed by the architects **Kjær & Richter**, and completed in 1982. The glass-fronted concrete structure houses a main concert hall, one of the finest in Denmark, and a chamber music hall. There are free performances on the foyer stage throughout the year, and the lobby has a café and a restaurant.

Musikhuset is the focus of the annual Århus Festival, held in early September. The festival draws performers and audiences from all over the world, presents theatre, opera and music of practically every genre, including jazz and rock, and the old streets are

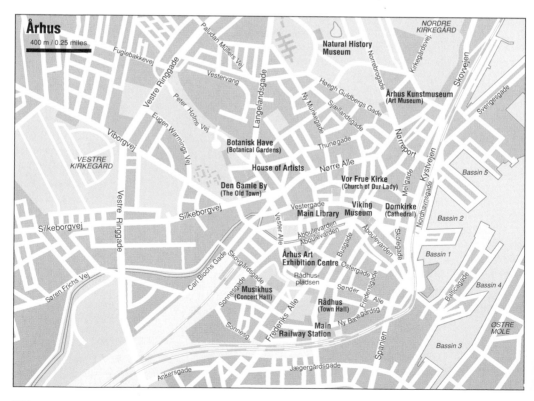

thronged with performers, from clowns to musicians and acrobats, each surrounded by its own audience.

Aarhus Kunstmuseum (the Århus Art Museum) has one of the oldest collections of Danish art outside the capital. It contains 18th, 19th and 20th-century Danish paintings as well as a large international collection. The museum has as many as 10 special exhibitions each year, so there is always a reasonable chance of finding something interesting to see.

Visit **Huset** (literally, The House), at the corner of **Museumsgade** and **Vester Allé**, which was the first of many small institutions (some of which were publicly funded) set up to provide for the creative needs of younger members of the community. Today, Huset offers everything from pottery workshops to free film evenings and music and theatre performances. A small café serves inexpensive meals.

One aspect of social life that does change frequently in Århus is the character of its nightlife. There are a number of venues for rock, jazz and other forms of popular music in and around the city centre. **Ridehuset** (near the city hall) is often used for large rock concerts as well as theatre productions. Other rock music venues include **Vestergade 58** and **Motown**. Live jazz can be seen and heard at **Bent J** in Nørregade, at **Cassiopeia** in Skolegade and the **No No Jazzclub** in Klostergade.

There are innumerable cafés in Århus, ranging in style from the hi-tech to the mundane: try **Café Mozart** at Vesterport, and **Øst for Paradis** (East of Paradise) in Paradisgade, or **Cafés Englen, Kindrødt** and **Drudenfus**, all within a stone's throw of each other in Studsgade. Skolegade has too many to mention, and Mejlgade (which continues northwest from Skolegade) sports both **Musikcafeen** and **Fru Jensen**, where one can often hear high-standard live jazz and rock.

Of course, it is always possible to get something to eat. Visit **Æsken** in Anholtsgade, or **Gyngen** in Skolegade, which serves a vegetarian menu. The

Harbour view.

atmosphere of the late 1960s and early 1970s lives on in this fair city, although nowadays it is thoroughly mixed up with the modern.

Travelling about the city is easy enough, with frequent buses and several pedestrian streets in the city centre. Various free maps are available – from the pictorial map included in the official guide (available at the tourist information bureau at City Hall) to the more comprehensive ones found in banks and at the railway station and port.

Århus offers facilities rather different from those of the capital, and people who visit the city do not come to find Little Mermaids or Tivoli Gardens (although Århus does have a small amusement part with the same name). Visitors who have the time and inclination may even wish to use the tourist bureau at City Hall to meet local residents, who are keen to exchange opinions with travellers and to keep their English up to scratch.

The Old Town: Just to the northwest of the city centre is one of Århus's proudest attractions, **Den Gamle By** (the Old Town). People come from all over the country to visit the collection of nearly 70 reconstructed urban buildings which make up this typically Scandinavian open-air museum. Most of them are from Jutland, and some from Sealand (the old theatre from Helsingør, for example) and Funen. The museum is centred on the first building to be opened on the site in 1914, the Mayor's residence, originally built in 1597 on the corner of **Immervad** and **Lille Torv** in the city centre. The museum has been under continual development and is still growing. The most recent addition is the **Lemvig Hus**, which is from 1839 and was moved and rebuilt in the Old Town in 1982.

The museum's basic philosophy is to present old market-town buildings in typical surroundings. The site could hardly be better suited to the purpose. Many of the buildings are open to the public, some as information centres and shops, and others have exhibits or workshops set up just as they were when

Gnags are one of the best-known groups in Århus.

the houses were in use. Many of the rooms not open to the public are used as workshops or to store artefacts. The museum has its own staff of craftworkers and conservators, and is also a research centre. Each individual building has its own commercial sponsor who pays for repair and maintenance. During the Århus Festival, Den Gamle By is alive with dozens of performances and thronged with spectators. It is open to the public throughout the year, but consult the tourist information bureau at City Hall for more detailed information.

Back to prehistory: The number 6 bus route takes passengers into the past as it leaves the southern suburbs of the city via narrow lanes and over the hilltops by the bay to the **Museum of Prehistory** at Moesgaard. Everything from arrowheads made of fish bones to the naturally-preserved and remarkable 2,000-year-old body of the **Grauballe Man** is displayed here. Housed in the outbuildings of a mansion, the museum not only serves as an exhibition centre for prehistoric finds from all over Denmark, but also has its own research facilities and often hosts exhibitions from other parts of the world.

Take in the indoor exhibit before setting out to walk the grounds along the "Prehistoric Trackway". In early May the greening beechwood shows Denmark at its prettiest. The path leads through fields of sheep past a variety of reconstructed buildings and **Skovmølle** (the mill in the woods). The 200-year-old mill still functions, and the restaurant next door is open all year during normal museum opening hours. Continue to **Århus Bay** at the mouth of the narrow **Giber brook**, or cut back along the brook to the road and the main house. Those who choose to take the long walk should follow the track, which is well marked. Guidebooks in a variety of languages are available at the entrance to the museum, where postcards and the like are also for sale.

The **Viking Settlement**, with several reconstructed buildings from the period, is the final stop on this walking

Browsing in the second-hand shops. Following pages: the Old Town.

tour into the past, which ends next to the main house.

In addition to its open-air museums, Århus has a multitude of parks and other open spaces. During the summer months there are open-air concerts and free entertainment for adults and children. Behind **Botanisk Have** (the Botanical Gardens) the university greenhouses can provide a welcome break from the music and noise of the gardens. The greenhouses shelter a collection of tropical and sub-tropical flora from the northern hemisphere, and are open only during the middle of the day.

There is an amusement park, **Tivoli Friheden**, near **Marselisborg** (one of the royal residences), and the city's symphony orchestra presents summer concerts in **Marselisborg Hallen**. The beaches north of Århus are highly recommended, but most visitors will find that the weather in Denmark is not always conducive to sunbathing.

Take a bike: The Århus area is ideal for cyclists, with a number of interesting rides within easy reach of the city – depending, of course, on the weather and the enthusiasm of the individual. One highly recommended tour takes the visitor south of the city through the grounds of Marselisborg Palace, past **Skovriddergården**, now the home of the forester and the site of an old water mill. There are deer and wild boar (safely enclosed) in the **Dyrepark** (Animal Park) which borders the bay.

Within easy reach are the forests **Riis Skov** to the north, and **Havreballe** just south of the city. To the west is **Brabrand Lake**, in a protected area, surrounded by a 10-mile (17-km) path for both cyclists and walkers.

Cycling within the city is easy as there are many specially designated cycle paths. If you are looking for other means of transportation, the buses are frequent and provide access to most of the city and its immediate vicinity. Board the bus through the rear doors and either use a multi-ride ticket (stamped in the machine), or insert the necessary coins into the ticket dispenser. The driver will change your notes if you are out of coins.

NORTH JUTLAND

It only takes a few minutes in the small town of Skagen to understand why this most northerly point of Denmark was an irresistible lure to the Skagen painters, who made it their home in the second half of the 19th century.

The narrow strip of land where Denmark ends in a pointing finger is so close to the sea and the vivid changing light of a wide, endless sky that it seems to be part of both. The "Nordic Light" (the name which the painters gave themselves) is characteristic of many parts of Scandinavia but its quintessence surrounds Skagen. This is what, in the 1880s, brought together artists such as Anna and Michael Ancher, Christian Krogh, P.S. Krøyer, and the marine artist and poet Holger Drachmann to flout the mainstream European Impressionist tradition and form their own school of "Reality Painting".

They took their inspiration from wide stretches of silver-white sands spiked with marram grass, in raging seas and threatening clouds that stormed across a metallic sky, and changed swiftly to peace where sea and sky seemed to meet, or in the white fleeces of mackerel skies and the cumulus clouds that locals use to predict the weather.

Summer nights: This radiant light, the sea and shore still draw painters to Skagen and North Jutland but, in addition, the area has become one of Denmark's most popular family holiday spots. The beaches and light summer nights are among the best in Northern Europe and a trickle of the more daring began to arrive as early as the middle of the 19th century. At that time, only the *very* daring actually swam but, more than 100 years later, a hot sunny day means that the cities of the north are deserted and everyone is swimming in, or sun-bathing beside, the sea.

Not just Danes are attracted. Today, North Jutland is a magnet for holidaymakers from all over Scandinavia, as well as Germany, Holland and other parts of Western Europe, and holiday-cottages have mushroomed in the sheltered areas behind the dunes and defensive tree plantings of the west coast. This is especially true of the northernmost area of **Vendsyssel**, which few realise is actually an island, cut off from the rest of Denmark by the Limfjord, just north of the town of Ålborg (*see pages 263–64*). But it is almost as accurate a description of the more southerly district of **Himmerland** which takes in the eastern areas of Jutland down as far as the **Mariager Fjord**, and the Limfjord waterway to the west (covered in West Jutland chapter, *pages 269–79*).

Its very popularity can make the Danish high season, from late-June to mid-August, a time to avoid unless you enjoy being part of a crowd. But the beaches are so endless along these northern coasts that, even at high season, it is relatively easy to find somewhere uncrowded, particularly on the less populated eastern side facing the Kattegat, which some claim is marginally warmer. Small coastal towns and villages such as Ålbæk, Sæby, Aså, and

Hals, an old fishing village that guards the eastern gateway of the Limfjord, are certainly much calmer and quieter. The east also has more holiday marinas than the less sheltered northwest.

If the clarity of the air and changing sea makes it easy to understand why the Nordic Light painters were conspicuous for the shimmering light of their pictures, it is no surprise to see that their influence continues: in **Skagens Museum**, which also has works from later periods, in **Anchers Hus**, bought by the Anchers in 1884, and **Drachmanns Hus**, the Villa Pax, a 19th-century villa which became Drachmann's home at the beginning of the 20th century. A little further south at **Hjørring**, the **Museum of Art** focuses on modern art and shows work by Poul Anker Bech, Svend Engelund, and Johannes Hofmeister. For an even better idea of how the "Nordic Light" continues, visit the exhibition held in August each year in **Vrå Folk High School** (not far off road 13 heading south). This started in 1942 to show the works of Svend

254

Engelund, who was born in the town, but has grown to include many younger artists. There is also a parallel exhibition on architecture.

Skagerak and Kattegat: Today, **Skagen** is a fishing port with some 12,000 inhabitants, which still has the characteristic yellow fishermen's houses that also inspired the Skagen painters. Less than 3 miles (5 km) further north, the road runs out at Grenen, where the trick is to stand with one foot in the Skagerak and the other in the Kattegat, a temptation few can resist.

Skagen Fortidsminder is another of the open-air museums, much beloved of Scandinavia, which shows life and work from the past. Just west of the town, peeping out of the dunes, is **Den Tilsandede Kirke** (the sand-covered church) with only the steeple visible. In the 17th century, the church was the largest in Vendsyssel but the dunes began to drift and reached the church 100 years later. Though generations of parishioners fought to save it, there was nothing they could do against the end-less drifts. In 1795, King Christian VII gave them permission to abandon their church. Who knows how long it will be before the top vanishes under the remorseless sand?

To understand how this could happen you need go no further than **Råbjerg Mile**, the largest example of "migrating sand dunes" in Denmark. Pushed by the wind and sea, the dunes travel a little further east every year, as tireless as the sands that overwhelmed the church. This Danish desert is very beautiful, can only be entered on foot, and is protected by law. The usual entrance is from **Kandestederne**, and the low-ceilinged church which has survived here has unique baroque wood carvings.

South of the migrating dunes, between Tversted and Ålbæk on the east coast, is one of Denmark's greatest natural attractions, the **Eagle Sanctuary** at Tuen. Here, some of the world's shyest eagles fly free and the Wenzel family, who own the sanctuary, have succeeded in getting large eagles and falcons to breed. Though the birds have

The northeast coast is often quieter than the busy western shore.

complete freedom, visitors are certain to see white-tailed eagles in flight and can watch golden eagles being fed. To avoid disturbing the birds, opening times are limited – only a couple of hours a day for a three-month summer season. As the Wenzel family's aim is also to educate, they provide information on the eagles' lives and habits, and a superb photography exhibition.

Ålbæk, on the east coast, is an old fishing port, surrounded by the typical moor and open countryside of North Jutland, and popular with those who want to avoid the summer crowds. **Frederikshavn**, a few miles south, is the leading port and ferry station in North Jutland, which grew from a fishing village to a fortified town. Traces of that period lie around the harbour and **Krudttårnet**, the Gun Tower Museum, which dates from 1686, has collections of weapons and uniforms, and thick walls to show its original purpose.

Holiday isle: Today, Frederikshavn's main function is as a busy port with connections to Sweden and Norway and, most important for visitors, to the island of **Læsø**, whose population of less than 3,000 expands like a balloon at holiday times. It is less than two hours away by ferry from Frederikshavn. Two-thirds of the island is uncultivated land with pools, heaths and scrub, and the northern coast has fine beaches. Many of the island houses are thatched with seaweed, some now restaurants and small hotels; there are also lots of holiday cottages, camping sites, and beaches with the blue flag that, in Denmark, indicates squeaky clean sea water and unpolluted sand.

A bicycle is an ideal way to get around and it is easy to hire one. An organised island tour combines nature and cycling in a five-day holiday. It includes both children and adults and is led by an experienced natural historian who can explain the mysteries of plant, bird and animal life.

In the past, while the men of Læsø fished and sailed, the women worked the land, and the **Museum of Fishing**

Skagen Song Festival takes to the streets.

and Shipping in Vesterø, where the ferry arrives, recalls their roles. There are two other communities, **Østerby** on the northeast coast and **Byrum** in the south, which has a viewing tower overlooking island and sea.

Sæby, 10 miles (17 km) south of Frederikshavn, is a town for strolling. It is said to have inspired the dramatist Henrik Ibsen but, judging by the small, spiteful societies he usually portrayed, this is not necessarily a compliment. This is an old town, founded in the early 16th century around **Vor Frue Kirke**, which dates from 1460, with an altarpiece, choir stalls and frescoes added over the next 100 years. There is also **Konsul Ørums Gård** from the 18th century, now a museum. **Sæbygård**, from the 16th-century, which lies just north of Sæby in a small forest, is one of the loveliest manor houses. **Voergård Castle**, along the river Voerså, also not far from Sæby, is a beautiful Renaissance building with a large collection of antiques and paintings, including works by Goya, Raphael and Rubens. **Voer**

Kirke stands nearby and has an imposing monument to Ingeborg Skee, who founded the Voer estate in 1586.

Small churches and religious houses are scattered widely in Northeast Jutland. **Borglum Monastery**, on a hill outside Lækken, is one of the most interesting buildings. Built by monks, it later became the Bishop's House and, along with many other religious buildings in the area, became a manor house after the Reformation, an event that gave North Jutland an abundance of beautiful mansions.

Vrejlev Kloster, once a convent, has a church built around 1200. **Vennebjerg Kirke**, with the tallest steeple in Vendsyssel, is used as a navigating mark and can be clearly seen from far out to sea. But the largest cluster of old churches is in Hjørring. The town itself is 13th-century but **Skt Olai Kirke** predates it by 100 years, and **Skt Catharinæs Kirke** is 13th-century Romanesque with three aisles and transepts. **Skt Hans Kirke**, erected around 1350, has some fine murals, rivalled by

The shifting sands of the north, wild enough to bury a church.

those in **Bindslev Kirke**, not far to the northeast, which boasts one of Denmark's finest pieces of medieval art, a Madonna painted in the early 13th century, and murals with a strong Byzantine influence.

The varied Jutland landscape is not just used for pleasure and leisure. It is also working land. The richer soil of the south produces crops of wheat and barley, as well as cows and pigs, while further north, farmers grow potatoes, rye and oats. Even the bog areas can be of use. **Paukjærgård** in the northern town of **Brønderslev** is a museum devoted to the moorland bog known as **Store Vildmose**, some way to the southwest of the town; it shows the agricultural machines and implements used in peat-digging, and the flora and fauna of the area. It also holds the largest flock of fallow deer in Vendsyssel. Below the Limfjord further south, **Lille Vildmose** is the largest raised bog in Denmark. Alongside a sphagnum moss industry, it has acres of unspoiled landscape, with herds of wild boar and deer. Although the public is not admitted, it is possible to get a view of the bog from the nearby Mullbjergene (hills).

Precious stones: Amber has been found and traded in North Jutland since the Stone Age and the area still has stone-cutters and jewellers who specialise in amber. **Gerå Amber Museum** lies 4 miles (6 km) south of the small fishing port of **Aså** on the east coast. At Gerå, Osvald Højer works with the stones, and at **Mygdal** (between Hjørring and Uggerby to the northwest) his son Benni Højer has Jutland's largest amber workshop. Both centres have exhibits that trace the history of the "gold of the north" and include shops.

Relics of early times are everywhere, for this northern peninsula was, not surprisingly, Viking territory. Even before the days of these great seafarers, the lives of prehistoric people can be traced through the relics they left. The long barrow at **Blakshøj**, just inland from **Gærum** on the east coast, is one of

Buying fish from the boat.

258

the country's longest passage graves. Also among the best preserved passage graves are the 5,000-year-old specimens at **Snæbum**, west of **Hobro** right in the south of Himmerland, which indicate how widely these primitive people were spread. For closer inspection, visitors can clamber through one of the passage graves here, **Snibhøj**. One thousand years ago, also near Hobro, the Vikings built **Fyrkat**. Four earth fortifications enclosed 16 large houses and one of these longhouses has been rebuilt. Hobro Museum houses some of the finds from Fyrkat.

North Jutland may be best known for swimming, sunning, sailing, windsurfing and other sea sports, but the countryside is also remarkable inland, with many special conservation areas and bird territories. Cycling or walking is a good way of getting close to nature and many districts hire out horses for the day. It goes without saying that the long coastline, and the rivers and lakes, small and large, make for good fishing. Lake and river fishing call for a licence.

The sea and fjord are free. Ask at the local tourist offices for details of all these services.

One of the best cycle tours consists of seven gentle days around the **Mariager Fjord**, which starts and finishes at **Hobro**, and takes in historic ruins and stately homes as well as the countryside. The route also covers the fjord towns of Assens and Hadsund, and the idyllic town of the roses, Måriager, half-way along the fjord.

One of the most popular areas for cycling and walking is the Jutland Ridge. The 21 miles (30 km) between the **Forest of Dronninglund** and **Pajhede Wood** at **Øster Vrå** further northwest has a special cycling and walking track, which wends its way through beech woods, fir trees, heath and bogland, typical of the area. In Dronninglund itself is **Dronninglund Castle**, a former convent later used by Charlotte Amalia, the wife of King Christian V. Today it is a conference centre but the chapel is open to the public and its frescoes worth spending a

A gathering of swans and coot in a quiet fjord. Following pages: a forest stream in full flood.

little time over. **Dronninglund Art Centre** on the edge of the forest has visiting exhibitions.

Further north, the **Tolne Hills**, some 8 miles (12 km) west of Frederikshavn, are clad in beech and fir trees with a number of small lakes. A good starting point for a walk is the old pavilion near Tolne station. In Himmerland, you find Denmark's biggest forest, **Rold Skov**, around the town of **Skørping**. The area includes the **Hills of Rebild**, a national park, and Rebild car park makes a good point for starting a walk in the heather hills, beech woods and conifer forests. A good target are the springs of **Lille Blåkilde** and **Ravnkilde**, or to Denmark's second largest spring at **Store Blåkilde**, where 30,000 cu. metres of water come gushing out each day. On 4 July each year, Rebild National Park celebrates American Independence Day, the only celebration outside the United States.

Wild woods: One of the delights of the forests, which all Scandinavians enjoy, is picking berries. The woods yield wild raspberries, lingon, multer, and strawberries and the heath areas are rich in cranberries and blueberries. Both hold many more with names guaranteed to produce confusion in translation. Late summer is also the time for mushrooms and, though local mushroomers may be reluctant to disclose their secret locations, sharp eyes will certainly pick out boletus and ink cap mushrooms.

But the best informed visitor will keep a sharp look out for *pors* (bog myrtle or sweet gale) and juniper berries, according to season and location. (Bog myrtle grows best in the west coast soil). It's well-known that Ålborg produces excellent aquavit. But Vendsyssel claims to have given the world an even better drink, *bjesk*. For an unusual souvenir, there are two recipes. For Juniper Bjesk, put a dozen, dried, black juniper berries in a half bottle of aquavit and leave them to soak for a week. Strain the juice off and throw away the berries. For Pors Bjesk, put a twig of "Pors" into a half bottle of aquavit and leave to soak for a week until the twig is golden. Then just pour. *Skål*!

ÅLBORG

When the bustling, succesful commercial town of Ålborg was at its most prosperous in the Middle Ages, its rich merchants enjoyed the ostentatious display of their considerable wealth. None enjoyed it more than Jens Bang, whose opulent six-storey **Stenhus** (stone house) was built in 1642 to show off his wealth. It is still the largest preserved citizen's house from the Renaissance period.

Today, Ålborg, Denmark's fourth largest city (population 155,000), is still a busy commercial centre, owing much of its success to its position at the narrowest point on the south bank of the Limfjord. This advantageous site was the reason the Vikings settled here, and it soon became one of Denmark's busiest trading centres and a focal point for communications.

Jens Bang, as well as being rich, was an argumentatitve and obstinate man who made enemies and was not averse to taking revenge on them. This, they say, is why he cariacatured them in the grotesque carvings on the front of his house. He was also annoyed that he had never become a town councillor and, again, his house shows his anger at that omission in no uncertain terms. On the south facade of the Stenhus is the clear carving of the merchant himself, sticking his tongue out at the town hall across the street. Inside this historic house is a basement wine bar, open to the public.

Another well-preserved house in a city of well-preserved merchant mansions is **Jørgen Olufsen's Gård**, a three-storey, half-timbered building from 1616, complete with its hoists and doors where the storekeepers once hauled the merchant's newly-bought grain up to the loft.

The 15th-century **St Budolfi Cathedral** is dedicated to the English saint, St Botolph, the seamen's patron saint. It has a richly furnished and colourful interior, a large altarpiece from 1689 and a carved pulpit dated 1692. The baroque baptismal font was completed in 1728, and the impressive spire (1779) has a carillon of 48 bells. Just as interesting is the Monastery of the Holy Ghost (**Helligåndsklosteret**) with 15th-century cloisters. It is Denmark's oldest welfare institution and is still in use as a home for the elderly. Nearby is the **Church of Our Lady** and the little houses of Jjelmerstaid and Peder Barkensgade, old traders houses much as they have always been.

Ålborg Castle is 16th-century but only the eastern of the three original wings remains, along with the fortress wall. A new northern wing was built in 1633 and is now the residence of the Lord Lieutenant.

This old townscape lends itself to exploration by foot and the tourist office has a useful booklet, *Good Old Ålborg*, to guide visitors around all the key attractions. Ålborg has long had Scandinavia's largest cattle market, at Nyhavnsgade, on Tuesday and Friday.

Commerce has always been the bedrock of the city's existence and today three industries dominate: cement, tobacco, and aquavit. The latter is probably Ålborg's best known product – many claim the best aquavit of all – and has been distilled here since 1846. Two statues are closely associated both with the city and with two of these major industries. *The Goose Girl* by Gerhard Henning was presented in 1937 by C. W. Obel's Tobacco Company; the *Cimbrian Bull* by A. J. Bundgaard, which has a poem by Nobel prize-winner Johannes V. Jensen on its base, was presented in the same year by Danish Distilleries.

A little art, a lot of industry and some history are not the sum total of Ålborg. More recently there has been a greater emphasis on culture in its broadest sense. The **Ålborg Halls** were built between 1949 and 1953 with the aim of providing a suitable venue for the well-patronised concerts, theatrical productions, sporting events, congresses and art exhibitions.

The opening of the **Nordjyllands Kunstmuseum** in 1972 provided an outstanding centre for international art. Designed by a Finnish architectural couple, Elissa and Alvar Aalto, and a Dane, Jean-Jacques Baruël, it houses a permanent collection of Danish art from 1890 to the present day and distinguished works by foreign artists such as Picasso, Chagall, Le Corbusier, and many others, which are supplemented by visiting exhibitions. The city also holds concerts in the Museum and popular summer outdoor entertainment in the amphitheatre.

A new attraction is the **Ålborg Shipping and Naval Museum** (Ålborg Søfarts og Marinemuseum), opened in 1991 and sited near the western end of the harbour area. Its star attraction is *Springeren*, the last submarine to be built in Denmark. It is installed on dry land; openings in the bow and stern allow visitors to walk through.

On the outskirts is the **Danish Science Museum**, while the **Museum of History** in the city centre covers the past in all its aspects. It includes finds from Scandinavia's largest burial ground from the Germanic Iron Age and the Viking period at **Lindholm Høje**. This lies across the Limfjord to the northwest of **Nørresundby** and, with more than 600 graves, is well worth a visit.

Nørresundby has grown from an old village to become one of the largest towns in the north with 37,000 inhabitants. The church is the original 13th-century village church and the **Nørresundy Local Collection** has a large garden area of aromatic and medicinal herbs. Today, this north side of the fjord is linked to the city by road and rail bridges and a six-lane underwater tunnel for the E3 motorway. The area of Jutland north of the Limfjord is, in fact, an island, although this is not immediately apparent.

Between 1 and 5 July, some 20 miles (30 km) south of Ålborg, you will find the only celebration of American Independence Day to be held outside the United States. On those days, **Rebild National Park** is packed with Danish-Americans, back to "the old country" to celebrate with (or to trace) their kith and kin, at a festival often attended by the Danish royal family.

Preceding pages: Lindholm Høje, a Viking site just north of Ålborg. **Right,** Jomfru Ane Gade.

WEST JUTLAND

Distances rarely seem long in Denmark. It takes just five hours to cross the country from west to east, and you could tour round the island of Funen in a day. Western Jutland is a bit different, with a sense of space and long coastlines which have beautiful, almost unbroken beaches stretching ahead.

Much of this western coastline is still in a state of movement. Sand dunes and narrow land strips change at the whim of the North Sea tides, to form and reform and to build up into great hills, more than 200 ft (60 metres) high. These silver-white beaches are frequently backed by sand hills with marram grass.

Inland, the scenery is a mixture of fertile farmland and heath, moor and planted forests which the Danes call "plantage". There are slow-moving rivers and streams and placid lakes. The Limfjord, like an inland sea in the northwest, is a sailing paradise.

Although parts of Western Jutland cannot be called anything but flat, stretches of gently undulating hills help to avoid monotony. In winter, the weather can be rugged, with storms blowing in off a turbulent North Sea and the prevailing westerlies bending the trees towards the east. In summer, the combination of wind and sun can easily burn a sensitive skin, which needs protection but this part of Jutland is popular with holidaymakers, as one can see from the countless summer cottages, each with its flagpole, frequent camping sites, and holiday centres.

The loss of South Jutland to Germany in the war of 1864 led to the development of **Esbjerg** on the west coast. From a village with a handful of inhabitants, it has become a major port, the country's biggest fishing harbour and Denmark's fifth largest town (population 81,000). It is also the principal gateway for British ferries.

Fishing first: The importance of the fishing industry is reflected in the **Fisheries and Maritime Museum and**

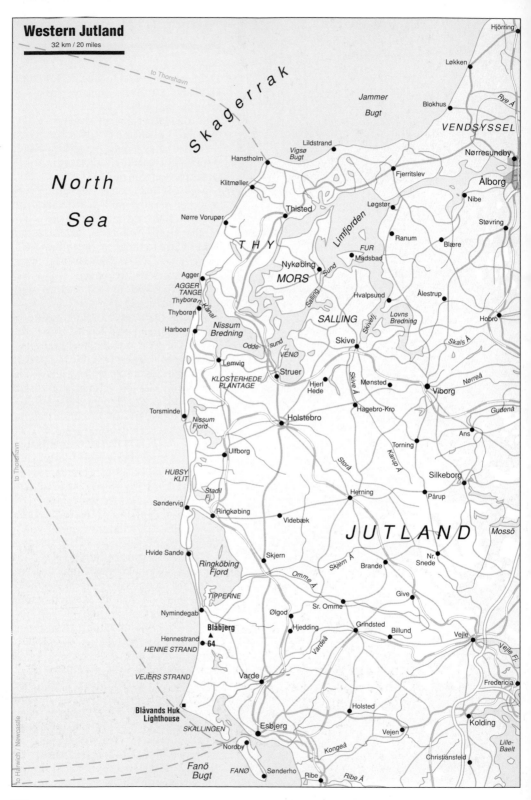

to Thorshavn

Skagerrak

North

Sea

Jammer
Bugt

Hjörring

Løkken

Blokhus

Rye Å

VENDSYSSEL

Lildstrand

Hanstholm

Vigsø Bugt

Fjerritslev

Nørresundby

Klitmøller

Løgstør

Ålborg

Nibe

Thisted

Nørre Vorupør

Limfjorden

Ranum

Støvring

T H Y

Blære

FUR

Madsbad

Nykøbing

Hvalpsund

Ålestrup

Agger

MORS

AGGER TANGE

Thyborøn

Salling Sund

SALLING

Lovns
Bredning

Hobro

Thyborøn

Kanal

Nissum Bredning

Harboør

Skive

Skals Å

Odde-

VENØ

sund

Skive Å

Mønsted

Lemvig

Skjern

Norreå

KLOSTERHEDE PLANTAGE

Struer

Hjerl Hede

Viborg

Gudenå

Hagebro-Kro

Torsminde

Nissum Fjord

Holstebro

Torning

Ans

Karup Å

Ulfborg

Storå

Silkeborg

HUBSY KLIT

Stadil Fj.

Herning

Pårup

Søndervig

Ringkøbing

Videbæk

JUTLAND

Mossö

Hvide Sande

Ringköbing Fjord

Skjern

Skjern Å

Brande

Nr. Snede

TIPPERNE

Omme Å

Give

Nymindegab

Ølgod

Sr. Omme

Hennestrand

Blåbjerg ▲
● 64

Hjedding

Grindsted

Billund

Vejle

HENNE STRAND

Vardeå

VEJERS STRAND

Varde

Fredericia

Vejle Fj.

Blåvands Huk Lighthouse ■

SKALLINGEN

Holsted

Esbjerg

Vejen

Kolding

Nordby

Kongeå

Christiansfeld

Lille-Baelt

Fanö Bugt

FANØ

Sønderho

Ribe

Ribe Å

to Thorshavn

to Harwich / Newcastle

Aquarium with its collection of fishing gear and models of boats. The salt-water aquarium has 200 species of fish found in Danish waters and a sealarium where you can watch the seals under, as well as in, the water. The development of the town from 1900 to 1950 is shown in the **Esbjerg Museum**, where a complete urban environment has been created, with shops, houses, workshops and other town features.

The town history archives have a large collection of documents, maps and old photographs, while the **Printing Press Museum** illustrates the craft of printing over 500 years. The **Modern Art Museum** features the work of contemporary Danish artists.

A monument in the fishermen's **Memorial Grove** is dedicated to the many local fishermen who have lost their lives at sea. There are also monuments to allied airmen, German refugees, and military personnel who were killed in World War II.

Guarding the entrance to Esbjerg harbour and a 20-minute ferry ride away is the 11-mile (18-km) long island of **Fanø**. Fanø must be the first example of a successful "buy-out". Until 1741, the island belonged to the King of Denmark; then, when he was short of cash, he offered it for sale by public auction. Fanø's inhabitants bought the island and also obtained the right to build ships. In one move, they had kept their island and created a major industry, which constructed 1,000 sailing ships between 1741 and 1900.

Today, Fanø has long forgotten its busy industrial past and relaxed into a role as a holiday island. The only town is **Nordby**, which has narrow streets and typical thatched Fanø houses. The **Seamen's Church** (1786) includes ship models, and there are more in the **Shipping and Costume Museum** (Fanø Søfarts og Dragtudstilling). The **Fanø Museum** is a typical seaman's house with a 17th-century interior.

Sønderho is the jewel in Fanø's crown, with its old cottages, inn, and **Seamen's Church** (1782). The local museum, **Hannes Hus**, also reflects the great days of sail. For today's holiday-

makers, the west coast has a superb 11-mile (18-km) stretch of white sandy beach backed by sandhills, and the rest of the island is characteristic West Jutland scenery: dunes, heath, forest.

North of Esbjerg, **Blåvands Huk Lighthouse** is Denmark's westernmost point. There are many summer cottages here, seemingly oblivious to the Danish Army's noisy training area nearby. Good beaches line the coast, two at **Vejens Strand** and **Henne Strand** being excellent examples. Here, too, you find yet more signs of the ways of the North Sea.

North of Henne Strand on the way to Nymindegab is the **Blåberg Klitplantage**, a 210-ft (68-metre) high sand ridge that changes its shape as the wind blows and the tides wander to form what is called a "migrating dune". **Varde** has some preserved houses but a visitor gets a better idea of how the town looked in 1800 from the 1:10 miniature town model which has some 150 buildings.

From **Nymindegab** to **Søndervig**, the sea is also still forming the coastline.

A narrow strip of land runs north, separating the sea from the expanse of the **Ringkøbingfjord**, a broad, shallow expanse the direct opposite of the conventional idea of a fjord. Once, this saltwater "lake" was part of the sea with an entrance at its northern end. Today, the shifting sands have left only a narrow channel half way along at the fishing village of **Hvide Sand** (appropriately translated to white sand) big enough to allow a small boat through.

From the road that runs along the sandhills, the view of the fjord is interesting, with reeds and water plants pushing up above the surface. But from this road, the sea view is rather disappointing, scarcely visible through the dunes with their many cottages and camping sites. At **Tipperne**, at the southern end of Ringkøbingfjord, is an important bird sanctuary on a peninsula jutting out into the fjord.

All the way north, this natural coastal phenomenon repeats itself again and again and has left stretches of salt water cut off from the sea. The strip that divides the Nissumfjord from the North Sea is at one point wide enough to allow for the attractive small village of **Torsminde** and gives better sea views than the Ringkøbing "strip".

North again, you come to **Nissum Bredning.** To the east, Nissum Bredning becomes the westernmost part of the marvellous **Limfjord**, which winds and wriggles right through to the east of Denmark and eventually empties into the Kattegat, east of Ålborg. This effectively turns North Jutland into an island although, without a map, it is not easy to realise it. Nissum Bredning opens into the sea at what is called the **Thyborøn Kanal** – even if it looks more like a narrow, natural opening than a canal.

Ringkøbing, once one of the west coast's busiest ports, is now on the inner coastline of the fiord, 6 miles (10 km) from the sea. This ancient port was founded in 1250 and has retained much of its old atmosphere, with typical West Jutland houses along the little streets. A few miles away, Stauning airport has a

Esbjerg Harbour, one of Denmark's busiest ports.

Veteran Aircraft Museum, and 5 miles (8 km) to the north at Hee is Sommerland West. This children's activity park has more than 40 attractions and is crowded all summer.

Heading north past beaches and sand dunes, stop at Husby Klit for Strandgården, a museum which includes all the first editions of the poet-vicar Kaj Munk, who was also a staunch member of the resistance movement in World War II. He is buried not far away at Vedersø Kirke.

First co-operative: For good fishing, turn inland from Ringkøbing, which has some splendid angling rivers. The Skjern, for example, has over 60 miles (100 km) of river banks which give good sport. Late in the 19th century, Danish farmers were pioneers in forming agricultural co-operatives and at Hjedding, near Ølgood, is Denmark's first co-operative dairy with its original 1882 machinery; it is now a museum.

Herning is an ancient settlement which in the past 100 years has expanded from a few houses to become the centre of the Danish textile industry. It is also an exhibition and congress town, which means that at times it is full to overflowing.

The town museum includes a delightful series of 57 detailed little dioramas depicting "A year at Jens Nielsen's Farm" created by the artist Inge Fauertoft. Another collection of 46 called "A September day at Jens Nielsen's Farm" are at Hemingsholm, an old mid-Jutland manor house (1579) which is now a museum. It has a period interior and is dedicated to the moorland poet, Steen Steensen Blicher.

The Herning Art Museum has an important contemporary collection and there is a large sculpture park and a photographic museum, with the Foto Galleriet featuring exhibitions by Danish and international photographers. Herning may have risen from the Jutland moorland, but it is not being left behind in the race for culture.

Forming the apex of a triangle made up of Ringkøbing and Herning is Holstebro, a busy commercial town.

Spøttrup Castle.

Lacking historical associations, it has also decided to make a cultural name for itself as an art centre. There is an impressive range of sculptures and fountains throughout the town, the latest being the high-tech laser sculpture of Frithoff Johansen – the first permanent example of its kind in the world.

Holstebro has a whole raft of museums covering art and graphics, including the **Museum of Miniature Art**, containing 400 international works each no longer than 4 by 6 inches (10 by 15 cm). Collections of pipes and dolls and the history of a Dragoon regiment and World War II Resistance are other subjects. To the east of Holstebro, at **Ulfborg**, the church has an unusual preaching chair which runs from wall to wall. The surrounding countryside to these three towns seldom rises over 300 ft (90 metres) above sea level and, apart from a scattering of villages and hamlets, there is little to take the eye.

The coastline north, with almost continuous beaches, eventually thins to a finger at the fishing village of **Thyborøn**, where there is a ferry (12-minute crossing) over the Thyborøn Kanal to another spit of land, **Agger Tange**. In the south, the **Nissum Bredning** narrows sufficiently at **Oddesund** for there to be road and rail bridges, and the waters then continue northeast to become the great waterway known as the Limfjord.

World of water: All this complicated area around, or even part of, the Limfjord has islands with narrow sounds between, and peninsulas which project into the fjord itself. A spit of land may have the fjord on both sides, an island may be linked by a bridge. If sailing is not possible, this is an area for slow, leisurely driving on roads that link the fjord towns and villages and wind across farmland and heath, and you are never far from water. On these twisting roads, directions are difficult and a map is essential.

Struer is another of Denmark's "young towns" and has major industries. The local **museum** is in an old farmhouse and vicarage next to the

Two moods on the changeable west coast: peaceful summer...

home of the poet Johannes Buchholtz (1882–1940). Near the Oddesund bridges are two major windmill farms; without the benefit of oil or hydro-electric power, Denmark has experimented hard with many forms of alternative energy and these are modern windmills for the generation of electricity. The island of **Venø**, with 150 inhabitants, lies to the northeast of Struer (connection by ferry); it has the smallest village church in Denmark, from the 16th century.

West of Struer, the **Klosterhede Plantage** is the biggest planted forest in Denmark and covers an area of 25 sq. miles (65 sq. km). To the east is **Hjerl Hede**, one of the country's most impressive natural areas covering 2,000 acres (810 hectares) and all preserved since 1934. Hjerl Hede has a large collection of historical buildings which have been moved from other parts of Jutland. They range from a smithy to a dairy, and an inn to a rope walk. There is a forestry museum and a bog farm museum. Nearby **Sahl Kirke** has a so-called golden altar made of delicately beaten copper plates on oak.

Skive on the River Karup, is old-established, and today a busy road and rail junction and makes a good base for exploration. It is at the base of the Salling peninsula, a pleasant rural area of farmland and rolling hills which reaches out into the Limfjord. Historically the most interesting building is **Spøttrup Castle**; this is one of Denmark's finest medieval fortresses, surrounded by a double moat, and has a well-preserved interior. Adjoining it is a medieval herb garden and rose park.

To the west, the peninsula is linked to the island of **Mors** by an impressive bridge spanning the Salling Sund. At the northern tip is the island of **Fur** (five-minute ferry crossing). Erosion by the sea has created steep molar cliffs on Fur and the museum at **Madsbad** has a rare collection of fossils.

Facing the Sondersø and Nordsø lakes is the town of **Viborg**, a junction of six main roads where east and west meet and a town that either East or West

...and wild waves in autumn.

Jutland can claim. Although the cathedral was founded in 1130, the present building was completed only in 1876. Nevertheless it has some beautiful frescoes by Joakim Skovgård while there is a museum to Skovgård and other artists.

Viborg Museum has workshops and products of the town's craftsmen and two exhibitions: "Our daily needs" and "The town and its citizens". The pews at **Søndersogn Church** are covered by some 200 paintings. At Thorning, south of the town, is the **Blicher County Museum** which covers 19th-century peasant culture.

Underground concerts: West of Viborg is an area of disused limestone mines (*kalk gruber*). Those at **Mønsted** are open to the public, with galleries 114 ft (35 metres) below ground. Some galleries are used to mature cheese because of their even temperature. At **Daugbjerg** the galleries (also open) go down as deep as 230 ft (70 metres) and there is a bat museum. The mine owner is also an enthusiastic violinist who holds concerts underground. Limestone was first

extracted as long ago as the 10th century and was used in the building of Ribe **Domkirke** (Cathedral).

To the east of the Salling peninsula is **Himmerland**, a region of gently rolling farmland with some wide swathes of moorland and heath. On two sides, the waters of the Limfjord vary from narrow sounds and sheltered coves to broad stretches of open water with islands and peninsulas. They are a pure delight for the sailing enthusiast.

Hessel, near Hvalpsund, is the last completely thatched manor house in Denmark, now an agricultural museum with a period interior and a collection of implements. **Ålestrup** has the **Danish Bicycle Museum**, with more than 100 machines as well as some early sewing machines and radios.

Between **Ranum** and Trend are the remains of what was intended to be a great church and monastery. It was given to the Cistercian monks in 1157 by King Valdemar. Only ruins now remain and the monastery, which became a manor house in 1668, is a centre for young criminals.

A small town with a long history is **Løgstor**, on the east of the Limfjord, which was a Viking fortress in AD 1000. In the 16th century it was the centre of the herring fisheries, but the disappearance of the fish meant a change to commerce and shipping. This was at first thwarted by the shallow waters of the Aggersund but resolved in 1861 by the construction of the Frederik VII's canal, 3 miles (5 km) in length. It continued in use until a new channel was made through the shallows at the turn of the century.

Today, part of the canal is a yacht harbour and the **Limfjord Museum** is in the former canal warden's house. Løgstor has reverted to being a quiet town very different from its past as Viking fortress or commercial port. **Nibe** was also founded because of the herring fisheries and, like Løgstor, is a quiet little place and the best preserved community in the Limfjord area.

The island of **Mors**, the largest in the Limfjord, lies between the Salling peninsula and that part of West Jutland

At Nørre Vorupør fishermen drag their boats up on to the sand.

traditionally called **Thy**. Mors includes a microcosm of all West Jutland's landscape, from salt marshes to great molar cliffs. **Hanklit** is 215 ft (65 metres) high and embodies tertiary flora and fauna and layers of black volcanic ash. Nearby is **Salgjerhøj**, 293 ft (89 metres) high, offering panoramic views over the waters of Limfjord.

The principal town, **Nykøbing**, grew up around the Abbey of St John (1370) and the **Morsland Historical Museum** is in the former Dueholm Monastery. To the south is **Jesperhus Blomster Park**, the largest flower gardens in Scandinavia with over 500,000 blooms.

The narrow peninsula of **Thy** is like a long pincer, with its jaw at the Thyborøn Kanal, to the northwest of the Limfjord. At **Ydby Hede**, overlooking the Skibsted fjord, there are 50 grave mounds from the Bronze Age. Vestervig has Scandinavia's biggest village (12th-century) but the scenery is more likely to catch the visitor's attention.

Swimming beaches: From the fishing village of **Agger**, in the south, to Hanstholm in the north of Thy, there is a splendid coastline with good beaches. Inland are extensive areas of heath, forest and lakes. At the village of **Nørre Vorupør** the fishermen still draw their boats up on the beach; but at **Klitmøller**, fishing has given way to holiday cottages. Between Klitmøller and Hanstholm is a stretch of spectacular scenery, the **Hansted Reservat**, a treeless heathland which is rich in bird and wildlife. It is closed to the public during the breeding season.

In 1917 the Danish government decided to build a harbour at Hanstholm but work proceeded very slowly and in World War II the German forces turned it into a heavily fortified zone and installed long range guns. Work resumed in the 1960s, with the harbour built out of sight at the base of steep cliffs and the town spread out above. There is a museum near the lighthouse and another one in a former wartime bunker.

Thy's principal town is **Thisted**, a commercial centre to the south of the peninsula. The Gothic church dates

Jutland waters, lake, fjord or river, make for fine fishing.

from about 1500 and the local museum honours two famous townsmen, the poet J. P. Jacobsen and the educator Kristen Kold.

Beyond Hantshom at the northern end of the Vigsø bay is **Bulbjerg**, a limestone cliff 130 ft (40 metres) high which affords widespread views of the area and is known as the "shoulder of Denmark". Inland, **Fjerritslev**'s claim to fame is its preserved brewery, which is now a museum.

Blokhus, further north and on the coast, is now a lively holiday centre with a superb broad sandy beach which makes it possible to drive along to the next holiday resort of **Løkken**, 10 miles (16 km) away. The latter is both a fishing port and holiday centre and has a museum. Near Saltum the pioneer Danish activity park, **Fårup Sommerland**, offers a huge range of children's activities. Inland from Løkken is **Børglum Kloster**, an 11th-century episcopal residence and monastery which became a manor house after the Reformation and was restored in 1750–56.

A feature of this part of Jutland are the large sand drifts; those at **Rubjerg Knude** are impressive, with steep cliffs rising 240 ft (74 metres) from the sea. The disused lighthouse is now a **Sand Drift Museum** and, when the wind blows, the sand is whipped up like a whirlwind. The disused Mårup church near **Lønstrup** has a large anchor from the British frigate *Crescent*, which ran aground here in 1808. Two hundred and twenty-six people died and are buried at Mårup. **Lønstrup**, once a busy fishing village, is now popular, particularly with Danish holidaymakers.

In 1804 the citizens of **Hirtshals** wanted to build a harbour but were rebuffed by the government. Despite that, they stubbornly pursued their aims and in 1917, 113 years after the first application, the harbour received approval; even so, it was not finished until 1930. It is now an important fishing centre with ferry connections to Norway. There is a salt-water aquarium and a local museum but the harbour is Hirtshals' best monument – to the triumph of persistence.

SOUTH JUTLAND

The half-timbered and gabled houses in the marshes of South Jutland indicate that this is an historic area. It holds Denmark's oldest town, Ribe, and has played an important part in Danish history. In 1864 the Danes lost southern Jutland (which became part of Slesvig-Holstein) to Prussia, after a heroic battle at Dybbøl, and recovered it only in 1920. At that time, in a plebiscite, North Slesvig voted with an overwhelming majority to return to Denmark, and the border was redrawn to form the area that is now southern Jutland.

Though the landscape is basically flat and alternates between heath, marshland, dunes and forest, with a network of well-stocked rivers to keep the anglers happy, history gives this area, closest to mainland Europe, an added interest.

Ribe, the first town as you travel south along the west coast, ranks high on the list of historic centres in Scandinavia with 560 buildings included in a municipal preservation project. The small houses and courtyards and the old *kros* (inns) are much as they were hundreds of years ago. But Ribe is no museum; the houses are homes to local people, their windows colourful with pot plants and bright curtains.

Ribe began as a Viking settlement in the 9th century and was of great importance in the Middle Ages. Its days of glory ended in the 17th century when economic and political power moved to Copenhagen, and its industries foundered in the 19th century when South Jutland was lost to Germany after the decisive battle at Dybbøl.

Ribe Domkirke (Cathedral), which dates back to 1150, stands on the site of one of Denmark's earliest wooden churches, built around AD 860. It has five aisles. The red brick tower is 14th-century and the 234 steps to the top are worth climbing for the splendid views over the surrounding countryside. In days past, that high tower had a very practical use. Before the building of

dykes and barriers, this low-lying area was periodically terrorised by flood and the church bell in its high tower tolled out as a warning of danger. The "Cat Head Door" was said to be the entrance for the Devil.

Quedens Gaard, a four-winged, half-timbered merchant's house, is now a museum of interiors with exhibits which reflect local crafts, trade and industry. The old grammar school was in use from the early 1500s to 1856, and the 15th-century town hall was the seat of local government from 1709 to 1966. The art museum includes works by well-known Danish artists from the so-called "Golden Age" of the early 19th century.

In the marketplace is an ancient inn called the **Weiss' Stue**, panelled with biblical pictures, where the courtyard makes a fine outdoor restaurant in summer. The town continues the Middle Ages tradition of *vægter* (night watchman). Each evening at 10 p.m., he walks around singing the old *vektor* songs which once told the people that

they could sleep soundly. All was well. In summer, he is most often accompanied by a crowd of visitors.

Floods and whales: Ribe was once a seaport and the old quay has a flood column whose highest watermark shows the height of the 1634 flood which reached as far as the Cathedral. The silting up of the river means that now Ribe Harbour can be used only by small pleasure craft. Off the coast is the tiny windswept island of **Mandø** which can be reached by a tractor bus at low tide (your own car is not recommended). It is an isolated community of some 100 inhabitants.

To the south, the larger island of **Rømø**, accessible along a 5½-mile (9-km) causeway is a favourite of German visitors. It has wide sandy beaches on the west coast and Havneby has a ferry connection to the island of **Sylt**. The island was once the home of prosperous whaling fleet commanders and one of their houses (*circa* 1746) at Toftum is now a museum, **Nationalmuseets Kommandøgård**. In summer, this

house is the setting for folk dancing, lace-making and similar demonstrations of traditional skills.

Nearer the German frontier, **Højer** is one of the oldest villages in Denmark where 250 houses and farms are preserved, though still lived in. Højer's windmill, now a museum, is the tallest in northern Europe.

Inland areas, once little more than marsh and moor, have few major centres of population, but South Jutland is easy driving and, like so many areas in Denmark, good for cycling. You are rarely far from the sea. The little town of **Gram**, surrounded by moors, heath and pine forests, is typical, an old market town which grew up around its castle, today a sleepy little place. The present castle dates from 1664 and the west wing houses a geological museum.

One characteristic sight in this marshland area is the isolated farms built on high mounds to protect them from floods that came frequently and suddenly before the dykes and sluices were built. The little village of **Rudbøl**

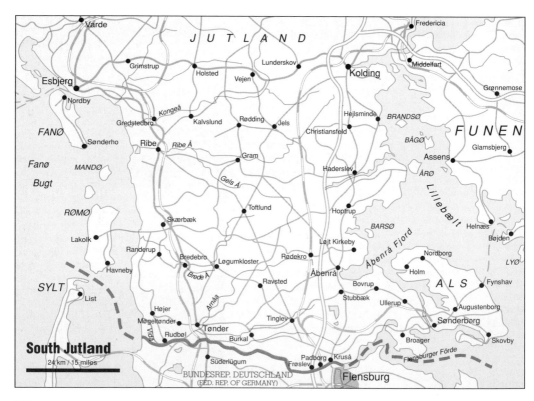

South Jutland

24 km / 15 miles

straddles the frontier and provides the amusing sight of Danish locals wheeling their shopping trolleys back over the border after a visit to the German supermarket. This area is famous for its local produce and a good place to try the town specialty of a marsh sausage is the **Rudbøl Gransekro**, an inn that has been serving them since 1791.

Møgeltønder's village street, lined with lime trees, can with justification claim to be one of the most beautiful in this part of Europe. The little houses are of typical Friesian design and at one end of the village, the church has Denmark's oldest working organ (1679). At the other is **Schackenburg Palace**, built as a church property and now a royal possession.

Nearby **Tønder** is the "capital" of this southwestern country. This former port, which received its charter in 1243, is now a considerable distance from the sea. It became famous as a lace-making centre and in its heyday 12,000 young women were employed on this work. An excellent museum covers the history of the area and in particular the lace-making industry, as well as its collection of silver and tiles.

There is a well-preserved and attractive 17th and 18th-century townscape and many houses have distinctive painted doorways. In the 12th century, Cistercian monks established a church and monastery at **Løgumkloster**. The present church combines Romanesque and Gothic styles and the old buildings now house a retreat and a school for bell ringers (*carillonneurs*).

Reminders of war: Moving on east towards Kruså, **Frøslev** has a reminder of World War II, as parts of a German internment camp have been kept as a museum. Some 16,000 Danes were imprisoned here; for many it was only a temporary stay along the road to the concentration camps. The key frontier town is **Padborg**.

Kruså is the gateway to **Sønderborg** and the island of **Als** which stretches east at the mouth of the Lillebælt, looking across to Funen. For the motorist – the most likely way to travel –

A long narrow neck of land at Feggerklit, Mors.

the best road is the secondary coast road alongside Kobbermølle Bugt which is much prettier and more enjoyable than the bigger road. On the outskirts of Gråsten is the magnificent white-painted Gråsten Palace. Apart from the chapel with its impressive floor to ceiling altarpiece, the original 17th-century buildings burned down in 1759. The palace was rebuilt and, in 1935, was presented to the Danish Crown Prince and Princess of the time. It is now the summer residence of the Danish royal family but, when the royals are not there, chapel and parkland are open to the public.

Almost on the outskirts of Sønderborg is another dramatic area, **Dybbøl**, which played such a major role in the war of 1864. The area is a national park and includes the ramparts and old cannon from the battle which resulted in southern Jutland disappearing off the map for 50 years, to become part of Germany. All over the area museums have reminders and relics from this time and the **Dybbøl windmill**, restored and

painted white, and its museum are open to the public.

Sønderborg (population 30,000) calls itself the largest town in South Jutland – although, to be pedantic about it, the majority of the town is across the sound on the island of Als. The town has grown up around the castle, which has a central core and four wings and was begun by King Valdemar the Great about 1100 as a defensive fortress. Today it houses a major **Museum of Danish History**, which, unsurprisingly, relates to the wars of 1848 and 1864 as well as World Wars I and II and the area's general history and culture.

Als is a pleasant if unspectacular island designed for pottering around, with some good, sandy beaches in the north and south. At Mommark there is a ferry to Søby on the island of Ærø, across the other side of the Belt, while at Fynshav another service runs to Bøjden on Funen.

The only other centre of any size on the island is **Nordborg** which has a castle, with one of Denmark's major industrial concerns as a rival on the approaches to the town. There is a graceful twin-spired church at **Broager** which has interesting frescoes from 1250. **Egen Church** has a wooden bell tower – unusual in Denmark.

On the hoof: At the height of the farming way of life, from the 16th century to the middle of the 19th century, South Jutland's best-known drove road was called **Hærvejen** and ran south to north through the area from Bov to Jels-Rædding, and then up through Jutland to Viborg. Along this drove road, the farmers herded their cattle on the hoof, stopping overnight as the cattle grew thinner on the long road to market. A section of the old road is still preserved near **Immervad Bro**, an old granite boulder bridge, and the local authorities are making strenuous efforts to have the whole of Hærvejen reinstated as a walking and cycling route.

Going north on the eastern side of the peninsula, the first town of importance is **Åbenrå** (population 20,000). The town, set on the Åbenråfjord, should in theory have a beautiful location and **Haderslev Domkirke**.

outlook but, alas, the view is spoiled by the spectacle of oil storage tanks and a massive power station.

Granted a charter in 1333 by Duke Valdemar, the town became a major port in the 17th and 18th centuries. Its maritime heritage is reflected in the museum which has all kinds of marine artefacts from ships in bottles to shipbuilders' tools. Impressive houses around the town and on the Løjt Kirkeby peninsula are reminders of the good shore life enjoyed by the sea captains in days gone by. The church at **Løjt** has South Jutland's longest late-Gothic triptych (1520). In Åbenrå the oldest church is the 13th-century **St Nicolai** which has a baroque altarpiece, pulpit and baptismal font. In the town are some attractive cobbled streets and preserved houses.

The last town in an area which has always been vulnerable from the south is **Kolding**, with Koldinghus Slot (Castle). Over the centuries it has been involved in many wars and not much is left of the original building from 1208.

Its last burning in 1808 was caused not so much by direct attack as through the sensitivity to cold of Napoleon's Spanish troops, stationed there during Denmark's confused alliance with the French Emperor. Faced with the chill of a Scandinavian winter, the Spaniards stoked up their fires so well that the old royal castle went up in flames. Nevertheless, the Spaniards were popular in Kolding and are credited with, or blamed for, teaching the Danes to smoke cigarettes.

Today, Koldinghus is restored and furnished with collections of wartime memorabilia as well as arts and crafts. The town itself is a junction on the route across Denmark. The main rail line runs through the town, though the motorway now bypasses it.

Southern Jutland may once have been torn by war, but today this gentle area is better summed up in Kolding's Geographical Garden where over 2,000 varieties of trees and shrubs from all over the world have brought about a more peaceful invasion.

Hærvejen, the ancient military road that runs through Jutland, now a good walking path.

The most essential – perhaps even the only – word you need to know in Greenlandic is *imaga*. It means "maybe" or "some time, perhaps". The nearest is the Spanish *mañana*, but that has too great a precision for Greenland where most things are dominated by the weather. In a climate which changes from hot sun and clear bright air to a veil or deluge of rain in a moment, the weather decides what one will do and whether it will be possible to keep to a plan made the day before. Will it be so good that everything must wait for jobs that can only be done outside, will the plane be able to land or, almost more important, will it take off again?

Many a visitor has "overnighted" at Narsarsuaq in the extreme south of this massive island because the incoming aircraft could not land, and the airports all have transit hotels used for just these occasions. The record is held, so the story goes, by a plane load that waited three weeks at the "all-weather" airport, **Søndre Stromfjord** – but that was during the worst of the winter weather, they add reassuringly.

Greenland, called *Kalaallit Nunaat* (Land of Man) in Greenlandic, is the world's largest island with an area of 840,000 sq. miles (2,175,600 sq. km). It is almost as large as Saudi Arabia. The distance between the south and north is 1,660 miles (2,670 km), and the longest distance between the west and the east coast is a good 1,700 miles (2,735 km). The southernmost point at Cape Farewell is on 59° 46' N, the same latitude as Oslo, Norway's capital. Greenland's closest neighbour is Canada, separated by the Davis Strait to the south and by the small Nares Strait in the north.

Ice cap: More than four-fifths of Greenland is covered by the Ice Cap, or inland ice, which stretches down to a depth of some 2 miles (3 km). The Greenlanders live in small settlements around the coast. This green ice-free strip is only a few miles wide before the land climbs steeply to the Inland Ice, a permanent mask which turns the interior into a vast, rumpled white cap of age-old glacier ice. The Ice Cap and the deep-cut fjords make sea or air the only links between the isolated settlements and the longest metalled road in Greenland is no more than around 10 miles (17 km) long at Søndre Stromfjord. Here the airport runway separates a civilian community of around 400, who lead a transitory working life at this outpost of the jet age, from the United States airbase, where US servicemen and Danes watch the skies for any emergency. In summer the temperatures here reach 80° F (25° C) and in winter it can be down to –50° F (–10° C), and this largely male community has a curious sense of impermanence.

The Danes came to Greenland in 1721, when the priest Hans Egede founded a mission and trading station in the west of the island. New stations proliferated in the next 150–200 years. Greenlanders sold skins, blubber and walrus tusks through a Danish-controlled trading company and, as a Danish colony, the island was all but isolated from the rest of the world right up to World War II.

At the start of the war, links with Denmark were severed as the Germans occupied the Danish mainland. The United States sent military forces to Greenland, set up radar stations and airfields, and Greenlanders were suddenly exposed to the good and bad influences of modern Western civilisation. The results were frightening. Tuberculosis and other diseases previously unknown to the indigenous people blighted the population, and the military had to make strenuous efforts to safeguard the Greenlanders' health and reduce high infant-mortality rates.

As the war ended and resumption of contacts with Denmark began, the Greenlanders had no desire to return to their enforced days as a closed society. They petitioned the United Nations for more autonomy, and the transition from old to new gathered pace in education, hospital facilities, fishing industries and so on.

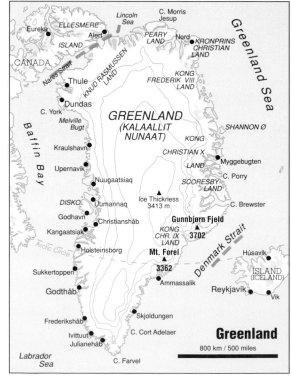

292

Home rule: In 1953, a constitutional amendment made Greenland an integral part of the Kingdom of Denmark, under the Crown, and in 1979 the island gained Home Rule with an elected Assembly (Landstinget) of 21 members (later increased to 27) and an autonomous government (Landsstyret) of six members. The Landsstyret's current chairman, and head of government, is Jonathan Motzfeldt, who leads the central administration from the capital **Nuuk** (Godthåb in Danish). Greenland received its own flag in 1985 and is a member of the Nordic Council. The population is around 53,000 of whom about 11,000 live in the capital.

Many of the declining number of Danes, up to some 10,000, who mostly date from the days before Home Rule, have continued to work for the Greenlandic government as administrators, teachers or advisers, but an increasing number of the duties previously entrusted to the Danish Ministry for Greenland have been transferred to the home government. The Royal Greenland Trade Department, which exercised a monopoly on trade to and from Greenland, has been replaced by a Greenlandic company, Greenland Trade (Kalaallit Niuerfiat).

As part of the development towards greater independence, the Greenlandic side places heavy emphasis on Greenlanders filling more of the positions hitherto occupied by Danes sent out to the country, hence the declining Danish population. Also in the search for their own identity, more Greenlanders now prefer to describe themselves as Innuits rather than Eskimoes, to underline their sense of common heritage with their counterparts in Canada, Alaska, and the Soviet Union.

Old seal-hunters: In North and East Greenland some of the people still follow the ancient ways of sealing by kayak. The sealing families still partly subsist on a barter economy and use every part of the seal, but they also earn money by selling seal skins. The early 1980s slump in prices caused by international campaigns against the use of

A fishing boat pushes its way out through the icebergs. **Following pages:** fishing at Eriksfjord.

sealskins as fur coats, was a near mortal blow to the hunters. The trade has only recently been partly restored by the grudging acceptance by the anti-fur lobby that Greenlandic sealing is humane and restricted to the hunting and killing with rifles of adult seals. In the past, skins were always exported in the raw but now Greenlanders and some Danes have set up tanneries and workshops so that the skins can be processed and manufactured, and sold as finished goods. The majority of export income, however, now stems from shrimp, salmon and cod fishing – often with the use of highly sophisticated trawlers – and several townships have modern fish-processing plants.

Though Greenland joined the European Community along with Denmark in 1973, the island had difficulty in accepting the Community's fishing quotas and a strong movement developed to end membership. In 1985, after a referendum, Greenland left the Community. Instead, it is associated with Europe through an Overseas Lands and Territories agreement which also applies to other countries.

Greenland has its own radio services and, since 1982, has also had nationwide Greenlandic television. The US still operates two airbases, at **Thule** in the north and Søndre Stromfjord in the central area, as well as several strategic early warning systems and radar installations on the Inland Ice. Danish-United States military co-operation in Greenland dates back to an agreement as long ago as 1951.

The Scandinavian airline SAS flies several times a week between Copenhagen and the large airport at Søndre Strømfjord and **Narsarsuaq** at the southern tip and, where it has been possible to construct airfields, the Greenlandic airline Grønlandsfly flies domestic routes. Air travel, as much as changing attitudes, has opened up Greenland in a way that would have been impossible 50 years ago, and tourists from all over the world and scientific expeditions are drawn in growing numbers to the island's grandiose, unique and often mysterious nature.

THE FAROE ISLANDS

The sea is serious business in the Faroe Islands and nothing shows that more clearly than **Tórshavn**'s harbour. It is stuffed with boats of all kinds – visiting ships, inter-island ferries, sailing boats and other pleasure craft and, most numerous of all, the fishing boats which disgorge their cargoes at one of the big fish processors scattered around the islands' coasts.

The fishing fleet is one of the most modern in Europe. Fish products make up more than 95 percent of the country's export earnings and the not-to-be missed tang of fish permeating the harbour is also the smell of money.

The islands lie far to the north of mainland Europe, halfway between Iceland and the Shetland Islands, some 320 miles (450 km) south of the former, and 225 miles (300 km) north of Scotland's northernmost outpost. The sailing distance between Faroe and Copenhagen is around 900 miles (1,500 km).

But though the Faroe Islanders are prosperous with a high standard of living – they claim to have more cars and more video recorders per head than anyone else in Europe – everything is relative. Only 45,000 live on the 18 inhabited islands (there are a dozen more which are home only to the huge colonies of birds) and most are clustered in coastal communities. As though to contrast with the muted blues, greens and greys of rocks, sea and hills, modern Faroeses favour brightly painted houses of the most unlikely hues. The old tradition was black paint, which helped to preserve the timber, with roofs of living green turf, and this is becoming popular once more.

Warm and wet: Far north as the islands are and feel, the Gulf Stream, which also brings useful warmth to mainland Scandinavia on the other side of the North Atlantic, keeps the climate maritime and mild. The seas do not freeze and in the coldest month the average temperature is around +3° C (36° F). In the warmest, it reaches 11° C

(52° F). Yet this maritime climate is changeable; one minute the sun is hot against the back, followed by driving rain as the mist comes down.

No self-respecting tree could grow to reasonable height against that constant wind – though, as a joke, the Faroese call the small copse in the shelter of the park in the capital, Tórshavn, the islands' "forest". Faroe's other name is the Sheep Islands – even today, there are thousands more sheep than people. They live on the blanket of grass and their meat is used for home consumption. The islands are scattered with a type of Arctic willow, and some heather and bilberry.

Birds everywhere: Though Faroe has few mammals, the rich bird-life is outstanding, especially on the cliffs. The towering faces of the stacs and cliffs are home to thousands of sea birds and in the sheltered pools live phalaropes and red-throated divers. The stiff-winged flight of the fulmars follows the boats without ever tiring and clown-faced puffins gaze solemnly from cliff bur-rows. The Faroes' national bird, the black and white oyster catcher, calls worriedly from every small hillock and makes good use of the turf roofs to seek its breakfast. Collecting birds' eggs has been an important source of income since ancient times, and the luckless puffin is a delicacy, caught during the open season in July with a curious instrument of pole and net, and served stuffed and cooked in many households. The island of Mykines is its great stronghold and attracts birders from many lands.

The islands' first substantial settlers came from Norway in the 9th century. Even before that time, an early township, **Kirkjubøur**, had been the centre of life for a group of Irish friars who colonised the islands around the 8th century. In 1380, as Norway came under Danish Rule, the islands too became part of Denmark and, when the union dissolved in 1814, the Faroese continued as a Danish county, under the Danish crown. Gradually a strong movement for independence arose, with

Preceding pages: village life on the remote westerly island of Mykines; **Suderø**, every harbour in the Faroe Islands is full of boats of every type. **Left**, well clad for the changeable Faroese weather.

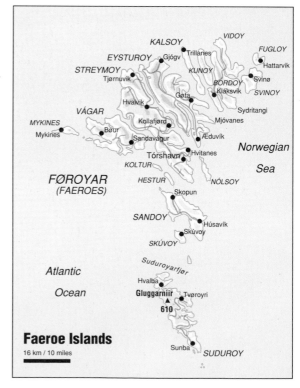

FØROYAR (FAEROES)

Atlantic Ocean

Norwegian Sea

KALSOY
VIDOY
EYSTUROY   Gjógv   FUGLOY
STREYMOY   Trillanes   Hattarvik
Tjørnuvik   KUNOY   Svinø
BORDOY   Klaksvík   SVINOY
Gøta
Hvalvik   Sydritangi
VÁGAR   Mjóvanes
MYKINES   Kollafjørd
Mykines   Bøur   Æduvik
Sandavágur
Tórshavn   Hvitanes
KOLTUR
HESTUR   NÓLSOY
Skopun
SANDOY   Húsavík
Skúvoy
SKÚVOY
Suduroyarfjør
Hvalba
Gluggarniir   Tvøroyri
610
Sunba   SUDUROY

Faeroe Islands
16 km / 10 miles

demands for more self-government.

This was intensified during World War II when Britain occupied the islands from 1941 to 1945 and, for that period, Faroe had little or no contact with a Denmark occupied by the Germans. After the war, a strong faction favoured total separation from Denmark and, though the demand for full independence has rumbled on, negotiations between the two governments resulted in the present system of Home Rule from 1948.

Self-government is by a democratically elected Assembly (*Løgting*) made up of 32 members and with legislative powers in all local affairs. Executive power is entrusted to a local government (*Landsstyret*), headed since 1985 by a Social Democrat, Alti Dam. The Faroe islands also send two representatives to the Danish Parliament.

The dominant industry is fisheries, accounting for more than 95 percent of the islands' exports. Fishing is traditionally concentrated on cod, which is processed into split, dried or salted cod, but the modern boats also catch large quantities of blue whiting, coalfish and shrimp. Drastic changes in fishing have taken place, first from fishing in local waters to deep-sea fishing, with ocean-going trawlers that travel throughout the North Atlantic, and then back to local fishing with the use of sophisticated equipment. This long seafaring history is traced in Torshavn's **Maritime Museum** and also in the museum at **Klaksvik**, the second largest town, on Bordoy island. As well, Torshavn has the Nordic Centre, which aims to bring together the best of Nordic culture in art exhibitions and concerts, and other performances.

Need to trade: The Faroes, together with Denmark, belonged to the European Free Trade Association (EFTA) from 1967 but the islands declined to follow Denmark into the European Community in 1973 largely at the insistence of the fishing industry. Relationships with the EC have since been regulated by a series of agreements similar to those applying to Norway and

Torshavn, capital of the islands.

Sweden, and good relations prevail.

Thanks to the fishing income, the Faroese live well. Around 85 percent of families own their own houses, with well stocked modern facilities. The Faroes have had a radio station since 1957 and their own television since 1984. Life is very much home and family-centred, particularly in the smaller communities. A wandering child is everyone's concern, neighbours work together, and Faroese often set off over long distances to visit friends at a time when most people might be thinking of going to bed. Precise time-keeping is not something that worries the Faroese unduly, and this draws its logic from the past. Then and (still to a large extent) now, the priority is to do what must be done when the weather is right.

Besides the fishing industry, there are shipyards and other trades aimed almost exclusively at the fishing industry. Faroese manufacturing has specialised in production machinery and equipment for fishing, fish-farming and fish-processing. Computer systems developed for the monitoring of fish-processing are exported to several countries. Of late, however, to counter-balance their heavy dependence on fishing, the Faroese have sought to develop a more diversified industry and trade, based upon the domestic market, and have started a popular Philatelic Bureau which provides some monetary jam on the daily bread and butter. Due to the modest size of the Faroes, there is a limit to the scope of such industries and the authorities currently face a financial crisis; the islands are now the most heavily indebted country in Europe.

The Faroese are proud of the rich culture and traditions of their islands, where the language, old costumes and customs are kept very much alive. On festive occasions, all still join in the special Faroese chain dance, which can last all night. Theatre and music abound and, based on the size of the population, the Faroese must be the world's most eager buyers and readers of books and newspapers. But what else are they to do in the long, dark winter, unless it be the chain dance?

GETTING THERE

BY AIR

Flights arrive daily from most European countries, North and South America and the Far East at Copenhagen Airport, half an hour's drive by shuttle bus (departing every 15 minutes) from central Copenhagen. The airport has recently been remodelled and has a large duty-free shopping area. International traffic also reaches the airport at Billund in west-central Jutland. The national carrier is **SAS**, Scandinavian Airlines System, for international traffic, and **Danair** (consisting of Maersk Air, SAS and Cimber Air) serves most domestic routes.

BY SEA

Reaching Denmark by sea can be a beautiful experience, and there are many routes to choose from. From West Germany ferries connect **Puttgarden** and **Rødby** (Lolland), **Kiel** and **Bagenkop** (Langeland), **Travemünde** and **Gedser** (Falster) and, in the summer, also **Rønne** (Bornholm). Ferries from East Germany ply the routes between **Warnemünde** and **Gedser** and, in the summer, **Sassnitz** and **Rønne** (Bornholm). **Swinoujscie** in Poland sends a daily ferry to **Copenhagen**.

Sweden has lines from **Helsingborg** to **Helsingør** (North Sealand) and from Helsingborg to **Grenå** (East Jutland); other ferries go from **Varberg** to **Grenå** and from **Göteborg** to **Frederikshavn** (North Jutland); ferries bound for Copenhagen go from **Landskrona** to **Tuborg Havn**, from **Malmö** to **Nyhavn** (Copenhagen), and from **Limhamn** to **Dragør**; from **Rønne** (Bornholm) there is a ferry to **Ystad**.

Lines from Norway go from **Oslo** to **Copenhagen** or to **Hirtshals** and **Frederikshavn** in North Jutland; from Hirtshals there are also ferries to **Bergen**,

Egesund, **Christiansand** and **Stavanger**. Ferries from **Larvik** and **Moss** (Norway) reach **Frederikshavn**.

Departure harbours in Britain are **Harwich**, which has ferries to **Esbjerg** and, in the summer, **Newcastle** has another line to Esbjerg.

BY ROAD

Traffic across the German border can be heavy at times, and some waiting time should also be anticipated at the car ferries. Friday and Sunday evenings are worst, but midweek usually poses few problems. It can pay to make reservations for a vehicle for both domestic and international ferry routes as early as possible.

BY RAIL

Trains arrive daily from Germany, Britain and Sweden, and several travel agencies sell package coach tours to Denmark. There is no well-organised system for travelling Europe by bus, but a large number of private tour operators make coach travel readily available.

TRAVEL ESSENTIALS

VISAS

Most travellers are not expected to present a visa on arrival, provided that their stay is of three months or less. Tourist visas are not required for citizens of European Community countries, Canada and the United States. Other nationalities may be required to obtain a visa before arriving. If in doubt, ask at the nearest Danish Embassy or Consulate.

PASSPORTS

The rules for travelling within the European Community are changing. Check with a Danish embassy or consulate before you go, if you want to use identification other than passport. Travellers from the Scandinavian countries have hitherto not needed to show any identification, but that practice might change as the borders to the south become more open. Travellers from countries outside Scandinavia or the EC are required to show valid passports when they enter Denmark.

CUSTOMS

Cigarettes, spirits, perfume, cameras and other luxury items are relatively expensive in Denmark, and customs officials have learned all the tricks used by amateur as well as professional smugglers. The rules about how much one can bring into Denmark are quite complicated. They depend upon which country one arrives from, and whether duty and taxes have already been paid. Always check in advance.

To be safe, bring only one litre of spirits **or** two litres of wine; 200 cigarettes **or** 50 cigars **or** 250 g of tobacco; 500 g of coffee; 100 g of tea; 50 g of perfume; 250 ml of eau de toilette; and goods/gifts not exceeding a value of 350 Dkr. (2,750 Dkr. if bought in EC countries, tax paid). These limits are also changing; once again, check with the local Danish Consul before packing your bags with gifts.

In addition, "travel requisites" for personal use only are permitted. These may be, for example, jewellery, cameras, perfume, fishing equipment, medicaments (but bring along the prescription if they contain narcotics), a tape recorder or a personal computer. People under 17 are not allowed to carry alcohol or tobacco, and one must be 15 to bring in coffee. Special permission is required to bring in meat, narcotics, poisons, fireworks, weapons, products made from plants or animals protected by the Washington Convention, and gold and securities. Money and cheques may be brought in freely.

Cats and dogs need to be accompanied by a certificate of vaccination (check for details at an embassy or consulate) and may be examined by a frontier veterinarian. No certificate is required if the animal comes straight from other Scandinavian countries or from Great Britain, Ireland, Japan, New Zealand or Australia.

WHAT TO BRING

The average mean temperature in July, the hottest month of the year, is 60° F (16° C), so even if you are lucky enough to travel in a year with a *real* summer, expect to find cold and rainy days as well. Yet it can also be very hot, well above 70° F (20° C). The only time of year with consistently good weather is from mid-May to mid-June. In any case it is wise to bring a sweater and an umbrella or rain jacket. Shoes that can stand a little water are a good idea.

Many Danes find it practical to dress in several layers: a shirt over a T-shirt and a cardigan casually swept around the shoulders will be appropriate for an early autumn night or a cool summer night. Temperatures as low as 0° F (–17° C) are not uncommon during winter. A flexible wardrobe is often necessary.

Danes dress casually on the beach, at the restaurant and at work. Young people are generally fashion-conscious, spending great sums on designer sweatshirts and tennis shoes or carefully assembling their own look from second-hand shops. When going out for the evening it isn't necessary for men (for all but a very few night spots) to put on a suit and tie.

MONEY MATTERS

The Danish currency unit is the *krone*. One krone (crown) is divided into 100 øre (from the Latin *aureus*, for gold coin). There are notes for 50, 100, 500 and 1000 kroner and coins for 25 and 50 øre and 1, 5, 10 and 20 kroner. Between the summer of 1989 and 1993 new coins are being introduced, so if you haven't visited in a few years expect some changes.

Until recently, credit cards were not commonly used in Denmark. But a mutual Danish banking card, the Dankort, paved the way for Visa cards, which are held by many people today. With a Visa or MasterCard you can go quite a long way in the shops. Diner's Club cards are accepted in many, but not all restaurants. American Express cards can be used in major hotels and shops, but are not very popular in general. All banks and a few shops take traveller's cheques.

GETTING ACQUAINTED

GOVERNMENT

Denmark has been a democratic country since 1849. The constitution allows any party which can gather 4 percent of the vote representation in parliament, the **Folketing**. At some times as many as 11 parties have been represented, but the Social Democratic Party has remained the most influential throughout most of this century.

The Folketing has 179 members, four of whom are elected in Greenland and the Faroe Islands (Færøern). Both are former colonies of Denmark, but today have status as counties. Both have their own languages, and Greenland gained home rule in 1979; the Faroe Islands became self-governing in 1948.

Denmark has been ruled by minority governments for a long time, and the political fluctuations have been rather limited. But a new scepticism and lack of trust in the "system", the government and its administration, is evolving. Though most people make money enough to get by, many miss the little luxuries that seem to make all the trouble worthwhile, and they (like everyone else) blame the situation on politicians. The changing structure of the European Community, which will become an open "inner market" in 1992, also creates uncertainty about the future politics of the country.

It is certain, however, that for many years to come the state will have to pay close to 30 billion Dkr. annually in interest on old debts. The Danish economy suffers from a severe budget deficit, accumulated over the course of many years, and one of the tasks for the present government is to change the habits of what have been called "Europe's most optimistic consumers." The fact that the public administration has one-third of all Danish workers on its payroll adds to the problem.

The goal for Danish politicians has for many years been to create a society where "few have too much and fewer have too little" and, even if the political debate has sharpened in recent years, the average income and the benefits of the social welfare system are still among the highest in the world but so are personal income taxes. The latter means that a growing number of people feel that they have too little left for themselves when the rent and union dues have been paid. The average family spends about 30 percent of its net income on rent, 20 percent on food and 15 percent on transportation.

GEOGRAPHY

Denmark consists of 406 islands and the peninsula of Jutland, the northernmost part of Western Europe. The area is about 27,280 sq. miles (70,655 sq. km), or about that of Vancouver Island on the west coast of Canada.

Altogether the coastline adds up to some 4,500 miles (7,300 km). The landscape is varied but mostly flat, and nowhere more than 490 ft (150 metres) above sea level. Denmark borders Germany to the south and is only a 25-minute ferry ride away from Sweden to the east. Standard time is GMT + 1.

The total population is slightly more than 5.1 million, a quarter of whom lives in Copenhagen. Not one of them is more than 33 miles (52 km) away from the ocean. About 90 percent are members of the Evangelical Lutheran Church.

Consider the weather before you to go:
Mean temperature
January 25° F, –4° C
February 30° F, –1° C
March 30° F, –1° C
April 43° F, 6° C
May 50° F, 10° C
June 57° F, 14° C
July 61° F, 16° C
August 59° F, 15° C
September 54° F, 12° C
October 48° F, 9° C
November 41° F, 5° C
December 36° F, 2° C
Falling night time temperatures account

One of the first Scandinavian countries to
attract travellers, Norway offers fjords and
mountains, a seemingly endless coastline
of inlets, islands and summer nights that
never darken. The **Insight Guide**
captures both nature's
abundance and the
cosmopolitan capital,
Oslo.

VI SEES SNART!

Another new **Insight Guide**
shows you around Denmark:
from Copenhagen's Tivoli
pleasure garden to Legoland,
from rich farmland to
fascinating islands.

And **Insight Guide:**

Sweden not only introduces you to the
stunning expanse of the country, but also
portrays the people of modern Sweden.

Denmark
Norway
Sweden

(at least in part) for the low average. The swimming season starts (except for true masochists) in the middle of May and ends in September. The best part of the summer usually falls between 10 May and 20 June with short, light nights. Sometime around the summer equinox (23 June) it often starts to rain, and sometimes does so until August, when school begins and most natives have already spent their summer holidays on a Mediterranean island. But other summers bring beautiful sunshine and warm nights. It seldom rains all day long; one will frequently have a couple of hours to dry off between showers. Remember to dress for cold and wet weather in the winter.

WEIGHTS & MEASURES

The Danes use the metric system and measure temperature in degrees Celsius. To convert from Centigrade scale to Fahrenheit, multiply by 1.8 and add 32 to the result. To convert from Fahrenheit to Centigrade, subtract 32 and divide by 1.8. For example, normal body temperature (98.6° F), becomes 37° C.
The following conversion table may also help:

To convert:	Multiply by:
Inches to Centimetres	2.540
Centimetres to Inches	0.393701
Feet to Metres	0.3048
Metres to Feet	3.2808
Yards to Metres	0.9144
Metres to Yards	1.09361
Miles to Kilometres	1.60934
Kilometres to Miles	0.621371
Gallons (US) to Litres	3.785
Litres to Gallons	0.2642
Pounds to Kilograms	0.4536
Kilograms to Pounds	2.20462

The standard **electrical current** supplied in Denmark is 220 AC.

CULTURE & CUSTOMS

Tipping: Tips are included in all bills. There are, of course, a few situations where a sign of appreciation will be welcomed. When arriving at the hotel, give the porter 5 to 15 Dkr. for carrying luggage to the room.
At a restaurant it is a friendly gesture to pick up the notes but leave the coins for the waitress. Excellent service should be rewarded a little more generously. It is unusual to tip a waitress in a bar or café, and never tip the hairdresser. Cab drivers will appreciate it if the fare is rounded up to the nearest 5 or 10 Dkr., but they may not ask for a tip. They may, however add 3 Dkr. per bicycle transported and 2 to 4 Dkr. for carrying luggage at the destination.
When in doubt, the best solution is usually to ask people directly if a tip would be appropriate. Tipping is the exception rather than the rule, and some might feel offended if you try to give them money for a service they have provided for nothing.

COMMON COURTESY

The sexual revolution so frequently associated with Denmark went hand in hand with women's liberation and the raising of social consciousness in general. Bear in mind that an hour's conversation with a stranger doesn't mean a commitment to spending the night together. Public information campaigns to limit the spread of AIDS have worked well, and most Danes will have the means and desire to use some form of protection against it and other sexually-transmitted diseases.

BUSINESS HOURS

Most offices are open from 8 or 9 a.m. until 4 or 5 p.m. Rush hours can be tiresome, but the traffic is usually moving. The heaviest hours are 7.30–9 a.m. and 3.30–5.30 p.m.
Most shops close at 5.30 p.m. Monday–Thursday and at 7 p.m. (8 in Copenhagen) on Fridays. Supermarkets remain open until 7 p.m., at least in Copenhagen. Opening hours on Saturday are 9 a.m.–2 p.m. in Copenhagen, but 9 a.m.–noon in most other places. On the first Saturday in each month, most shops remain open until 4 or 5 p.m. All shops are closed Sundays. Exceptions are the bakeries and kiosks, some of which are open round the clock. In addition, the supermarket at the **Central Railway Station** and **Steno Apotek** (the pharmacy across Vesterbrogade from the train station) are open all day, every day. Keep the closing hours in mind when planning day trips.
Banks are open 9.30 a.m.–4 p.m. Monday–Friday, but add two hours on Thursday and

stay open till 6 p.m. The same goes for most public offices. In Copenhagen, the bank in the Central Railway Station stays open till 10 p.m. in the summer and 9 p.m. in the winter, but only as a service to travellers who need to exchange currency.

Official time is based on the 24-hour clock.

HOLIDAYS

Denmark observes a few national holidays. June 5th is Constitution Day, and shops and offices close at noon. A floating holiday is Prayer Day (**Store Bededag**), which falls on 15 May in 1992, 7 May in 1993 and 29 April in 1994. Around Easter, Maundy Thursday, Good Friday and the following Monday are observed. So are Ascension Day and Whitsun Monday. Christmas is celebrated on the evening of 24 December and continues through the 26th. All shops are closed on holidays.

RELIGIOUS SERVICES

Services are normally conducted Sundays at 10 a.m., and they are often repeated at 2 p.m. There are several foreign congregations in Copenhagen. **The English Church** is located at Esplanaden near Amaliegade, **Sankt Petri Church**, with ceremonies in German, can be found on the corner of Nørregade and Skt. Pedersstræde, and the **Church of the Reformation**, which is shared by a German and French congregation, is located at Gothersgade across the street from Rosenborg Castle. **Jewish Synagogue** is at Krystalgade, 1172 Copenhagen. Tel: 33 12 88 68.

COMMUNICATIONS

POST & TELEPHONE

A shortage of telephone numbers in Copenhagen made a transition from 6 to 8 digit numbers necessary some years ago. In May 1989 all telephone numbers in the country were changed by the addition of one digit, and visitors who may have been accustomed to the previous system will doubtless be a little confused at first. The Danes certainly were.

Calls cannot normally be charged to credit cards. "Calling card" customers of an American company may have their calls charged in the US, however, by dialling 04 30 00 10 (toll-free) to reach an American operator. The same number should be used for collect calls to America. For information on other telephone services dial 0030.

Post offices are open 9 a.m.–5 p.m. on weekdays, and 9 a.m.–12 noon on Saturdays. There are some exceptions to the rule, however; some offices open later and close earlier and some stay closed on Saturdays. For urgent matters, the Customer Service at the Mapn Post Office, Tiltensgade 39, 1500 Copenhagen V, tel: 33 33 89 00 can direct you to the nearest office. In general, the solution in case of emergency is to go to the Central Railway Station. Poste Restante letters should be collected at the main post office in the region you are in, unless they are specifically addressed to a local post office.

Money orders can be collected or dispatched at all post offices during normal business hours, and **telegrams** can be sent by phone (0028 for information) or from any post office. Ask for assistance at a post office or at the hotel to send a **telex** or **fax**.

In addition, phone calls to foreign countries can be placed from **Statens Teletjeneste** offices, above the post office in the Central Railway Station, and next door to the post office in Købmagergade in Copenhagen.

MEDIA

If the craving for a foreign newspaper or magazine cannot be denied, try the railway station or the largest neighbourhood kiosk. Otherwise, there are the news broadcasts in English, German and French on weekday mornings (Programme 3) from 8.15–8.30.

It may also be comforting to know that movies in foreign languages are not dubbed but shown in the original language with Danish subtitles.

Many public libraries have a good selection of books in English and Copenhagen has bookshops which specialise in foreign literature. Try any of the large bookshops for literature in English, or **Deutsche Buchhandlung** (Vester Voldgade 83) for German books, and **The French Bookshop** (Badstuestræde 6) or **Haase** (Løvstræde 8) for books in the Romance languages. Other titles in the *Insight Guides* series can be found in most large Copenhagen bookshops.

EMERGENCIES

In case of fire or severe accident, or when police assistance is required immediately, dial 0-0-0. The call is free from all telephones.

MEDICAL & DENTAL

Health care is generally free in Denmark. Acute illnesses or accidents will be treated at the emergency room of the nearest hospital. Travellers with chronic diseases should be aware of international rules and the policies of their insurance company before arriving in Denmark. It may be possible to have costs reimbursed on return. If one is too ill to go out, it is still possible to have the assistance of a physician. In this case one may be asked to pay for the consultation on the spot.

Pharmacies are open during normal business hours, but there is a 24-hour pharmacy in every region. The names and addresses are posted on the door of every local pharmacy (or look in the yellow pages under **Apotek**). In Copenhagen use **Steno Apotek** on Vesterbrogade, across the street from the Central Railway Station. Prescriptions are required for most drugs other than aspirins and pain relievers of similar strength.

Dental care is available by appointment only. Check the listings under **Tandlæger** in the business directory to find the closest. Dentists' fees are paid in cash, and the same guidelines for reimbursement apply as for other health care. Outside normal business hours one can go to **Tandlægevagten** (no appointment necessary). In Copenhagen the address is Oslo Plads 14 near Østerport Station.

LOST PROPERTY

It may be possible to recover lost or stolen property, but don't count on it. Contact the nearest police station for assistance, or try the lost-and-found offices at the train station.

Beware of pickpockets: Gangs of professionals roam the streets in the tourist season, working the crowds and unsuspecting tourists. Remember to notify credit card firms immediately if the cards disappear. Holders of MasterCard, Visa, Eurocard, Access and Eurocheque should get in touch with their own bank or with the Danish bank associated with their bank.

American Express card holders should contact: American Express International, Amagertorv 18, 1160 Copenhagen K, tel: 33 11 50 05 (9 a.m.–5 p.m.) or Freecall 80 01 01 00 24-hour service.

GETTING AROUND

BY AIR

Danair has daily flights from Copenhagen to Bornholm, Odense, Århus (Tirstrup) and several other destinations in Jutland. All flights are in or out of Copenhagen – there are no flights between the other destinations. Prices vary single 515–610 Dkr. (There is also a special return fare at same cost, with some restrictions).

BY BUS, TRAIN & FERRY

You can get almost anywhere in Denmark by using a combination of train, bus and ferry. A trip from Copenhagen to Northern Jutland takes about 8 hours, to Southern Jutland 5–6 hours. Though it is still less expensive than flying, prices have gone up lately. Ask about prices and reservations at any railway station. Be sure to make reservations for trips during weekends and holidays – as far in advance as possible, as train seats and ferry space are quickly booked.

BY BICYCLE

The best way to enjoy the landscape is a trip by bicycle. Bring your own bike if you want to tour the country, but for transportation around the city, a rented one will do. The local tourist information office can tell you where to pick one up. For information on routes and practical advice, contact Dansk Cyklistforbund (Danish Association of Cyclists), Rømersgade 7, 1362 Copenhagen K, tel: 33 32 31 21. Open: Summer, Monday–Friday 9.30 a.m.–5 p.m. Winter, Monday–Friday 9.30 a.m.–3 p.m. Late night Thursdays to 6 p.m. winter or 7 p.m. summer.

BY CAR

Travel time in Denmark is not great but a car gives the freedom to go anywhere quickly. It pays to shop around when renting a car. Ask the travel agency if they have a special offer, or try the yellow pages. Avis and Hertz have offices all around the country, but it is often possible to make a better deal with local companies. Be prepared to present a valid international driving licence and you must be 20–25 years old to rent a car. When coming to Denmark from the south, be sure to fill the tank before crossing the border as petrol is *very* expensive (7+ Dkr. per litre in 1991), and to make reservations for ferries ahead of time (at any railway station). Taxis are expensive and sometimes hard to find; most people use them within city limits only.

Driving: It is neither easy nor cheap to get a driving licence in Denmark, and most drivers have had at least 20 hours of classroom and behind-the-wheel training. They know the rules of the road, and expect that everyone else does also. Use turn signals and drive politely, and traffic will be safe. *Always* yield at pedestrian crossings and *always* look out for bicycles when turning right. *Always* look over your left shoulder when opening the doors on the driver's side – bicycles are everywhere.

Speed limits are enforced. In cities the limit is 50 kph, in the country 80 kph. A rectangular white sign with a black silhouette of buildings and towers indicates densely populated areas and the maximum speed limit of 50 kph. Be aware that the 50 kph speed limit is also enforced in towns along a country road. The speed limit on main roads is 100 kph (80 for buses, 70 for trucks and cars with trailers). Overtake on the left only.

Drinking and driving: Alcohol is involved in one-third of all traffic accidents resulting in fatal injuries in Denmark. The best advice is not to drink alcohol at all when driving; but if you must, one beer or drink an hour is the absolute maximum. A blood alcohol level of 0.08 percent will cost you the right to drive in Denmark, and 0.12 percent can take you to jail for at least a week. Danish police frequently set up road blocks (unannounced and at different locations) to test all who drive past for alcohol and to conduct a cursory inspection of their vehicles. Remember that public transportation is reliable, cheap and easily available – use it as an alternative to the car if you've been partying.

WHERE TO STAY

HOTELS

Danish hotels are good in a clean, well-run Scandinavian way. They are not cheap, but have first-class facilities and are very much business-oriented; more recently, they have also been keen to attract conferences. As more and more hotels go in for extensive refurbishment, it is harder to find the small, traditional hotel with character.

Nevertheless, as in other Scandinavian countries, almost all hotels slash their rates in the summer months when business visitors are scarce, and offer fine value if you visit from June to late August, when the Danes take to their summer cottages. Watch the dates though, a difference of a week can almost double the price. Always ask. Scandinavian hotels, including Danish, more often have showers than baths. If you want a tub, ask before you book.

In Greenland, which until recently had only a few hotels, the move into modern hotels aimed at the conference market has been rapid and the list of hotels is now longer than you might expect in such a remote, snow-covered area. In general, these hotels come into the expensive category and there is not a wide selection of alternatives. Make sure of your accommodation before you go, and do not expect to rent rooms in private houses.

In the Faroe Islands, hotels were until recently largely designed for visiting seamen. Apart from a few in Torshavn (of which at least two have good facilities), modern hotels are not plentiful. Private houses and youth hostels provide an alternative. Details from: the Danish Tourist Board in your home country or contact Tourist Information in Copenhagen, H. C. Andersens Boulevard 22A, 1553 Copenhagen V. Tel: 33 11 13 25.

KRO/INNS

For character, turn to the *kro* (inn), once 17th and 18th-century stagecoach inns and scattered throughout Denmark. Most preserve the past by leaving the original inn intact and building on extra accommodation motel-style. They are usually outside the main towns. Nearly 70 *kro* combine to provide Inn Cheques (*Dansk Kroferie*), bought in advance and valid for an overnight stay at very reasonable prices. Details from: Dansk Kroferie, Søndergade 31, DK-8700 Horsens, Denmark. Tel: 75 62 35 44, fax: 75 62 38 72.

SELF-CATERING & CAMPING

This is always popular in Denmark, particularly for people who bring their own cars north from Germany or across the North Sea from Britain, and is an ideal way of seeing the country in summer. Summer houses are reasonable to rent but normally require a guest to stay at least a week. Whether it is rented out centrally or not, the house may well belong to a Danish family. Danes, known homemakers, often spend even more money and thought on their holiday home than they do on their permanent dwelling, and the standard will be high.

You can hire stationary caravans or huts on many campsites, or take your own tent. There is also a camping voucher, similar to the Inn Cheque. Details from: Camping Club Denmark, Horsens Tourist Bureau, address and phone as above under *Kro*/Inns.

FARM HOLIDAYS

Danish farmers were the first to try the idea of inviting guests to stay as one of the family on their comfortable farms, where the steading looks more like a well-kept courtyard garden. You get an excellent and inexpensive insight into Danish life and can sometimes volunteer to help when needed, popular with children, also with the farmer during harvest! The main centre is Jutland. Contact: Horsens Tourist Board, Søndergade

31, DK-8700 Horsens, Denmark. Tel: 75 62 35 44, fax: 75 62 38 72.

BED & BREAKFAST

Danes are relative newcomers to the idea of entertaining bed and breakfast guests, and you should check that breakfast is included in the price. Even when it is not, it can usually be arranged. In Danish "bed and breakfast" is *Logi/Morgenmad* and you should, therefore, be certain of getting breakfast if you ask for details from Skandinavisk Logi/Morgenmad, SLM, Kongensgade 94, DK-1264 Copenhagen K. Tel: 33 91 91 15, fax: 42 18 72 53.

YOUTH HOSTELS

As in most countries, youth hostels cater for people of all ages, and Denmark has around 100 of them, with a high standard of facilities higher than in most European hostels. You need a valid membership of the Youth Hostel Association in your home country. Details from: Denmarks Vandrerhjem, Vesterbrogade 39, DK-1620 Copenhagen V, price 20 Dkr., plus postage. The Danish Tourist Office also has a free list of sites.

The YMCA and YWCA have two Inter-rail points in Copenhagen: at Inter-Rail Point, Store Kannikestræde 19, DK-1169, Copenhagen K. Open: July to mid-August. They offer accommodation around 50 Dkr. plus breakfast; and at Inter-Rail Point, Valdemarsgade 15, DK-1663 Copenhagen V, tel: 31 31 15 74. For information on youth hostels and inexpensive accommodation, enquire also with the Youth Information Centre – USE IT, Rådhusstræde 13, DK-1466 Copenhagen. Tel: 33 15 65 18, fax: 33 15 75 18. Open: year round. Outside hours, consult the outdoor notice board for information.

GENERAL

The Danish Tourist Board publishes a guide each year, which gives overnight accommodation in Denmark, covering hotels, inns, holiday hotels and holiday centres. Available from: Danish Tourist Board in individual countries or, failing that, from: Copenhagen Tourist Information, DK-1553 Copenhagen V. Tel: 33 11 13 25.

If you arrive in Copenhagen without a booking, the Accommodation Service is at Kiosk P at Central Station. Open: 9 a.m.– midnight, 1 May to mid-September (shorter hours, off season). By post: Hotel Booking, Copenhagen, Hovedbanegården, DK-1570, Copenhagen V.

It is difficult to divide Danish hotels into precise price bands; the Moderate category in particular often overlaps at both ends. Prices given are average, for two in a double room and *usually* breakfast, with bath or more often a shower, which you find in the bulk of Danish hotel and inn accommodation. Without private facilities, all categories will be cheaper. Enquire. Remember rates may be lower in summer, particularly in large business hotels. Away from the centre of Copenhagen, prices are lower.

Copenhagen hotels listed below in categories as follows: Expensive: 900–2,240 Dkr; Moderate: 675–900 Dkr; Inexpensive: under 300–675 Dkr.

Outside Copenhagen: Expensive: 800–1,700 Dkr; Moderate: 600–800 Dkr; Inexpensive: under 300–600 Dkr.

COPENHAGEN

Hotel d'Angleterre: Kongens Nytorv 34, DK-1050 Copenhagen K. Tel: 33 12 00 95, fax: 33 12 11 18. This is Copenhagen's "Royal" hotel, which has many times entertained European royalty and famous people. Its pavement café is popular with the less exalted. 243 Beds. Suites. Expensive.

71 Nyhavn: Nyhavn 71, DK-1051 Copenhagen. Tel: 33 11 85 85, fax: 33 93 15 85. A Romantik Hotel. An unusual, atmospheric hotel built into a converted warehouse along the waterside at Nyhavn, near the quay. 110 beds, most with splendid harbour views. Expensive.

Savoy Hotel: Vesterbrogade 34, DK-1620 Copenhagen V. Tel: 31 31 40 73, Fax: 31 31 31 37. 133 beds in a 1906 building in a garden courtyard off Vesterbrogade. Carefully restored in the mid-1980s with advice from the National Museum. Just edging into the Expensive category.

Copenhagen Admiral Hotel: Toldbadgade 24–28. Tel: 33 11 82 82, fax: 33 32 55 42.

Another delightful conversion of an old building, this time a 1787 granary with excellent facilities. 815 beds. Moderate.

Hotel Excelsior: Colbjørnsgade 14, DK-1652 Copenhagen V. Tel: 31 24 50 85, fax: 31 24 50 87. 100 beds in an old building, well modernised, it has a plant-filled atrium were you can sit for drinks. No restaurant but choice of many nearby. Rooms well furnished in cool Scandinavian style. Moderate.

Sophie Amalie Hotel: Sankt Annæ Plads 21, DK-1250 Copenhagen K. Tel: 33 13 34 00, fax: 33 32 55 42. Not far from the quayside near Nyhavn, some rooms with a harbour view. Quiet. An old building well renovated. Moderate.

Skovshoved Hotel: Strandvejen 267, DK-2920 Charlottenlund. Tel: 31 64 00 28., fax: 31 64 06 72. About 5 miles (7 km) from the centre in a row of old fishing cottages. 36 rooms, the larger ones facing the sea. Idyllic spot with a conservatory restaurant of high gourmet repute. Hotel: Moderate. Restaurant: Expensive.

Hotel Amager: Amagerbrogade 29, DK-2300 Copenhagen S. Tel: 31 54 40 08/54 50 09, fax: 31 54 90 05. On the way to the airport, but only 5 minutes' bus ride to the centre. A traditional "pension" hotel, rooms without private facilities. Inexpensive.

Copenhagen Capriole Hotel: Frederiksberg Alle 7, DK-1820 Frederiksberg C. Tel: 31 21 64 64, fax: 33 25 64 60. Old "pension" hotel converted from a block of flats. 45 beds in fairly basic rooms but most with private facilities. Fifteen to 20 minutes' walk to centre, three to four stops by choice of buses. Inexpensive.

ODENSE

Hotel H.C. Andersen: Claus Bergs Gade, Odense. Tel: 66 14 78 00, fax: 66 14 78 90. Good, modern hotel in the old part of Odense, next to museum. 250 beds all with private facilities, also conference facilities. Expensive.

Motel Brasilia/Blommenslyst Kro: Middelfartvej 420, DK-5491 Blommenslyst.

Tel: 65 96 70 12, fax: 65 96 79 37. Beautiful motel added to old *kro* (inn) in lovely garden. Excellent traditional food at the inn. Five miles west of Odense. Moderate.

Missionhotellet Ansgar: Østra Stationsvej 32, DK-5100 Odense C. Tel: 66 11 96 93, fax: 66 11 96 75. The old mission hotels nowadays have all facilities and are usually very good value. 70 rooms. Inexpensive.

ÅRHUS

Hotel Royal: Store Torv, Box 43, Århus. Tel: 86 12 00 11, fax: 86 76 04 04. Beautiful building, more than 150 years old. Modernised in character with a fine conservatory restaurant, Queen's Garden. 186 beds with private facilities. Expensive.

Hotel La Tour: Randersvej 139, DK-8200, Århus N. Tel: 86 16 78 88, fax: 86 16 79 95. 200 beds, all private facilities. Moderate.

Hotel Ritz: Banegårdsplads 12, Postboks 37, Århus. Tel: 86 13 44 44, fax: 86 13 45 87. Very central and close to station. 110 comfortable beds, all private facilities. Inexpensive.

THE FAROE ISLANDS

Torshavn
Hotel Borg: Oggjarvegur, PO Box 105, FR-110 Torshavn. Tel: 0298-17500, fax: 0298-16919. A big, modern hotel but built in traditional style with dark timber walls and turf roof, in a beautiful position above the hill behind Torshavn, looking across the harbour to the island of Nolsoy. All private facilities. Just into the Expensive category.

Hotel Hafnia: Aarvegur 6 1B, FR-110 Torshavn, some 100–200 metres from the harbour. 76 beds all with private facilities. Sauna. Moderate.

Torshavn Sjomansheim: Torsgata 4, PO Box 97, FR-110 Torshavn. Tel: 0298-13515, fax: 0298-13286. Comfortable hotel with 72 rooms, some with private facilities. Restaurant with good, simple fare. Inexpensive.

Eystoroy, Eidi
Hotel Eidi: In the north of this northern

island on the Sundini Channel. 31 beds without private facilities but with mini-bars, an asset in a country without licensed restaurants and bars. Inexpensive.

Eystoroy also has two youth hostels, as do many other islands.

Bordoy, Klaksvik
Klaksvikar Sjomansheim: Vikavegur, FR-700 Klaksvik. Tel: 0298-55333. The main accommodation in the Faroe Islands second largest community, handy for the ferry to Leirvik. 61 rooms, some with private facilities. Restaurant. Moderate.

GREENLAND

Nuuk (Godthalb)
Hotel Hans Edede: Aqqusinersuaq 1–5, Box 289 DK-3920 Nuuk. Tel: 0299-21029, fax: 0299-24487. Big, modern conference hotel in Greenland's capital has 250 beds with private facilities. Expensive.

Narsarsuaq
Hotel Narsarsuaq: The Airport, DK-3921 Narsarsuaq. Tel: 0299-35253, fax: 0299-35370. The airport hotel, 10 miles or so from the start of the Inland Ice, with a good view of the icebergs in the fjord. 192 rooms, all private facilities. Expensive.

Narsaq
Narsaq is a good holiday base on the southwest coast, some two hours by boat/20 minutes by helicopter from Narsarsuaq.

Hotel Perlen: Box 8 DK-3291 Narsaq. Tel: 0299-21533, fax: 0299-31520. Comfortable, family-run hotel with good food and beautiful view of the Narsaq sound and its icebergs. 60 rooms, some with private facilities. Ideal for fjord and iceberg tours and of mountains behind. Moderate.

Illulisaat (Jakobshavn)
This town is much further north on the west coast, opposite Disko Bay.

Hotel Arctic Illulissat: Box 501, DK-3852 Illulissat. Tel: 0299-44153, fax: 0299-43924. Good quality modern hotel at the top of the hill, with a superb view overlooking the bay and Disko island. Best reached by helicopter

from Søndrestrømfjord Airport, the all-weather airport that is part of the US Air Force base. Expensive.

Qaanaaq (Thule)
Hotel Qaanaaq: Box 88, DK-3971 Qaanaaq. Tel: 0299-50120, fax: 0299-50064. A small, simple hotel on the remote northwest coast of Greenland, reached through Thule air base. 10 rooms without private facilities. Inexpensive.

FOOD DIGEST

Within the past couple of decades the Danish kitchen has gone through a quiet revolution. Not only have the traditional hearty meals of pork and beef seen new low-calorie, high-fibre varieties, but words like pizza, pasta, quiche and kebab have also gone into the everyday vocabulary. These days one can eat in a variety of languages and still not be exotic.

But the food that is usually associated with Denmark has not suffered from this clash of cultures: Open sandwiches, *smørrebrød*, are still most common for lunch. If you don't count calories, try a lunch buffet of cold dishes, (*smörgåsbord* is originally a Swedish word, but the tradition is Danish, too) where you can pick and choose from a range of Danish specialties. A beer and an *aqvavit* are traditional and go well with lunch.

Check the prices before entering a restaurant or inn. It is hard to judge from the exterior alone if the prices will be reasonable. The least expensive food is often found in cafés with only a few dishes on the menu. Most cafés serve chili con carne, quiche, a salad and soup and several kinds of sandwiches. Among the money savers are also many Oriental restaurants, especially those with Chinese menus, 80 Dkr. or less will cover a main course and a beer (all prices are from 1991).

Many restaurants offer "a two-course meal

of good, Danish food" – meal of the day – for 80 Dkr. This is where one finds pork roast, minced beef, meat or fish balls, and other traditional dishes with ice cream for dessert. Drinks are not included.

When in Denmark take advantage of the varieties of fish available from the Baltic and North Seas. Freshwater fish, whether from the rivers of northern Scandinavia or the fish farms of Jutland, is excellent. Relatively inexpensive meals can be prepared easily, and are common in restaurants. Fowl and game are common, especially in autumn, and should by all means be sampled.

COPENHAGEN

A couple of good cafés to visit for lunch or dinner are **Zeze** and **Café Dan Turell** in Store Regnegade and **Krasnapolsky** in Vestergade, but you will easily find your own favourites.

For lunch try **Risotto** on Nytorv. Old-fashioned open sandwiches are served at **Café Sorgenfri** in Knabrostræde, at **Bjørnekælderen** at Frederiksberg Alle 55, and in many other bars; but the queen of *smørrebrød* is **Ida Davidsen** at Store Kongensgade 70. One of the best cold buffets can be found at the **DSB Restaurant** in the Central Railway Station. **Den Sorte Ravn** is possibly the best (and most expensive) fish restaurant in town.

Some restaurants with attractive settings, good food and reasonable prices are **Peder Oxe** on Gråbrødretorv, the restaurant in **Nikolaj Church** on Nikolaj Plads, **Joanna** in Læderstræde 11 and **Din's** in Lille Kannikestræde. Try **Sjatodulak** at Lille Triangel. If you are willing to pay for high quality, visit **Lumskebugten** at Esplanaden 21, **Kong Hans** at Vingårdsstræde 6 or **La Saison** at Hotel Østerport across from Østerport Station. Vegetarians will be pleased to find their interests considered at the latter but they should also try **Greens** in Grønnegade. Visit **Pasta Basta**, Valkendorfsgade 22 (between Strøget and Gråbrødretorv) for a first-rate buffet of hot and cold pasta dishes at reasonable prices.

Ostehjørnet in Store Kongensgade is a cheese shop, and serves good, sharp Danish cheeses during normal business hours. An excellent market with pasta, fish, meats, vegetables and fruit – in addition to excellent take-out items – is **Køkkenes Torvehal**, on Strøget at Bremerholm (across from Magasin du Nord, which also has a good grocery).

ÅRHUS

Although there isn't much room in **Café Casablanca** in Rosensgade, there are a few tables for diners. If they are occupied try **Den Høje** in Skolegade, where the food is somewhat heartier. Stop at **Underground** in Nørregade 38 or in the pedestrian street, where they serve sandwiches, but the main attraction is the ice cream. **Jacob's Bar BQ** claims to be the first restaurant to bring the charcoal grill to Denmark, and its location in the courtyard of an old merchant's house makes it a nice place to go on a summer night. Vegetarians should visit **Huset** in Vester Alle. For an expensive but memorable culinary experience try **De Fire Årstider** (The Four Seasons) at Åboulevarden across from Magasin or **Mahler** at Vestergade 39.

ODENSE

There are several good cafés in the area around **Brandts Klædefabrik**, and restaurant **Amfita** is just inside. **Café Birdy's** at Nørregade 21 is a nice combination café/restaurant and features vegetarian dishes. Traditional Danish food is served at **Frank A** at Jernbanegade 4; walk from the restaurant to one of the city's best bars next door.

THINGS TO DO

COPENHAGEN

We recommend the purchase of a "Copenhagen Card" at your hotel or at the tourist bureau. The card is good for free entry at Tivoli and 50 other places, and it can be used as a bus/train ticket as well (sample prices 105 Dkr. for one day, 170 Dkr. for two days, 215 Dkr. for three days; children pay half price). If you want to take a package tour, pick up a brochure in the tourist bureau at Rådhuspladsen. Sightseeing tours in and around Copenhagen start right across the square on the east side of City Hall. Tours of the harbour start from, among other places, Nyhavn and Gammel Strand every 15 minutes.

Amalienborg Slot: The Queen's residence. Changing of the guard every day at noon.

Arbejdermuseet (Workers' Museum): Rømersgade 22. Tel: 33 13 01 52. Open: Tuesday–Sunday 10 a.m.–3 p.m., Saturday and Sunday 11 a.m.–4 p.m. Closed: Monday.

Bakken: Dyrehavevej in Klampenborg. Tel: 31 63 35 44. Amusement park in the former royal hunting grounds (Dyrehaven). Open: April–August. An amazing assortment of rides and game booths and more than 30 restaurants and pubs.

Botanisk Have (Botanical Gardens): Gothersgade 128. Open: daily, April–September 8.30 a.m.–4 p.m., October–March 8.30 a.m.–6 p.m. Admission: free.

Carlsberg Breweries: Ny Carlsbergvej 140. Tel: 31 21 12 21. Tour of the brewery Monday–Friday at 11 a.m. and 2 p.m. (groups by appointment).

Carlsberg Museum, Valby Langgade 1. Tel: 31 21 01 12, ext: 1273. Open: Monday–Friday 10 a.m.–3 p.m. Admission: free.

Christiansborg (The Parliament): Christiansborg Slotsplads. Open: daily 9.30 a.m.–3.30 p.m. Guided tours in English.

Dansk Post – og Telegraf Museet: Valkendorfsgade 9. Tel: 33 32 30 63. Open: Tuesday–Sunday 1–4 p.m.

Danmarks Akvarium: Strandvejen at Charlottenlund Fort. Tel: 31 62 32 83.

Davids Samling (The David Collection): Kronprinsessegade 30. Tel: 33 13 55 64. European and Islamic handicrafts. Open: daily 1–4 p.m. Closed: Monday. Admission: free.

Den Hirschsprungske Samling: Stockholmsgade 20. Tel: 31 42 03 36. Impressionist painters. Open: Tuesday–Saturday 1–4 p.m., Sunday 11 a.m.–4 p.m.

Den Lille Havfrue (The Little Mermaid): Langelinje. Bronze sculpture by Edvard Eriksen.

Dukketeatermuseet (doll and marionette museum and shop): Købmagergade 52. Tel: 33 15 15 79. Open: Monday and Wednesday–Friday 12.30–5 p.m. Closed: April and Bank Holidays.

Frihedsmuseet (Danish Resistance Museum): Churchill Parken. Tel: 33 13 77 14. Open: May to mid-September, Tuesday–Saturday 10 a.m.–4 p.m., Sunday 10 a.m.–5 p.m; mid-September to April, Tuesday–Saturday 10 a.m.–3 p.m., Sunday 10 a.m.–4 p.m. Admission: free.

Frilandsmuseet (Open-Air Museum): Kongevejen 10, Lyngby. Tel: 42 85 02 92. Open: daily, summer 10 a.m.–5 p.m., winter 10 a.m.–3 p.m.

Geologisk Museum (Geological Museum): Øster Voldgade 5–7. Tel: 33 13 50 01. Open: Tuesday–Sunday 1–4 p.m.

Georg Jensen Museum (Silverware): Bredgade 11. Tel: 33 11 40 80. Open: Monday–Friday 10 a.m.–5.30 p.m., Saturday 10 a.m.–2 p.m.

Grundtvigskirken: På Bjerget. Tel: 31 81 44 42. Open: Monday–Saturday 9 a.m.–4.45 p.m., Sunday noon–4 p.m. (1 p.m. September–May).

Holografisk Museum (Holography Museum): main entrance of Tivoli, H. C. Andersens Blvd 22. Tel: 33 13 17 13.

Holmens Kirke (Naval Church): Holmens Kanal. Tel: 33 13 61 78. Open: summer, Monday–Friday 9 a.m.–2 p.m. winter 9 a.m.–noon; Saturday 9 a.m.–noon.

Jens Olsens Verdensur (Astronomical clock): City Hall, Rådhuspladsen. Tel: 33 15 38 00.

Kastellet (The Citadel): Grønningen. Tel: 33 11 22 33. Open: daily 6 a.m.–sunset.

Det Kongelige Bibliotek (The Royal Library): Christians Brygge 8. Tel: 33 93 01 11. Open: Monday–Friday 9 a.m.–7 p.m., Saturday 10 a.m.–7 p.m.

Det Kongelige Teater (The Royal Theatre): Kongens Nytorv. Tel: 33 32 20 20 (administration), 33 14 10 02 (ticket office). National stage for theatre, opera and ballet. Performances: Monday–Saturday from September–May.

Kunstindustrimuseet (Museum of Applied Arts): Bredgade 68. Tel: 33 14 94 52. Open: Tuesday–Sunday 1–4 p.m.

Københavns Bymuseum (Copenhagen City Museum): Vesterbrogade 59. Tel: 31 21 07 72. Open: summer, Tuesday–Sunday 10 a.m.–4 p.m., winter 1–4 p.m.

Københavns Rådhus (The Town Hall): Rådhuspladsen. Tel: 33 15 38 00. Open: Monday–Friday 9.30 a.m.–3 p.m. Guided tours.

Legetøjsmuseet (Toy Museum): Valkendorfsgade 13. Tel: 33 14 10 09. Open: Monday–Thursday 9 a.m.–3 p.m., Saturday and Sunday 10 a.m.–4 p.m. Closed: Friday.

Louis Tussaud Wax Museum: main entrance of Tivoli, H. C. Andersens Blvd 22. Tel: 33 14 29 22. Open: daily 10 a.m.–11 p.m. when Tivoli is open. November–March 10 a.m.–5 p.m., rest of the year 10 a.m.–4.30 p.m.

Marmorkirken (also **Frederikskirken**): Frederiksgade 4. Tel: 33 15 37 63. Open: Monday–Saturday 11 a.m.–2 p.m., admission to the cupola Saturday 11 a.m.

Nationalmuseet (The National Museum): Frederiksholms Kanal 12. Tel: 33 13 44 11. Danish history and prehistory. Open: summer, Tuesday–Sunday 10 a.m.–4 p.m., winter 11 a.m.–3 p.m.

Nationalmuseet i Brede: I. C. Modewegsvej near Ørholm Station. Tel: 42 85 34 75. Changing exhibitions. Has closed down, but *might* reopen in 1992.

Ny Carlsberg Glyptotek, Dantes Plads, H. C. Andersens Blvd. Tel: 33 91 10 65. Classical paintings and statuary. Open: summer, Tuesday–Saturday noon–3 p.m; winter, Tuesday–Saturday noon–3 p.m., Sunday 10 a.m.–4 p.m.

Ordrupgaardsamlingen, Vilvordevej 110. Tel: 31 64 11 83. Paintings. Open: Tuesday–Sunday 1–5 p.m.

Rosenborg Castle: Øster Voldgade 4. Tel: 33 15 32 86. The crown jewels. Open: daily, June–August 10 a.m.–4 p.m; September–October 11 a.m.–3 p.m; November–May 11 a.m.–2 p.m. Closed Mondays November–April.

Royal Copenhagen Porcelain: Smallegade 45, Frederiksberg. Tel: 31 86 48 48. Tour of the factory at 9.45 a.m. Tuesday and Thursday; winter 1991 Monday–Friday 9, 10 and 11 a.m. Parties of five or more should book in advance. Bus from the shop at Strøget in the summer.

Rundetårn (The Round Tower): Købmagergade 52. Tel: 33 93 66 60. Open: daily, June–August 10 a.m.–8 p.m; April–May and September–October 10 a.m.–5 p.m; November–March 11 a.m.–4 p.m. Shorter hours Sundays. Tycho Brahe's observatory at the top.

Statens Museum for Kunst (Museum of Fine Arts): Sølvgade 42. Tel: 33 91 21 26. Open: Tuesday–Sunday 10 a.m.–4.30 p.m.

Storm-P. Museet: Pile Alle & Frederiksberg Alle (Frederiksberg Runddel). Tel: 31 86 05 23. Open: Tuesday–Sunday 10 a.m.–4 p.m. (winter Wednesday, Saturday and Sunday only).

Teatermuseet (Theatre Museum): Christiansborg Ridebane 18. Tel: 33 11 51 76. Open: Wednesday and Sunday 2–4 p.m.

Thorvaldsens Museum: Porthusgade 2. Tel: 33 32 15 32. Open: Tuesday–Sunday 10 a.m.–5 p.m. Guided tours in English.

Tivoli Gardens: H. C. Andersens Blvd 22. Tel: 33 15 10 01. Open: daily May to mid-September, 10 a.m.–midnight.

Tobaksmuseet (Tobacco museum and shop): Amagertorv 9. Tel: 33 12 20 50. Open: Monday–Friday 9.30 a.m.–5 p.m., Saturday 9.30 a.m.–1 p.m.

Tuborg Breweries: Strandvejen 54 in Hellerup. Tel: 31 29 33 11, ext: 2215. Tour of the brewery, Monday–Friday at 10 a.m., 12.30 p.m. and 2.30 p.m.

Tycho Brahe Planetarium: Gammel Kongevej 10. Tel: 33 12 12 24. Open: Sunday–Monday 11 a.m.–10 p.m., Tuesday–Thursday 9 a.m.–10 p.m., Friday–Saturday 11 a.m.–10 p.m.

Tøjhusmuseet (Arsenal Museum): Tøjhusgade 3. Tel: 33 11 60 37. Open: summer, Tuesday–Saturday 1–4 p.m., Sunday 10 a.m.–4 p.m; winter Tuesday–Saturday 1–3 p.m., Sunday 11 a.m.–4 p.m.

Vor Frelsers Kirke (Church of Our Saviour): Sankt Annægade 29. Tel: 31 57 27 98. Open: June–August, Monday–Saturday 9 a.m.–4.30 p.m., Sunday noon–4 p.m; May–April and September–October, Monday–Saturday 9 a.m.–3.30 p.m., Sunday noon–3 p.m; November–March, Monday–Saturday 10 a.m.–1 p.m., Sunday noon–1.30 p.m.

Vor Frue Kirke (Church of Our Lady/Copenhagen Cathedral): Nørregade. Tel: 33 14 41 28. Open: Monday–Saturday 9 a.m.–5 p.m., Sunday noon–1 p.m. and 3 p.m.–4.30 p.m.

Zoologisk Have (Zoo): Roskildevej 32. Tel: 36 30 25 55. Open: daily, summer 9 a.m.–6 p.m., winter 9 a.m.–5 p.m.

Zoologisk Museum (Zoological Museum): Universitetsparken 15. Tel: 31 35 41 11. Open: summer, Tuesday–Sunday 11 a.m.–5 p.m.

NORTH SEALAND

Teknisk Museum (Technical Museum): Nordre Strandvej 23, Helsingør. Tel: 49 21 71 11. Open: daily 10 a.m.–5 p.m.

Fredensborg Castle: near Hillerød. Open: daily 1–5 p.m. in July only.

Frederiksborg Slot (Frederiksborg Castle and Chapel, Museum of Natural History): Hillerød. Tel: 42 26 04 39. Open: daily May–September 10 a.m.–5 p.m; October–December 10 a.m.–4 p.m; Jan–March 11 a.m.–3 p.m; April 10 a.m.–4 p.m.

Kronborg Castle: Helsingør. Tel: 49 21 30 78. Open: daily, May–September 10 a.m.–5 p.m; April and October, (closed on Mondays except during school autumn holiday) 11 a.m.–3 p.m; November–March, (closed on Mondays except between Christmas and New Year, closed Christmas Day) 11 a.m.–3 p.m. Maritime Museum, Royal Apartments and Chapel, Tours of the Cellar and Dungeon, site of Royal Shakespeare Company productions of *Hamlet*.

Louisiana (Museum of Modern Art): Strandvejen, Humlebæk. Tel: 42 19 07 19. Contemporary art. Open: daily 10 a.m.–5 p.m.

Nivågård Samlingen: Gammel Strandvej, Nivå. Tel: 42 24 10 17. Collection of 16th to 19th-century paintings. Open: Tuesday–Friday 1–4 p.m., Saturday–Sunday noon–5 p.m.

Selsø Herregårdsmuseum (manor house): Skibby/Skuldelev near Frederikssund. Tel: 42 32 01 71. Open: daily, July 11 a.m.–4 p.m; May and August Saturday–Sunday 1–4 p.m.

Sankt Mariae Kirke og Karmeliterklostret (Church of St Mary and Carmelite Abbey): Kirkestræde, Helsingør. Tel: 49 21 17 74. Guided tours daily, May–September 11 a.m. and 2 p.m; winter Saturday–Sunday at 2 p.m.

Sankt Olai Kirke (Cathedral Church of St Olai): Stengade and Skt Anna Gade, Helsingør. Open: daily 10 a.m.–4 p.m. Admission: free.

Vedbækfundene (Vedbæk Archeological Excavation): Gammel Holtegaard, Attemosevej 170. Open: all year Tuesday–Friday 2–4.30 p.m., Saturday–Sunday 11–4.30 p.m.

Willumsen Museum, Jenriksvej 4, 3600 Frederikssund. Tel: 42 31 07 73. Open: daily, April–September 10 a.m.–4 p.m; October–

March Monday–Saturday, 1–4 p.m., Sunday 10 a.m.–4 p.m.

Øresundsakvariet (Øresund Aquarium): Strandpromenaden 5, Helsingør. Tel: 49 21 37 72. Open: daily noon–4 p.m.

SOUTHWEST SEALAND

Frilandsmuseet (Open-Air Museum): Meinkesvej 5, Maribo. Tel: 53 88 11 01. Open: daily, May–September 10 a.m.–5 p.m.

Gavnø Park and Slot: Gavnø near Næstved. Tel: 53 80 02 00. Manor house with a large collection of paintings and rose gardens. Open: daily, May–August 10 a.m.–5 p.m.

Gåsetårnet: Vordingborg. Castle from the 14th century. Denmark's best-preserved ruin from the Middle Ages. Open: daily, summer 11 a.m.–5 p.m., winter 2–4 p.m.

Holmegård Glass Works: Fensmark near Næstved. Tel: 53 74 62 00. Open: Monday–Friday 9.30 a.m.–noon and 12.30 p.m.–1 p.m., (Saturday–Sunday 11 a.m.–3 p.m. summer only). Parties of 10 or more should call in advance.

Knuthenborg Safari Park: Bandholm, Maribo, Lolland. Open: daily, May–September 9 a.m.–6 p.m.

Køge Skitsesamling: Nørregade 29, Køge. Tel: 53 66 24 14.

Lejre Forsøgscenter: Lejre near Roskilde. Tel: 42 38 02 45. Open: daily, May–September 10 a.m.–5 p.m. Archaeological Research Center.

Lungholm Ulvemuseum: Rødbyvej 20, Rødby. Tel: 53 90 03 26. Open: daily, May–October 10 a.m.–5 p.m. World's only museum of wolves.

Nysø Herregård: Præstø. Manor house with sculptures by Bertel Thorvaldsen.

Roskilde Domkirke (Roskilde Cathedral): Tel: 42 35 27 00. Open: Monday–Saturday, 9 a.m.–5.45 p.m May–August; 10 a.m.–3.45 p.m October–April; Sunday noon–5.45 p.m. (summer only).

Sparresholm Vognsamling: Holme-Olstrup. Tel: 53 76 41 88. Collection of wagons and coaches.

Trelleborg, Slagelse. Viking fortress. Open: daily, April–September 10 a.m.–6 p.m.

Vallø Castle: southeast of Køge. Admittance to the park daily.

Vikingeskibshallen (Viking Ship Museum): Roskilde Harbour. Tel: 42 35 65 55. Open: daily, summer 9 a.m.–5 p.m., winter 10 a.m.–4 p.m.

Aalholm Castle: Nysted. Tel: 53 87 10 17. Restored manor house with a large exhibition of old automobiles. Open: daily, late-May to early-September 11 a.m.–6 p.m.

BORNHOLM

Bornholms Dyre- og Naturpark: Borrelyngvej 45, Allinge. Tel: 53 98 15 65. Deer park for children. Open: daily, May–September 10 a.m.–5 p.m.

Bornholms Lokalhistoriske Arkiv (Local history archives): Central Library, Rønne. Tel: 53 95 07 04. Open: May–September, Monday–Friday 10 a.m.–7 p.m., Saturday 10 a.m.–2 p.m; October–April, Monday–Friday 10 a.m.–8 p.m., Saturday 10 a.m.–2 p.m.

Bornholms Museum & Bornholms Kunstmuseum: Sct Mortensgade 29, Rønne. Tel: 53 95 07 35. Open: summer, Monday–Saturday 10 a.m.–4 p.m; winter Tuesday, Thursday and Sunday 2–5 p.m.

Erichsens Gaard: Laksegade 7, Rønne. Tel: 53 95 07 35. Arts and crafts. Open: summer, Monday–Friday 10 a.m.–4 p.m; winter Tuesday, Thursday and Sunday 2–5 p.m.

Forsvarsmuseet (Defense Museum): Galløkken, Rønne. Tel: 53 95 65 83. Open: Tuesday–Saturday 10 a.m.–4 p.m.

Gudhjem Museum: Stationsvej, Gudhjem. Tel: 53 98 54 62. Open: mid-May to mid-September, Monday–Saturday 10 a.m.–4 p.m., Sunday 2–5 p.m.

Hammershus (ruins from the Middle Ages): northwest Bornholm. Free admission all year.

Melstedgård Frilandsmuseum (Open Air Museum): Melstedvej 25, Hasle. Tel: 53 98 55 98. Working museum of farming history. Open: mid-May to October, Tuesday–Sunday 10 a.m.–5 p.m.

Nexø Museum: Nexø Harbour. Tel: 53 99 31 32. Open: June–September, Monday–Friday 2–5 p.m., Saturday 9 a.m.–noon.

Østerlars Rundkirke: Østerlars. Tel: 53 99 82 64. Open: April–September, Monday–Saturday 9 a.m.–5 p.m.

ODENSE

Purchase the "Adventure-pass" (adults 70 Dkr., child 35 Dkr. in 1991, half-price out of season) at hotels or the tourist bureau for free admission to 24 different attractions. The pass is valid for two days only and may also be used as a bus ticket.

Carl Nielsen Museet: Claus Bergs Gade. Tel: 66 13 13 72. Memorial to the Danish composer and his wife.

City Hall: Flakhaven. Open: May–September, Monday–Friday at 2 p.m., guided tours.

Danmarks Grafiske Museum (Denmark's Graphic Arts Museum): Brandts Klædefabrik. Tel: 66 12 10 20. Open: Monday–Friday 10 a.m.–5 p.m., Saturday–Sunday 11 a.m.–5 p.m.

Funen Kunstmuseum (Funens Art Museum): Jernbanegade 13. Tel: 66 13 13 72. Danish painters. Open: daily 10 a.m.–4 p.m., Wednesday also 7–10 p.m.

Funen Stiftsmuseum: Jernbanegade 13. Tel: 66 13 13 72. Funen in prehistory. Open: daily 10 a.m.–4 p.m., Wednesday also 7–10 p.m.

Funen Tivoli (amusement park): Sdr. Blvd 304. Tel: 66 11 49 75. Open: daily April–August.

H.C. Andersens Barndomshjem (the childhood home of Hans Christian Andersen): Munkemøllestræde 3–5. Tel: 66 13 13 72. Open: daily, summer 10 a.m.–5 p.m., winter noon–3 p.m.

H.C. Andersens Hus (Hans Christian Andersen Memorial House): Hans Jensens Stræde 39–43. Tel: 66 13 13 72. Open: daily, June–August 9 a.m.–6 p.m; April–May and September 10 a.m.–5 p.m; October–March 10 a.m.–3 p.m.

Hollufgård, Hestehaven 201. Tel: 66 13 13 72. Former manor house turned cultural activity centre.

Jernalderlandsbyen: Store Claus 40. Tel: 66 18 09 87. Rebuilt village from the Iron Age. Contact the tourist bureau for further information.

Jernbanemuseet (Railroad Museum): Dannebrogsgade 24. Tel: 66 12 01 48, ext: 238. Open: daily, May–September 10 a.m.–4 p.m; October–April Sunday 10 a.m.–4 p.m.

Kunsthallen (gallery): Brandts Klædefabrik. Tel: 66 13 78 97. Open: daily 10 a.m.–5 p.m.

Museet for Fotokunst (Museum of Photography): Brandts Klædefabrik. Tel: 66 13 78 97. Open: daily 10 a.m.–5 p.m.

Møntergården: Overgade 48–50. Tel: 66 13 13 72. Museum of cultural history. Open: daily 10 a.m.–4 p.m.

Skt Albani Kirke: Albanitorv. Tel: 66 12 16 64. Roman Catholic Church.

Skt Hans Kirke, Nørregade 42. Tel: 66 12 43 88. Open: Monday–Saturday 10 a.m.–4 p.m. (June–August also Sunday).

Vor Frue Kirke: Overgade/Frue Kirkestræde. Tel: 66 12 65 39. Open: daily, June–August 9 a.m.–3 p.m; October–March 10 a.m.–noon.

Zoologisk Have (Zoo): Sdr. Blvd 320. Tel: 66 11 13 60. Open: daily, May–August 9 a.m.–6 p.m; April and September 9 a.m.–5 p.m; October–March 9 a.m.–4 p.m.

FUNEN AND ITS ARCHIPELAGO

Egeskov Castle: Kværndrup. Tel: 62 27 16 25. Vintage cars in a castle from 1554. Open: daily, June–August 9 a.m.–5 p.m; May and September 10 a.m.–5 p.m.

Flaskeskibsmuseet (Bottle Ship Museum): Ærøskøbing, Ærø. Open: daily, May–September 9 a.m.–5 p.m; October–April 10 a.m.–4 p.m.

Fåborg Museum: Fåborg. Tel: 62 61 06 45. Painters from Fyn. Open: daily, April–October 10 a.m.–4 p.m; Saturday–Sunday 11 a.m.–3 p.m. (November–March).

Hindemae: South of Ullerslev. Tel: 65 36 22 05. Manor house from 1787, arts and antiques. Open: daily, June–August 11 a.m.–5 p.m; September–May, Sunday 11 a.m.–5 p.m.

Nyborg Castle: Tel: 65 31 02 07. Open: daily, June–August 10 a.m.–5 p.m; September–October, Tuesday–Sunday 10 a.m.–3 p.m.

Skovsgård: Humble, Langeland. Manor house with wagon museum. Open: 15 May–September, Monday–Friday 10 a.m.–4 p.m., Sunday 1–5 p.m; September–3rd week in October, Monday–Friday 10 a.m.–5 p.m., Sunday 1–4 p.m. Closed: Saturdays.

Terrariet: Vissenbjerg. Tel: 64 47 18 50. Largest vivarium in Scandinavia. Open: daily, summer 9 a.m.–6 p.m; winter 9 a.m.–4 p.m.

ÅRHUS

Århus Festuge (Festival Week) in the beginning of September is one of the best known in Denmark. Opera, ballet, concerts, performance art and street happenings are on the programme, be sure to make hotel reservations months ahead to visit during the festival. If you visit at other times there are still many places to go:

Botanisk Have (Botanical Gardens): Peter Holms Vej. Tel: 8821 06 77. Open: Monday–Saturday 1–3 p.m., Sunday 11 a.m.–3 p.m.

Den Gamle By (The Old Town): Viborgvej. Tel: 86 12 31 88. Open: daily, summer 9 a.m.–6 p.m., shorter hours in the winter.

Friheden Tivoli (Amusement Park): Skovbrynet. Open: daily May–August.

Moesgård Museum (Archeology Museum): Open: daily, April–September 10 a.m.–5 p.m; October–March 10 a.m.–4 p.m., closed Monday.

Kunstnernes hus (Arts Centre): Saltholmgade. Tel: 86 20 20 66. Open: Monday–Friday 10 a.m.–5 p.m., Saturday–Sunday noon–5 p.m.

Kvindemuseet (The Women's Museum): Domkirkeplads 5. Open: Tuesday–Sunday noon–5 p.m.

Marselisborg Castle: Summer residence of the Royal Family. Changing of the guard at noon, when the Family is in residence.

Musikhuset (Concert Hall): Frederiks Allé. Open: daily 11 a.m. till the last performance.

Naturhistorisk Museum (Museum of Natural History): Universitetsparken, Bygning 210. Tel: 86 12 97 77. Open: daily, July–August 10 a.m.–5 p.m; September–June 10 a.m.–4 p.m. Closed: Monday October–April.

Rådhuset (City Hall): Tel: 86 13 20 00. Admission to the tower for groups only, permission needed.

Videnskabshistorisk Museum (History of Science Museum): Observatorievej 3. Open: Wednesday–Sunday noon–4 p.m.

Vikingemuseet (Viking Museum): Skt Clemenstorv 6. Open: Monday–Friday 9.30 a.m.–4 p.m., Thursday 9.30 a.m.–6 p.m.

Vor Frue Kirke: Vestergade. Tel: 86 12 12 43. Open: May–August, Monday–Friday 10 a.m.–4 p.m., Saturday 10 a.m.–2 p.m; September–April Monday–Friday 10 a.m.–2 p.m., Saturday 10 a.m.–noon.

Århus Kunstmuseum: Vennelystparken. Tel: 86 13 52 55. Museum of modern art. Open: Tuesday–Sunday 10 a.m.–5 p.m.

EAST JUTLAND

Gammel Estrup Herregårdsmuseum: Auning, Djursland. Tel: 86 28 30 01. Manor house and agricultural museum. Open: May–October, Tuesday–Sunday 10 a.m.–5 p.m; November–April 11 a.m.–3 p.m.

Jellinghøjene: Jelling. Denmark's birthplace. Burial mounds and rune stones from the Viking Age.

Koldinghus: Kolding. Tel: 75 50 15 00. Newly restored castle from the 13th century. Open: daily, May–September 10 a.m.–5 p.m; October–April, Monday–Friday noon–3 p.m., Saturday–Sunday 10 a.m.–3 p.m.

Legoland: Billund. Tel: 75 33 13 33. Amusement park with miniature Lego world. Open: daily 26 April–15 September 1991.

Løveparken (the Lion Park): Givskud. Tel: 75 73 02 22. Open: daily, May–September 10 a.m. until 2 hours before sunset.

Silkeborg Kunstmuseum, Gudenåvej 7–9, Silkeborg. Tel: 86 82 53 88. April–October, Tuesday–Sunday 10 a.m.–5 p.m; November–March noon–4 p.m.

Silkeborg Kulturhistoriske Museum: Hovedgårdsvej 7, Silkeborg. Tel: 86 82 14 99. Glass works and prehistoric finds. Open: daily, mid-April to October 10 a.m.–5 p.m; November–March Wednesday, Saturday and Sunday noon–5 p.m.

Trapholt Kunstmuseum: Æblehaven 23, Trapholt (north of Kolding). Tel: 75 54 24 22. Open: October–April, Monday–Friday noon–4 p.m., Saturday–Sunday 10 a.m.–4 p.m; May–September, Monday–Sunday 10 a.m.–5 p.m.

Viborg Domkirke (Viborg Cathedral): Viborg. Tel: 86 62 11 07. Largest ashlar church in Europe. Open: daily, June–August 10 a.m.–4 p.m; April–May and September 11 a.m.–4 p.m., Sunday noon–4 p.m; October–March 11 a.m.–3 p.m., Sunday noon–3 p.m.

NORTH JUTLAND

Bangsbomuseet: Bangsbo near Frederikshavn. Tel: 98 42 31 11. Museum of cultural history. Open: daily 10 a.m.–5 p.m. (closed Monday November–March).

Børglum Kloster (Castle and Monastery): east of Løkken. Tel: 98 99 40 14. Open: daily, June–August 10 a.m.–6 p.m.

Danmarks Cykelmuseum (Bicycle Museum): Borgergade 10, Ålestrup. Tel: 98 64 19 60. Open: May–October Monday–Sunday 10 a.m.–5 p.m.

Helligåndshuset: C.W. Obels Plads, Ålborg. Oldest welfare institution in Denmark, founded in 1431. Monastery with frescos. Open: Monday–Friday at 2 p.m. (late June to early-August only).

Jens Bangs Stenhus: Østergade, Ålborg. Merchant's house from the Renaissance.

Michael & Anna Anchers Hus: Markvej 2, Skagen. Tel: 98 44 30 09. Open: daily, summer 10 a.m.–6 p.m; November–April, Saturday–Sunday 11 a.m.–3 p.m.

Nordjyllands Kunstmuseum: Kong Christians Allé 50, Ålborg. Tel: 98 13 80 88. Twentieth-century paintings. Open: daily 10 a.m.–5 p.m. (closed Monday September–June).

Nordsømuseet (North Sea Museum): Willemoesvej, Hirtshals. Tel: 98 94 44 44. Open: daily, July–August 9 a.m.–7 p.m; September–June, Monday–Friday 9 a.m.–4 p.m. and Saturday–Sunday 10 a.m.–5 p.m.

Rebild Bakker: near Skørping in Himmerland. National park founded in 1912 by Danish-American citizens. Site of annual 4th of July celebration.

Skagens Museum: Brøndumsvej 4. Tel: 98 44 64 44. Open: daily 10 a.m.–5 p.m. (summer), Sat-Sun 11 a.m.–3 p.m. & Wed 1-3 p.m. (winter). The Skagen School of Danish painters.

Vendsyssel Historiske Museum (Museum of Local History): Museumsgade 3, Hjørring.

Tel: 98 92 06 77. Open: daily, May–June 11 a.m.–4 p.m; July–August 10 a.m.–5 p.m; October–April, Monday–Sunday 1–4 p.m.

Vitskøl Kloster: south of Ranum. Herb garden open: June–August 10 a.m.–8 p.m. Monastery from 1158.

Voergård: east of Flauenskjold. Renaissance palace. Tel: 98 86 71 08. Open: Saturday 2–5 p.m., Sunday 10 a.m.–5 p.m. (late-June to early-August only).

Zoologisk Have (Zoo): Mølleparkvej, Ålborg. Tel: 98 13 07 33. Open: daily all year.

WEST JUTLAND

Carl-Henning Pedersen og Else Alfelts Museum: Uldjydevej 3, Herning. Tel: 97 22 10 79. Open: Tuesday–Sunday 10 a.m.–5 p.m.

Esbjerg Fiskeauktionshal, the harbour. Fish auctions all year round. The auction begins daily at 7 a.m.

Fiskeri- og Søfartsmuseet (Fishing and Maritime Museum): Tarphagevej, Esbjerg. Tel. 75 15 06 66. Open: June–August, Monday–Friday 10 a.m.–5 p.m. and Saturday–Sunday 10 a.m.–6 p.m.; daily, September–May 10 a.m.–4 p.m.

Fyrkat (Viking Fortress): southwest of Hobro. Tel: 98 52 10 65. Open: daily, April–August 9 a.m.–7 p.m; September–October 9 a.m.–5 p.m.

Hjerl Hede Frilandsmuseum (Open Air Museum): Herl Hedevej 14, Vinderup, southwest of Skive. Reconstruction of village life. Open: daily, April–October 9 a.m.–5 p.m.

Holstebro Kunstmuseum: Sønderbrogade 2, Holstebro. Tel: 97 42 45 18. Open: daily 10 a.m.–4 p.m. Closed: Monday.

Lundehøj: northeast of Hurup in Thy. One of the largest passage graves in Denmark. Ask for the key and a lantern at the farm nearby.

Spøttrup Borg, southwest of Rødding. Tel: 97 56 16 06. Fourteenth-century castle. Open: daily, May–August 10 a.m.–6 p.m; September 10 a.m.–5 p.m; April, Sunday 11 a.m.–5 p.m.

Venø and Vestervig Kirker: The smallest and largest Danish village churches, respectively.

SOUTH JUTLAND

Augustenborg Castle: Augustenborg. Classical palace from 1770. The park is open to the public.

Dybbøl Mølle: west of Sønderborg. Tel: 97 56 16 06. Perhaps the most important battlefield in modern Danish history. Open: daily, June–August 10 a.m.–5 p.m; September–May 1–4 p.m.

Haderslev Domkirke (Haderslev Cathedral): Tel: 75 52 51 31. Open: daily, May–September 10 a.m.–5 p.m; October–April 10 a.m.–3 p.m.

Møgeltønder: Slotsgade. A "living" museum of old houses.

Ribe Domkirke (Ribe Cathedral): Tel: 75 42 06 19. Open: May–September, Monday–Saturday 10 a.m.–6 p.m., Sunday noon–6 p.m; October–April, Monday–Saturday 10 a.m.–noon and 2–4 p.m., Sunday 2–4 p.m.

Sønderborg Castle: Open: daily, summer 10 a.m.–5 p.m., winter 1–4 p.m.

NIGHTLIFE

COPENHAGEN

Although most of this section describes night spots for young adults, there's much more to night life in Copenhagen and the larger cities. Film, theatre, dance (both the internationally famous Royal Ballet and various struggling modern companies), opera and music to suit any taste are alive and well in Denmark. Check the local newspapers or, as always, call the tourist information offices for information about what's currently on.

In 1977, three young men imported the French café to Copenhagen and opened **Café Sommersko** in Kronprinsensgade. It was an immediate success. With the best selection in beers and spirits seen for a long time, and one of the first cappuccino machines in Denmark, it soon became *the* place to be seen with friends. A year later, they expanded with **Café Dan Turell** (named after the popular author) in Store Regnegade. It too was a success, and other people picked up the idea. Today it is hard to find a neighbourhood in any city without a local café.

A key ingredient in the café life is talk. Anything from an enlightened discussion to plain gossip will do. The cafés drew a whole generation away from home, and many young people use their favourite café as a living room. They go there to meet friends, to have lunch or dinner, to read the paper or, incidentally, to have a good time.

Café Dan Turell is mostly frequented by artists and while some people love it others cannot find the charm. In the same neighbourhood is **Zeze**, where the average age of the guests is under 30, and **Café Victor**, which is both a restaurant and a café. **Café au Lait**, in Gothersgade, is the closest any café comes to being cosy. **Klaptræet**, at Kultorvet (both a cinema and bar/café) is frequented by both the up-and-coming and the down-and-gone.

Nyhavn has a whole bundle of cafés, some of which hide in the back streets. Try **Zeleste** in Store Strandstræde and **Café Blomsten** in Lille Strandstræde. Try also around Lars Bjørnsstræde – one of the good choices is **Sabine**. Just around the corner in Vestergade is the largest and trendiest café, **Krasnapolsky**, with changing exhibitions of modern art upstairs and the discotheque **Umatic** in the cellar; it's one of the few cafés where one should be prepared to queue to get in at night.

Den Lille Café on the second floor at the far end of Istedgade in Vesterbro specialises in cocktails. In Nørrebro, **Café Floss** at Sankt Hans Torv is a good pick, and **Café Pavillonen** in Fælledparken is worth a visit. Try also **Bananarepublikken**, on Nørrebrogade. In Østerbro, **Krut's Carport** in Øster Farimagsgade is a nice local place with a few tables outside in the summer. **Park Bio & Café** on Østerbrogade is another trendy cinema/café combination – visit both if you have time.

But even if the cafés have taken up many of the good locations recently, pubs can still be found in large numbers. The atmosphere here is often cosier, and the dim lights attract a crowd that is somewhat different from those who seek the limelight of the large cafés. **Universitetscaféen** in Fiolstræde at the corner of Skindergade is visited by many students and foreigners staying in Denmark and, despite its name, it is not a café. **Café Rex** in Pilestræde (across the street from **Pilegården**, and around the corner from **Bo-Bi Bar**) is frequented by journalists and others who like to stay on top of things, and the same is true for **Musen og Elefanten** in Vestergade. While in the neighbourhood, one may also wish to visit **Charlie's**, a clean and pleasant place where there's always someone to talk to.

The neighbourhood bars in Nørrebro and Vesterbro tend to be slightly sleazy, but if that sounds attractive, try **Andy's Bar** in Gothersgade. Andy's Bar is one of the places where people gather after 2 a.m., when many other bars and cafés close. Other possibilities are **Brønum** at Kongens Nytorv, **Rådhuskroen** in Løngangsstræde, **The English Pub** and **The Duke** (which stand side by side) in Gothersgade and **Kabyssen** at Christianshavn.

Though some night clubs and discotheques in Copenhagen can be compared to those of other large cities, they are generally fashioned after an international standard and miss either the madness or the local flavour that could make them interesting places. But try **Fellini** underneath the Royal Hotel in Hammerichsgade (very expensive), **Annabel's** in Lille Kongensgade, **Privee** in Ny Østergade or **On the Rox** in Pilestræde. **Exalon** on Strøget near Rådhuspladsen attracts soldiers and policemen, **Daddy's Dance Hall** near Vesterport Station and **Woodstock** in Vestergade caters for those who are old enough to remember when The Rolling Stones released their first hit single. For jazz fans **La Fontaine** in Kompagnistræde is the obvious pick when **Montmartre** (in Nørregade) closes.

Several nightclubs around the central railway station compete for the title of the sexiest in town – if strip-tease joints can be considered sexy.

After all this remember to pay attention to what's going on at **Huset** in Rådhusstræde. With a café, bar, live music club, restaurant (both good and cheap), theatre and video art centre, travellers and residents alike should consider the changing programme.

ÅRHUS

The night life is centered around Skolegade. A good bar is **Den Hoje**, but one can zig-zag down the street from bar to bar. (The same opportunity is also found in Ålborg in Jomfru Ane Gade.) Århus has fostered a great number of cafés in recent years. One of the oldest is **Café Casablanca** right behind the cathedral, and several others can be found in the old streets leading up to Guldsmedegade. One should stroll through Vestergade and Jægersgårdgade.

ODENSE

Frank A is recommended as the best bar; cafés are spread out in the city centre near the passage leading up to **Brandts Klæde-fabrik** but Odense was never famous for its night life.

In general, it is a good idea to hit the pedestrian street in any town, look for a café or a bar there and find a seat for a beer. Most Danes will welcome a chance to practise their English, and will be proud to unload an insider's view on the best places to go in their own city.

SHOPPING

Copenhagen never fails to appear on lists of the most expensive cities in the world. It is usually rated among the first 10, accompanied by the other Scandinavian capitals. Few people come to Copenhagen to find a bargain.

Part of the reason for the high prices is a value-added tax (called MOMS) of 22 percent, added to all sales and services. Visitors can avoid making this contribution to the Danish state by having their purchases shipped home.

Shops that cater to tourists know of this service, and will provide information about the procedures. If you buy something and want to take it with you immediately, look for a sign saying "Danish Tax-Free Shopping." About 1,500 shops are members of this association, and the VAT spent in them will be refunded on departure from Denmark. Show the tax-free invoice to the customs officer *before* checking in. He will return customs stamps which can be presented for cash at the Office for Repayment of VAT in the transit hall (minus a small service charge). If leaving by land, ask for the stamps and send the invoice back to "Danish Tax-Free Shopping" for a refund. A minimum purchase of 600 Dkr. is required (2,750 Dkr. for EC citizens and 1,200 Dkr. for Scandinavian citizens). These rules and restrictions change frequently – check for the latest information before arriving.

One may find it worthwhile to see what Danish shops have to offer. Bang & Olufsen TV and stereo equipment, Royal Copenhagen Porcelain, and duvets are among the best known goods, but also look for fashion and furniture. Pick up any of the free city guides for a list of shops. Below are just a few good places to browse:

COPENHAGEN

The main shopping areas are of course the pedestrian streets, and first among them

Strøget. When there, take a look inside **Illums Bolighus** (at Amagertorv). They sell everything from furniture to kitchenware, all of it high quality. Jørn Utzon, the designer of the Sidney Opera House, was invited to design the **Paustian** furniture store in Nordre Frihavn and it is also an interesting place to visit.

Visit **Krea** in Vestergade and **BR** across the street from **Magasin** ("the largest department store in Scandinavia") for toys and gifts for kids. Around the corner in **Lars Bjørnstræde** are street fashion and secondhand shops. **Pistolstræde** is more pricy, and one will find the name of **Birger Christensen,** the owner of Café Bee Cee, Birger Christensen Furs and several other food and fashion shops in the neighbourhood. **Georg Jensen**'s silver shop is at Strøget and Pilestræde, near Magasin, and don't miss **Køkkenes Torvehal**, on Strøget between Ny Østergade and Bremerholm, where you will find a collection of the best food and wine shops in town – not cheap, but you can't do better.

The department store Magasin is always crowded, no matter which city you browse in. Fashion bargains can be made in **Hennes & Mauritz**, originally a Swedish company, but now an enormous success with younger Danes.

Copenhagen is packed with antique shops; some are very exclusive and expensive while others do business on the pavement. They're fun to explore and spend money in – don't be afraid to negotiate a price, or to walk away from the shop if it seems too expensive. When away from the big cities look for potteries and local arts and crafts shops.

If it is necessary to complain about poor service or merchandise and the matter can not be straightened out on the spot, try using **Forbrugerrådet** (The Consumer Council). Their address is Købmagergade 7, 1150 Copenhagen K. Tel: 33 13-63 11 (10 a.m.–1 p.m. weekdays).

LANGUAGE

The old joke says that Danish is not so much a language as a disease of the throat, and so it sometimes seems. To make the language even more difficult, Danish has three extra letters – æ, ø, and å – plus unpronounceable sub-glottal stops, and a myriad of local dialects and accents. It almost seems like a conspiracy. No sooner have you got used to one set of sounds than the next town or village produces a new cacophony. Although the Danes are always helpful, a knowledge of a few basic pronunciation rules will also help to fathom out a notice, road sign or headline.

The roots of Danish and the other Scandinavian languages date back to around AD 200, when Old Danish (Norse) separated from the eastern and western versions of the Germanic tongue, to found a new independent group of languages on the Scandinavian peninsula. During the Viking era, 1,000 years ago, Danes, Swedes and Norwegians could understand each other without difficulty. The nearest visitors can get to this old language today is in Iceland, where isolation has enabled Icelandic to retain its old forms, sounds and letters, brought to the island by the Vikings.

Despite their clear differences of grammar, usage and vocabulary, Danes, Norwegians and Swedes are still able to understand one another. In a tripartite conversation, each will speak his or her own national language, and on an SAS (Scandinavian Air Services) flight the captain and head steward will make the flight announcements in their native tongue. The advent of cross-border television has helped inter-Scandinavian knowledge of all three forms, but claims to perfect understanding of each other's language are better taken with a pinch of salt.

Modern Danish is no more rational than English and has far fewer words. In essence, it is a pictorial language with a paucity of words, though not expressions. In addition to the many dialects and pronunciation in the different areas, another difficulty for foreigners is that many existing letters are pronounced in a different way from other European languages.

But there are a few simple rules of thumb for vowels which help a visitor at least to mutter a few words and possibly to be understood:

a - a, as in *bar*
å - aw, as in *paw*
æ - e, as in *pear*
e - as in *bed*
i - ee, as in *sleep*
ø - u, as in *fur*

None of this will help you to speak Danish within a few days, but it should help in getting place names right. It will also kindle a polite mirth in your hosts because all Danes love to hear a foreigner attempting to wrap a reluctant tongue round words such as *sikkerhedsforanstaltninger* (security precautions) or *anti-ubådskrigsførelse* (anti-submarine warfare) and not forgetting *rødgrød med fløde på* (a fruit dessert with cream).

Despite attempts to adapt them, Danish also includes many foreign words. Until the 1600s, these were usually borrowed from German because of close trading links with the Hanseatic States, and French also left its mark on the 18th century. Today, words such as "television" and "architecture" more often come from English, and over half the words in many trades are Danicised versions of English.

With just over 5 million speakers, Danish does not cover a wide linguistic territory but that does not mean it is not a vital and dynamic language. More than 1,200 novels come out each year. There are 1,000 new children's books, and 7,000 non-fiction titles. You can buy them in one of the 500 book shops or borrow them at one of the 150 public libraries in this highly literate country which, in all, has some 90 million volumes.

A quick look into any telephone book will reveal another quirk of the Danish language: the predominance of certain names. Around 7.7 percent of the population is called Jensen, 7.3 percent Nielsen and 6.2 percent answers to the name of Hansen. These are closely followed by umpteen Christensens, Andersens, Pedersens and Petersens. In all, two-thirds of the entire Danish population is a *-sen* of one sort or another.

The reason is historical, dating back to the days when the ancient Vikings and their descendants in small, limited societies, chose this way to distinguish between family clans. This means that any Scandinavian or Anglo-Saxon name ending in either "-sen" or "-son" has its roots in the Norse patronymic system (which also included *datter* for daughter). But, unlike Russia, where each person has a given name, a patronymic and a family name, Danes had no family names until 1828.

Before that time, sons and daughters took their surnames from their fathers. Thus, Anders Nielsen's son was called Jonas Andersen and his daughter Gudrun Andersdatter. Then, as the population grew, a new fad for fashionable names brought the whole system into chaos. In 1828, the government passed the Name Law, which stipulated that all families should choose and retain a surname for the future. Iceland is now the only country in the western hemisphere to use the old system, reintroduced in a spate of historical patriotism in the 1970s.

None of this makes Danish any easier to understand, let alone speak. But at least your efforts will amuse the Danes.

Visitors who plan to stay for a longer period will find several language schools for non-native speakers (the **Berlitz School** and K.I.S.S. in Copenhagen offer intensive training; **Studieskolen** provides a more humane alternative, and private tutors can be found), but the following words and phrases might ease your trip a little:

WORDS & PHRASES

Left *venstre*
Right *højre*
Street *(en) gade/vej*
Bicycle (path) *(en) cykel (sti)*
Car *(en) bil*
Bus/coach *(en) bus*
Train *(et) tog*
Ferry *(en) færge*
Bridge *(en) bro*
Traffic light *(et) trafiklys*
Square *(et) torv*
North *nord*
South *syd*
East *øst*

West *vest*

Yes/no *ja/nej*
Big/little *stor(t)/lille*
Good/bad *god(t)/dårlig(t)*
Possible/impossible *muligt/umuligt*
Hot/cold *varm/kold*
Much/little *meget/lidt*
Many/few *mange/få*
And/or *og/eller*
Please/thank you *vær så venlig/tak*
How much is it? *Hvad koster det?*

Can I pay with... *Må jeg betale med...*
Travellers cheques *rejsechecks*
Money *penge*
Notes/coins *sedler/mønter*

Please may I have the bill?
Må jeg få regningen?

May I have a receipt?
Må jeg få en kvittering?

Bank *(en) bank*
Exchange *veksle*
Exchange rate *kurs*
Business hours *åbningstider*
Open *åben*
Closed *lukket*

Pharmacy *(et) apotek*
Hospital *(et) hospital*
Emergency room *(en) skadestue*
Doctor *(en) læge*

Breakfast *morgenmad*
Lunch (break) *frokost (pause)*
Dinner *middag*
Tea *te*
Coffee *kaffe*

I *jeg*
You (formal) *du (De)*
He/she *han/hun*
It *den/det*
We *vi*
You (formal) *I (De)*
They *de*
Foreigner *udlænding*
Foreign *fremmed*

ABBREVIATIONS

A/S Ltd/Inc.
Dkr. Danish Kroner
DSB Danish State Railways
EF EEC
e.Kr. AD
f.Kr. BC
FNUN (United Nations)
HT Copenhagen Transit Authority
Kbh. Copenhagen
KFUK YWCA
KFUM YMCA
km/t. kilometres per hour
MOMS value-added tax

NUMBERS

1 *en/et*
2 *to*
3 *tre*
4 *fire*
5 *fem*
6 *seks*
7 *syv*
8 *otte*
9 *ni*
10 *ti*
11 *elleve*
12 *tolv*
13 *tretten*
14 *fjorten*
15 *femten*
16 *seksten*
17 *sytten*
18 *atten*
19 *nitten*
20 *tyve*
21 *enogtyve*
30 *tredive*
32 *toogtredive*
40 *fyrre*
43 *treogfyrre*
50 *halvtreds*
54 *firoghalvtreds*
60 *tres*
65 *femogtres*
70 *halvfjerds*
76 *seksoghalvfjerds*
80 *firs*
90 *halvfems*
100 *hundrede*

CALENDAR

The names of the months are similar to English and are easily recognised. The names of the days of the week are from Nordic mythology (also reflected in the English).

Monday *mandag* (moon day)
Tuesday *tirsdag* (from the Latin *dies Martis*)
Wednesday *onsdag* (Odin's day)
Thursday *torsdag* (Thor's day)
Friday *fredag* (Freja's day)
Saturday *lørdag* (from the Old Norse *laurgardagr*: "washing day")
Sunday *søndag* (from the Latin *dies solis*: the day of the sun)

Dates are written as: Day.Month.Year. The 11th of October, 1992, will be 11.10.1992 or 11. oktober 1992.

What time is it? *Hvad er klokken?*
Good morning *Godmorgen*
Good day/evening/night *Goddag/godaften/godnat*
Today *i dag*
Tomorrow *i morgen*
Yesterday *i går*
Morning (9–12) *formiddag*
Noon *Middag*
Afternoon *eftermiddag*
Evening *aften*
Night *nat*
What time is it? *Hvad er klokken?*
It's five *Den er fem*

PLACES

Copenhagen *København*
Elsinore *Helsingør*
Zealand *Sjælland*
Funen *Fyn*
Jutland *Jylland*

SPORTS

For information on athletics, badminton, bowling, boxing, bicycle races, fencing, hockey, judo, walking and more, telephone Idrættens Hus, Brøndby Stadion 20, 2605 Brøndby. Tel: 42 45 55 55.

Angling: Lystfiskeriforeningen, Store Kongensgade 59, 1264 Copenhagen K. Tel: 33 12 20 54.

Bird Watching: Dansk Ornitologisk Forening, Vesterbrogade 140, 1620 Copenhagen V. Tel: 31 31 81 06.

Golf: Dansk Golf Union, Golfvinget 12, 26 25 Vallensbæk. Tel: 42 64 06 66.

Soccer: Dansk Boldspil Union (for players), Ved Amagerbanen 15, 2300 Copenhagen S. Tel: 31 95 05 11. Københavns Idrætspark (for spectators). Tel: 31 42 68 60.

SPECIAL INFORMATION

The following addresses may prove helpful for visitors with special needs. This list describes services available in Copenhagen, but the local tourist information offices can help find equivalents throughout the country.

BABYSITTERS

Studenternes Babysitters: Lykkesholmsallé 33C, 1902 Frederiksberg C. Tel: 31 22 96

96. Rates are Dkr. 25 per hour plus a Dkr. 25 booking fee and transport. Open: Monday–Thursday 6.30–9 a.m., Monday–Friday 3–6 p.m., Saturday 3–5 p.m. Closed: Sunday.

BUSINESS SERVICES

Bella Center (trade shows and conventions): Center Blvd Copenhagen S. Tel: 32 52 88 11.

Dansk Industriråd (Frederation of Danish Industries): H. C. Andersens Blvd 18, 1553 Copenhagen S. Tel: 33 15 22 33.

Regus Business Centre: Regus House, Lars Bjørnsstræde 3, 1454 Copenhagen K. Tel: 33 32 25 25.

The Foreign Press Association in Denmark: Snaregade 14, 1205 Copenhagen K. Tel: 33 13 16 15.

Udenrigsministeriet (Ministry of Foreign Affairs): Asiatisk Plads 2, 1402 Copenhagen K. Tel: 33 92 00 00.

CLUBS

American Women's Club: P. O. Box 34, 2800 Lyngby. Tel: 31 29 12 32.

Copenhagen Rotary: Store Strandstræde 20, 1255 Copenhagen K. Tel: 33 11 00 46.

Lions Club International: Københavnsvej 19, 3400 Hillerød. Tel: 42 25 56 34. Between 10 a.m.–2 p.m.

FOR GAYS

Forbundet af 1948 (Association headquarters with club and disco): Knabrostræde 3, 1023 Copenhagen K. Tel: 33 13 19 48.

Pan-Information: P. O. Box 1023, Copenhagen K. Tel: 33 13 01 12.

FOR STUDENTS

DIS (Travel Agency): Skindergade 28, 1159 Copenhagen K. Tel: 33 11 00 44.

Danida Fellowship Centre/ISC: Frederiksborgsgade 52, 1360 Copenhagen

K. Tel: 33 15 32 16.

Use It (Huset, Information Centre),: Rådhusstræde 13, 1466 Copenhagen K. Tel: 33 15 65 18.

FURTHER READING

A History of Denmark, by Palle Lauring. (Høst; Copenhagen, 1986.)

An Account of Denmark as it was in the Year 1692: Robert Molesworth; (Wormanium Publishers, Aarhus, Denmark.)

An Outline History of Denmark: Helge Seidelin Jacobsen; (Høst; Copenhagen, 1986.)

Berlitz: Engelsk/Dansk, Danish/English: Editions Berlitz; Lausanne, 1981.

Copenhagen This Week: Folia Publishers, Copenhagen (monthly).

Country Report: Denmark: Reuters News Agency; London, (current electronic database).

Danmark Fra Luften (Denmark from the Air): Torkild Balslev; Bogan's Forlag A/S; Viborg, 1984 (in Danish, English edition available).

Danmarks Arkitektur: Kirkens huse (Danish Architecture: Churches): Hugo Johannsen and Claus M. Smidt, Ed. by Hakon Lund; Gyldendalske Boghandel, Nordiske Forlag A/S; Copenhagen, 1981 (text in Danish, captions in Danish and English).

Danmarks Oldtid på Moesgaard (Danish Prehistory at Moesgaard): Søren H. Andersen *et al.*; Moesgaard Prehistoric Museum; Aarhus, 1988 (in Danish).

Danmark 1:100 000 Topografisk Atlas: Geodætisk Institute; Copenhagen, 1982.

Denmark: An Official Handbook: Press and Information Department, Danish Ministry of Foreign Affairs; Kraks Publishers; Copenhagen, 1970.

Denmark – Praise and Protest: Alan Moray Williams; Høst; Copenhagen, 1969.

Denmark Today – The World of the Danes: Danish Ministry of Foreign Affairs; Copenhagen, 1979.

Environment DENMARK: Denmark's national report to the United Nations on the human environment: Danish Ministries of Foreign Affairs, Housing, Cultural Affairs and Environmental Protection; F.E. Bording, Ltd.; Copenhagen, 1972.

Facts About Denmark: Danish Ministry of Foreign Affairs (Press and Cultural Department); Danish Foreign Ministry/Forlaget Aktuelle Bøger; Copenhagen, 1987.

Historisk Atlas Danmark: Ed. by Jette Kjærulff Hellesen and Ole Tuxen; G.E.C. Gads Forlag; København, 1988 (in Danish and English).

Illustreret Videnskab: "Sådan genskabte arkeologerne Tollundmanden" (How archeologists re-created the Tollund Man); Vol. 12, 1987; Bonniers Specialmagasiner; Copenhagen, 1987 (in Danish).

Kraks kort over København og omegn (Krak's Map of Copenhagen and Environs), 63rd Edition, 1987; Kraks Forlag; Copenhagen, 1986 (in Danish, with museums and sights also listed in English).

Politikens Danmarks Historie, Vol. 1: Politikens Hus; Copenhagen, 1962 (and later editions, in Danish).

Prehistoric Denmark: National Museum of Denmark; Copenhagen, 1978.

The Art of Scandinavia, Volumes 1 & 2: Peter Anker and Aron Andersson (translated by Vivienne Menkes from the French original *L'Art Scandinave 1 & 2*); The Hamlyn Publishing Group, Ltd.; Middlesex, 1970.

The Proxemics of Danish Daily Life: Judith Friedman Hansen in *Studies in the Anthropology of Visual Communication* 3(1), 1976; Annenburg School of Communication, University of Pennsylvania; Philadelphia, 1976.

USEFUL ADDRESSES

TOURIST BUREAUX

Visitors and residents alike benefit from valuable service provided by the many local tourist offices. There is one in almost every city, with knowledgeable and friendly staff waiting to help and answer questions. They can assist in planning a trip and making the necessary reservations, or just by providing the needed directions and reference materials. Tell them about what you want to see or do: from fishing or bird watching, history, manor houses or 18th-century art, to organ or rock music, nouvelle cuisine, alternative life-styles or old locomotives; you name it – and there is a good chance they can find something of interest in the area you are visiting. Some of the tourist bureaux are:

COPENHAGEN

Turistinformation: H.C. Andersens Blvd 22, 1553 Copenhagen V. Tel. 33 11 13 25. (Located at the main entrance of Tivoli.) Københavns Turistforening: Nørregade 7 A, 1165 Copenhagen K. Tel: 33 13 70 07.

NORTH SEALAND

Helsingør Turistforening: Havnepladsen 3, 3000 Helsingør. Tel: 49 21 13 33.

SOUTHWEST SEALAND

Roskilde Turistforening: Fondens Bro 3, Postboks 278, 4000 Roskilde. Tel: 42 35 27 00.

BORNHOLM

Bornholms Turistbureau: Munch Petersensvej 4, 3700 Rønne. Tel: 53 95 08 10.

FUNEN

Svendborg Turistforening: Møllergade 20l, 5700 Svendborg. Tel: 62 21 09 80.
Odense Turistforening: Rådhuset, 5000 Odense C. Tel: 66 12 75 20.
Funen Archipelago: Ærøskøbing Turistforening, Torvet: 5970 Ærøskøbing. Tel: 62 52 13 00.

EAST JUTLAND

Århus Turistforening: Rådhuset, 8000 Århus C. Tel: 86 12 16 00 or 86 12 11 77.
Silkeborg Turistforening: Torvet 9, Postboks 950, 8600 Silkeborg. Tel: 86 82 19 11.
Turistforeningen for Ebeltoft og Mols: Torvet 9–11, 8400 Ebeltoft. Tel: 86 34 14 00.

NORTH JUTLAND

Skagen Turistforening: Skt Laurentiivej 22, 9990 Skagen. Tel: 98 44 13 77.
Ålborg Tourist Bureau: Østerå 8, 9000 Ålborg. Tel: 98 12 60 22.

WEST JUTLAND

Holstebro Turistbureau: Brostræde 2, 7500 Holstebro. Tel: 97 42 57 00.
Viborg Turistkontor: Nytorv 5, 8800 Viborg. Tel: 86 61 16 66.

SOUTH JUTLAND

Haderslev Turistforening: Søndergade 3, 6100 Haderslev. Tel: 74 52 55 50.
Ribe Turistforening: Torvet 3–5, 6760 Ribe. Tel: 75 42 15 00.

TOURIST OFFICES ABROAD

Danish tourist bureaux can also be found in Norway, Sweden and Finland. In Britain, Germany, Holland Italy, Japan, Canada and the United States of America. Some of the addresses are:

Britain: The Danish Tourist Board, U.K. Office, Sceptre House, 169/173 Regent Street, London W1R 8Py. Tel: 071-734 2637.

Germany: Dänisches Frendemverkehrsamt, Glockengiesserwall 2, Postfach 10 13 29, 2000 Hamburg 1. Tel: 40-32 78 03.

USA: The Danish Tourist Board, 6555 Third Avenue, 18th Floor, New York, NY 10017. Tel: 212/949-2333 or 2322.
Scandinavian Tourist Board, 150 North Michigan Avenue, Suite 2110, Chicago, Il 60601. Tel: 312/726-1120.
Scandinavian Tourist Board, 8929 Wilshire Blvd, Beverly Hills, CA 90211. Tel: 213/854-1549.

Japan: Scandinavian Tourist Board, Sanno Grand Building, Room 401, 2-14-2 Nagata-cho, Chiyoda-ku Tokyo, 100 Japan. Tel: 3-580 8360.

Canada: The Danish Tourist Board, P. O. Box 115, Station N, Toronto, Ontario M8V 3S4. Tel: 416/823-9620.

ART/PHOTO CREDITS

INDEX

L

M

N

T

U

V

W

A
C
D
E
F
G
H
I
J
a
b
c
d
e

g
h
i
j
k
l